How to Tune & Modify Your
CAMARO
1982–1998

JASON SCOTT

Dedication

For the apple of my eye, the light of my life —
For Jenna.

First published in 1998 by MBI Publishing Company,
729 Prospect Avenue, PO Box 1, Osceola, WI 54020-0001
USA

The information in this book is true and complete to the
best of our knowledge. All recommendations are made
without any guarantee on the part of the author or
Publisher, who also disclaim any liability incurred in
connection with the use of this data or specific details.

We recognize that some words, model names and
designations, for example, mentioned herein are the
property of the trademark holder. We use them for
identification purposes only. This is not an official
publication.

MBI Publishing Company books are also available at
discounts in bulk quantity for industrial or sales-promotional
use. For details write to Special Sales Manager at
Motorbooks International Wholesalers & Distributors, 729
Prospect Avenue, Osceola, WI 54020-0001 USA.

Library of Congress Cataloging-in-Publication Data
Scott, Jason, 1969–
       How to tune & modify your Camaro, 1982–1998 /
Jason Scott
          p.   cm. — (PowerTech series)
       Includes index.
       ISBN 0-7603-0436-X (pbk. : alk. paper)
       1. Camaro automobile—Maintenance and repair.   I.
Title.
       II. Series.
       TL215.C33S364   1998
       629.28'722—dc21   98–13191

On the front cover: Now this is high-performance. This
1992 Z-28 was built in the Chevy race shop with
cooperation from TDM Technologies. It houses a 510 cubic-
inch fuel-injected tuned port V-8 with competition cams for
stunning acceleration and top-end. The chassis has been
lowered one 1 1/2 inches, and 17-inch Ronal wheels with
Goodyear Eagle GSC tires have been added for stellar
handling.

Designed by Rebecca Allen

Printed in the United States of America

CONTENTS

ACKNOWLEDGMENTS:
SETTING THE RECORD STRAIGHT

If you were to look only at the cover of this book, you would understandably think that I wrote this book all by myself, without help from anyone. The truth of the matter, of course, is that projects of the size and scope of this book are never accomplished by one person working in isolation—I'm just the fortunate one who gets his name on the cover. Behind the scenes, under the cars, on the other end of the phones, and sometimes in front of the camera are a host of people who unselfishly provided their expertise, their time, and their enthusiasm to help me compile the vast assortment of information that spreads out over the next 160 pages.

Now, it would be nice to think that each of the contributors to this book helped me because I'm such a swell guy and they couldn't resist my charm, but they've actually got much more noble reasons—every single one of them is a Camaro enthusiast, first and foremost, and a good sport, too, ever anxious to help out a fellow enthusiast.

Unfortunately, it's impossible to thank everyone who got involved in this project in one way or another, but some people's assistance stood out as above and beyond the call of duty. Myron Cottrell is one of those people. As the head honcho at TPI Specialties, Myron has assembled more Chevy TPI engines than I can count and has also done a fair amount of racing on drag strips and road courses, too. Every word Myron shared about engine modifications, chassis setup, and even how to conduct the most realistic tests, was invaluable. To say I couldn't have

done this project without his help would be a gross understatement.

Myron's equivalent in the suspension world is surely Doug Nordin, at Global West Suspension. It's doubtful that anyone knows more about F-body suspension systems than Doug, who has trick solutions for problems that I didn't even know existed. He's spent years engineering and testing parts and modifications that not only make Camaros out-perform everything on the track, but make them survive the kind of punishment that sends most race cars to the trailer early on race day.

Complementing Doug's suspension know-how was Koni America's shock czar, Lee Grimes, who divulged volumes about the science behind shock damper action. More than just a slide-rule-packing engineer, though, Lee was able to point out the practical, real-world benefits of proper suspension setup and engineering that helped him garner his numerous SCCA Solo class wins.

Another man who showed me the proof in the pudding was Jim Hodgeman, Stillen's brake system guru. Jim was able to boil the complex physics of brake performance down to layman's terms.

It wouldn't be fair of me to overlook my behind-the-wheel engineering and driving lessons taught by an assortment of General Motors engineers, including Greg Peterson, Rod Michaelson, Jim Minniker, John Heinricy, Jim Ingles, John Moss, John Cafaro, and the new head of F-car development (and simultaneous Corvette Chief Engineer) Dave Hill. These guys eat, sleep, and breathe Bow Tie performance during the

work week. When the weekend comes, they put on their helmets and take to the track to test their latest theories by pushing Camaros and Corvettes faster and harder than GM executives might prefer. But some of their weekend discoveries really do get put to work back in "the office." Your Camaro—and this book—are proof of that. You won't meet a finer bunch of gearheads, and they've each been a true inspiration to me.

Those were just a few of the many people I relied upon to confirm what I suspected.

Speaking of being in the driver's seat, I also need to thank Scott Benedict and Stephanie Kapise for their assistance with photo shoots and testing, plus their attentive ears and helpful suggestions. I know it wasn't all fun and games for them darting through those road cones over and over and over . . . those grins were just for my benefit, weren't they? And whether they knew it or not, our endless conversations gave me insight into what parts of the book needed more clarification, and where I could cut some of the fat.

Most of all, I need to acknowledge the sacrifices of my daughter, Jenna, and my wife, Michelle. There was many a time when their plans were upset by my need to work on the cars, write, take photos, or make calls for this book. They gave up a lot over many more months than I had intended things to take (but since when have I ever been able to estimate time well, right, M?). Mere words can't express my gratitude, but suffice it to say that their gift of uninterrupted "quiet time" weren't unappreciated.

INTRODUCTION

My wife and I have a running joke when it comes to modifying cars: If it's louder, it must be better. So what if that new shifter transmits more gear whine into the cockpit? You never miss a shift anymore! And those new tires that hum and whir incessantly? They've got enough grip to turn on a dime and give you nine cents change! And your new exhaust? The poly bushings and those Heim joints? They're all louder, but provide measurable improvements in performance.

Of course, the reality of performance modifications is that any sounds that get louder—or new ones that appear—do so merely as side effects. The value of an upgrade can never be based upon how loud it makes your car . . . unless, of course, you're talking about stereo system components. And even when you are talking about stereo systems, you don't just want volume—you want *clear* volume, not distortion.

The point of this book isn't necessarily to point out what specific changes you should make to your Camaro, but rather to educate you on how to determine what modifications you should be considering, based on a number of factors including your budget, your skills, and your driving requirements. The key to race-winning performance is making smart decisions about modifications—determining the best way to spend your limited budget to get the best results. Sometimes you might need a few costly aftermarket performance parts, but in many cases the best value is to modify factory parts with specific inexpensive upgrades. That's the kind of knowledge I've struggled to provide you with, rather than just spoon-feeding you a list of parts to bolt on—parts that may or may not still be available when you get around to improving your Camaro's performance.

As you might expect, figuring out what your car is doing now, and how different changes affect it, involves thinking about many of the basic laws of physics. But don't let that scare you. Most of the principles of automotive physics are concepts that you've probably already thought about without realizing it.

Of course, theories are fine, but what you really want is to know what to do to make your Camaro faster. And while there's no one-size-fits-all answer to that sort of problem, I've tried, whenever possible, to present general suggestions for each of four basic "environments" in which you and your Camaro might operate: street high-performance driving, drag racing, autocrossing, and road racing. Each use has its own requirements, and rarely will what's right for one application be what's right for another. And it isn't safe to assume that the particular setup I might race with would be the same setup you would be comfortable or competitive with. But the ideas and information provided should get you into the ballpark (or race track, as the case may be), leaving just some fine-tuning to get the car working to your satisfaction.

Naturally, testing parts played a big part of putting this book together. I spent countless hours in the garage busting my knuckles, installing parts, and making modifications. I've been to race tracks testing changes. And I've tried living with those changes on the street. But given the immense assortment of parts and modifications available, it was impossible to test every part, let alone every possible combination of parts. To help fill in the blanks, I turned to various experts, like the racers and engineers mentioned in the "Acknowledgments" section, who all have valuable experience and knowledge of their own, most of which has been learned during years of exhaustive research, development, and testing of their own.

In the end, however, whatever modifications you choose to make are up to you. You alone can say what it is that you need your Camaro to be able to do. And, hopefully, after reading the following chapters, you'll have the knowledge that you need to make the necessary changes to attain those goals. Good luck!

In order to compete against
Ford's Mustang on the Sports
Car Club of America's Trans-
Am racing circuit, Chevrolet
engineers developed racing-
inspired performance
equipment and made it
available to buyers under RPO
Z28. By the time this photo
was taken in 1969, the Z/28
Camaro was already a legend.
Chevrolet photo

CAMARO PERFORMANCE HERITAGE

Long before the third-generation Camaro debuted in 1982, the model had an established reputation as a high-performance car. The 1967–1969 "first-generation" Camaros exemplified everything that "muscle cars" of the 1960s were about—huge engines and tire-shredding power. The Super Sport "SS" cars were terrors with high-performance 350s and a trio of 396 "big-block" engines, ranging up to 375 horsepower! Ultra rare COPO cars featured more powerful "Corvette" 427 big blocks in the L72 435-horsepower and all-aluminum ZL1 430-horse flavors. Meanwhile, the Z/28—the true sportscar Camaro—boasted a screaming 290-horse 302. During the 1960s, the engines were the stars of the show, and the Camaro's engine line-up gave it almost unbeatable acceleration and top speed.

As the 1970s dawned, the world was on the verge of major changes. The government and environmental advocates were pressuring auto makers to build more fuel-efficient, cleaner-running engines. Safety advocates teamed with the insurance industry to blacklist virtually every performance car rolling out of the Big Three's design studios. And a bunch of upset Arabians cut off America's normally free-flowing supply of crude oil, which, perhaps more than anything else, changed the public's view of gas-guzzling muscle cars. With gas prices soaring, interest in high-performance engines all but stalled. But performance enthusiasts still wanted more than just mundane transportation.

With ever-declining engine performance, Camaro's ride and handling began to take center stage. In tune with the growing interest in European sports cars, the new second-generation Camaro, which debuted late, in early 1970, was longer, lower and wider, and had a decidedly European flair. And the suspension system, though only marginally different from the first-generation car's independent coils up front and leaf-sprung live axle rear, performed remarkably well.

More than 30 years of performance history and tradition have made "late-model" Camaros the best pony cars ever! But there's always room for improvement. *Chevrolet photo*

Magazine tests of Camaros throughout the 1970s commented on the car's able handling abilities and comfortable ride.

Even by 1975, though, when GM's top executives gave the replacement F-car project the official "Okay," the handwriting was on the wall: The next-generation Camaro would have to be the best Camaro ever. A Camaro with only good handling characteristics wouldn't cut it, nor would one that only accelerated well. Buyers were becoming more picky—they wanted it all. And the all-new third-generation Camaro could be just the car to deliver it all, if it was designed properly.

Initially, GM executives considered the notion of a front-wheel-drive Camaro. They were intrigued by the economic bottom line of such a venture, because it would allow GM to utilize a number of parts from its X-car (Chevy Citation) line-up, thereby minimizing engineering costs.

Despite decreasing performance on the streets, Camaros only got quicker and quicker on race tracks. *Chevrolet photo*

The all-new third-generation Camaro debuted as a 1982 model and was immediately honored with the pace car duties at the 66th running of the Indianapolis 500. *Chevrolet photo*

Creating the Third Generation

But Tom Zimmer, Chevy's chief vehicles engineer, led the charge to keep rear-wheel drive, pointing to the enormous demand for the second-generation Camaro's performance handling options—the Z28. Zimmer's insistence that a front-wheel-drive car could never deliver the necessary ride and handling performance the Camaro's established market expected and demanded generated increasing support. The final nail in the front-drive coffin was the determination that the car had to at least offer a V-8 engine, but none of the X-car drivetrain gear would be able to withstand a V-8's torque—even a low-performance V-8.

As work progressed on the initial third-generation Camaro (and its Pontiac sibling, the Firebird), the suspension package began taking

By the mid-1980s, Chevrolet was hard at work on the fourth-generation Camaro, which was originally slated to arrive in the late 1980s as a front-wheel driver. Public outcry and concept cars like this 1985 GTZ Concept helped convince GM's top brass to stick with a rear-drive platform. *Chevrolet photo*

shape. A modified MacPherson strut front suspension was selected both for its cost effectiveness and its compact size. Out back, the live axle was retained, but now it featured coil springs, lower control arms, a Panhard (lateral track) rod, and massive torque arm to keep it located beneath the car. And unlike previous Camaros, the Z28's suspension was considered so essential to the car's success that the entire system was designed first for the Z's outstanding performance requirements, then that setup was toned down to create the base and Berlinetta models afterward.

The third-generation Camaro's incredibly popular body evolved from a 1976 sketch by Roger Hughet to the eventual Jerry Palmer production design created in Chevrolet Studio Three that was significantly smaller in size (by 18 inches in length), much more aerodynamically efficient, thoroughly modern, yet incredibly reminiscent of the previous Camaros, from its open grille nose to its wraparound, tri-color taillights. Additionally, two body styles were prepared: a hardtop coupe and a T-top roof. One of the Camaro's most dramatic features—its huge glass hatch—turned out to be a more difficult component to produce than expected, due to its complex compound curves.

The result was that the 1982 Camaro debuted to rave reviews. Of course, it helped that Chevrolet had little else to show off that year. With three models to choose from—the reserved base model, the up-scale Berlinetta with its unique nose and gold trim, and the Z28 with its deeper air dam and ground effects panel extensions—there was a Camaro for everyone. And while the bulk of Camaro buyers were males under the age of 36, a growing number were female, and the new car only sped up that trend.

While the base and Berlinetta models were more than capable of out-performing the majority of practical family sedans on the road, it was the Z28 that really got the enthusiasts' attention—and made even owners of expensive exotic sports cars sit up and take notice.

With grippy Goodyear Eagle GT tires and its specific suspension tuning,

Throughout the 1980s, Camaro continued its winning ways on race tracks of all types, including drag strips.

the Camaro was a delight to drive at speed down twisting, turning roads. And a pair of V-8 engines—one carbureted and one equipped with the Corvette's exotic-looking "Cross-Fire Injection" dual-throttle-body injection systems—let Z28 buyers choose just how much power they wanted. And for those Z28 buyers who fondly remembered the original Z/28s of the 1960s, there was even a fiberglass hood.

Camaro Indy Pace Car

In honor of the Camaro's rebirth as a leaner, meaner performance car, it was selected to serve as the official pace car of the Memorial Day weekend Indianapolis 500—Camaro's third time at the head of the greatest spectacle in racing, having led the field in 1967 and 1969. To commemorate the occasion, Chevrolet commissioned a run of special Pace Car Replicas. Remarkably, the actual Pace Cars (the Indianapolis Motor Speedway requires one pace car and a back-up car) and the 6,360 replicas of them were virtually identical. All featured a stunning silver paint scheme with blue lower body striping and red accents, Indy 500 decals, plus silver aluminum wheels with a red circumferential pinstripe and raised-white-letter Goodyear Eagle GT tires. Inside, each of the cars was equipped with blue cloth

and silver vinyl trim; adjustable "Conteur" seats, similar to popular Recaro seats of the day; a leather-wrapped steering wheel; an AM/FM stereo; and other amenities.

Attesting to the stock Z28's race-ready capabilities, the actual Pace Cars stuck with stock Z28 suspension and brake systems to keep the cars under control. But the Pace Cars and replicas did differ in two distinct ways: first, the Pace Cars' necessary strobe lights; second, the engines.

Pace Car Replicas had to make do with either of the normal Z28 305s—the carbureted LG4 or the LU5 Cross-Fire Injection version—but the real Pace Cars got real power under their hoods, courtesy of hand-assembled, all-aluminum, 350-inch V-8s built in the old-fashioned muscle car manner with a high-lift camshaft, high-rise aluminum intake manifold, four-barrel carburetor, custom tubular headers, and other traditional performance parts.

Ensuring that the new Camaro would continue to be synonymous with performance, Chevrolet renewed its sponsorship of the International Race of Champions (IROC) series, as it had done since 1974, which promoted race driver talents by pitting top drivers from several motorsports venues—NASCAR stock car racing, Indy car racing, sports car racing, and others—against each other in identically prepared, "race modified" (actually completely custom-fabricated) Camaro Z28s.

Appropriately, the IROC racing Camaros were rebodied with a variation of the production car's sharp new sheet metal, extended and bulged to cover the cars' tube frames, wide racing tires, and purpose-built small-block Chevy-based racing engines. The new IROC race cars looked so similar to their street counterparts that comparisons were inescapable, and Chevy wasted no opportunity to point out that the IROC racing Camaro was a Z28—just more of a Z28.

Despite an abbreviated sales year, 189,747 copies of the all-new 1982 Camaro rolled off the Norwood, Ohio, and Van Nuys, California, production lines and into owners' driveways—roughly a 50 percent gain over the previous year!

When the 1983 models hit the showrooms, buyers found little different, unless they happened to drive a Z28 equipped with the "High Output" 190-horsepower L69 H.O. 305 V-8 and its required five-speed manual transmission. Despite having 15 horses more than the complicated and equally priced Cross-Fire-injected 305, the L69—which relied on familiar performance parts: a big Rochester QuadraJet four-barrel carburetor, aluminum intake manifold, dual snorkel air cleaner with fresh-air ducting, and hotter camshaft—was specified by just 3,223 buyers.

Though there were few other "firsts" in 1983, there were several "lasts." Gone with the last of the 1983 models was the Z28's fiberglass hood, eight-track tape players, and the cantankerous LU5 Cross-Fire Injection 305 V-8, among other items.

Z28 Grabs Headlines

The 1984 model year was a study in opposites. On one hand, the Z28 was busy receiving awards from *Road & Track* magazine as the "Best Sport GT" in its price category, and from *Car and Driver* magazine as the best-handling American-built car. On the other hand, though, the Berlinetta—the luxury Camaro—was struggling. To help the model along, Chevrolet made a number of changes to the car, including a new, high-tech digital instrument panel, pod-mounted radio controls, an overhead console, and more. Most importantly, Chevrolet put some promotional muscle behind the Berlinetta. But in the end, Berlinetta production was a mere fraction of standard Camaro Sport Coupe and Z28 production—and the Berlinetta numbers plummeted in the two following years, before Chevy finally, mercifully, threw in the towel on its high-end Camaro.

Camaro performance took a quantum leap forward in 1985, when Chevy capitalized on its still ongoing IROC tie-in by releasing a special high-performance option for the Z28

Chevrolet's continued involvement in motorsports began to pay bigger dividends in the 1980s, too. Camaros were the sole model in the International Race of Champions (IROC) series for years, and GM finally created a street version to tie into that image. *Chevrolet photo*

that included a number of handling upgrades. Higher-rate springs lowered the ride height and thus the car's center of gravity, while revalved front struts and Delco-Bilstein rear shocks helped control wheel movements more precisely. Thicker stabilizer bars kept the car flatter than ever during even high-speed cornering, and special front subframe reinforcements gave the suspension a more solid platform against which to act. Increased steering caster and a higher-effort (faster ratio) steering box worked in conjunction with positively huge-for-their-day 16-inch aluminum wheels. Tires were lifted straight off the Corvette assembly line—massive 245/50VR-16 "Gatorback" Goodyear Eagles—to transform the IROC-Z into what was, to that point, the best-handling Camaro ever, capable of 0.92 g on the skidpad.

And while the F-car engineers were raiding the Corvette's parts bins for tires and suspension tuning tips, they saw fit to make off with the Corvette's new Tuned Port Injection fuel-injection system, which they then stuck on the LB9 305 V-8 engine to the tune of 215 horsepower. Suddenly, there was a horsepower war brewing, as Ford hurried to release its electronically fuel-injected 220-horse Mustang.

The Camaro line-up soldiered on in 1986, with mostly revisionary changes to the base and Z28 models, and the termination of the Berlinetta model during the year, as orders for only 4,479 trickled in.

Two hot items topped the Camaro option list for 1987. The first came in the form of a factory-optioned convertible, in both the base and Z28 lines. Camaro convertible conversions had been available for a number of years through independent modifiers, and in 1987 Chevrolet partnered up with one of the most successful of those—American Sunroof Corporation (ASC)—to have them perform the modifications to cars that were initially built on GM's assembly lines as regular sport coupes.

The Ferocious 350 TPI

The second item of note was the availability of the "Corvette" 350 Tuned Port Injection engine in Z28 models. Interestingly, Chevrolet

Production Camaros showed just how well-engineered they were by running circles around the competition in the IMSA Firehawk and SCCA World Challenge road racing series. Responding to racer's requests, Chevy released the 1LE performance package, which was the equivalent of the original RPO Z28 package, but better. *Chevrolet photo*

In the SCCA Trans-Am professional racing series, Camaros have more wins and championships than any other model in the series' history. *Chevrolet photo*

records indicate that one lonely Camaro had been built with the B2L/L98 engine in 1986, though it is believed to have been used solely as a prototype vehicle to prepare for the widespread 1987 availability of the engine.

The 350 V-8 had been absent from the Camaro line since the 1981 model, when it boasted just 190 horsepower. In TPI form and minus the Corvette's aluminum cylinder heads and more freely flowing air intake and exhaust systems, the new 350 belted out 225 horses under the twin-scooped Z28 hood. Though hardly earth-shattering power, the 350 was brutal enough to destroy the only manual transmissions Chevy had for the Camaro, so the option was limited to the four-speed automatic transmission.

On a somber note, the end of 1987 production marked the end of the line for the Norwood, Ohio, assembly plant, which had produced Camaros (and Pontiac Firebirds) since they were introduced in 1967.

Buyers breezing into their local Chevy dealer to order a 1988 Z28 were shocked to find that there, once again, was no such beast. In Chevy's infinite wisdom, it chose to cancel the Z28 model and replace it with the IROC-Z, which was no longer just an option, but its own model.

About this time, Showroom Stock racing was gaining in popularity, and the Camaro was always ready to make a good showing. But a handful of F-body engineers weren't content with seeing their life's work simply finish well.

In a move that harkened back to the good ol' days of the COPO Camaros of the late-1960s, they again raided the Corvette parts bins, this time to cobble together a competent brake system that was able to withstand the rigors of repeated race track abuse. While they were tinkering, the rebellious engineers took a page from the original Z28's manual and whipped up 1989's option code 1LE, which included a laundry list of high-performance parts that racers were crying for, including extra-stiff springs and shocks, oversize anti-roll bars, an aluminum driveshaft, and even a special, baffled, dual-pickup fuel tank to cure fuel starvation problems while cornering.

The catch to the 1LE cars was getting them—you couldn't just order a 1LE car. You had to order a specific combination of items that tricked the GM production scheduling computers into adding the 1LE option code. The combination required the B2L (350) or LB9 (305) TPI engines, the RPO G92 3.42:1 rear axle gear, G80 Positraction limited slip differential, and—the catch—no air conditioning. GM didn't promote the option to the general public because the car's suspension system would have been objectionable to most buyers, and would likely have resulted in bad publicity for the car company. Instead, only those racers "in the know" got their hands on what many enthusiasts considered to be, up to that point, the hottest-handling Camaro ever.

As the Camaro moved into the 1990s, the aftermarket "tuner" companies started, at long last, to take a look at the Camaro, and its Pontiac cousin, the Firebird. One company in particular, Street Legal Performance, went so far as to begin building highly modified Firebirds, known as SLP Firehawks. The Firehawk could be ordered from any Pontiac dealer, but somewhere between the factory and the selling dealer, the car stopped at the SLP shops for the Firehawk modifications, which included a custom-built 300-horsepower 350 engine, five-speed manual transmission, heavy-duty (1LE or extra-cost Brembo) brakes, 17-inch wheels and tires, special shocks, springs and stabilizer bars, a fiberglass hood, and even an optional roll cage, multipoint safety harness, and Recaro seat for the competition

This 1990 Camaro California design concept hinted at the shape of the new fourth-generation Camaro that was nearing production. *Chevrolet photo*

Intended to be a "last hurrah" for the third-generation Camaro, this modest-looking Camaro was planned for a production run of 602 units to match the number of 1967 Z/28s, and was to feature a hopped-up 350 engine and Corvette ZF six-speed manual transmission. Unfortunately, production costs killed the program and resulted in the 25th anniversary being marked with only "Heritage Edition" hood and decklid stripes and "25th Anniversary" emblems inside. Ironically, a hot 350 and six-speed would become standard equipment in the Camaro a year later.

models. Though no Camaro equivalent was available, SLP was happy to sell Camaro owners everything they needed to put their Camaro on an even footing with the Firehawk.

Fourth Generation Flyer

When the completely redesigned fourth-generation Camaro debuted in January 1993, it quickly became clear that SLP's efforts hadn't gone unnoticed by GM's F-body engineering team, as many of the Firehawk's advantages were incorporated into the new car, often with more impressive results than SLP had been able to achieve.

Under its familiar-looking twin-scooped hood, the new Z28 featured a 275-horsepower Corvette LT1 "Gen-II" 350-inch V-8 engine and a standard Borg-Warner T56 six-speed manual transmission, at long last letting F-body buyers have the "big" V-8 with a manual gearbox from the factory. A four-speed automatic, the

4L60 (formerly known as the 700R4), continued to be offered.

A completely new front suspension system did away with the third-generation's modified MacPherson struts in favor of a Short/Long Arm (SLA) design that featured upper (short) and lower (long) A-arms with a coil-over-shock damping system. Devoid of the struts' limitations, and thanks to a unique lower control arm design, engineers were able to tune the F-body ride and handling like never before. The rear suspension remained virtually unchanged from the third generation, aside from spring rates, shock valving, and anti-roll bar sizes.

And a redesigned base-level brake system gave the new-generation Camaro braking abilities nearly equal to the exotic (and expensive) 1LE systems of years previous. The new binders worked so well, in fact, that the 1LE cars no longer received any upgraded brake hardware!

As for the SLP Firehawk Firebird, it stuck around, boasting 300 horsepower thanks to freer flowing intake and exhaust systems, plus suspension tweaks, tasteful graphics, and a dynamite cold-air induction hood. It was shortly joined by a Camaro variation, the Z28-SS, which featured similar modifications. But now it was being given a run for its money by other "tuner cars." Callaway Cars built the C8 Camaro with knowledge the company developed while building its twin-turbo and SuperNatural Corvettes. Famed drag racer and engine builder John Lingenfelter, and successful road racer Doug Rippie were two others that put their respective names on highly modified F-bodies. And for the do-it-yourselfers of the world, GM saw fit to offer "bodies in white" (bare production car chassis minus any powertrain, suspension, interior, body glass, etc.) through its Performance

The new, fourth-generation Camaro hit showrooms in 1993 with a 275-horsepower 350 engine, a six-speed manual gearbox, radical new shape, outstanding handling, and a top speed over 152 miles per hour!

Parts catalog, which made excellent foundations for pro street and race-only projects.

Out on the professional racing circuits, the Camaro continued to regularly claim wins in the SCCA Trans-Am series, and eventually returned to illuminate the win lights at National Hot Rod Association (NHRA) events across the country.

And with the introduction of the 1998 Camaros, the models have again benefited from Corvette technological hand-me-downs. All mod-els, including the base coupes and convertibles, were given four-wheel disc brake components fashioned after those used on the 1997 "C5" Corvette. And while the base Camaro models continued to carry the Buick Grand National 210-horsepower, 3800 V-6, the Z28 featured the all-new, all-aluminum, third-generation Chevrolet small-block 350 V-8—the 305-horsepower 5.7-liter L51.

Time will tell what's in store for Camaro performance. But if the past is any indication—and it usually is— the Camaro should continue to thrive against its competitors well into the twenty-first century, thanks to an energetic engineering team at GM, a creative aftermarket performance parts industry and enthusiastic owners such as yourself.

The 1998 Camaro again reset the standard of what a pony car should be, when it appeared with an aggressively styled new front fascia and a 305-horsepower all-aluminum V-8 under hood! *Chevrolet photo*

BASIC BUILD-UP GUILDELINES

CONTENTS

In stock, as-new form, the 1982–1998 Chevrolet Camaro (known by its GM platform designation as an "F-body") offers drivers an impressive performance envelope. Equipped with a number of hot V-8 or even V-6 engines, a Camaro can out-accelerate the majority of other cars on the road. Its responsive suspension system enables it to cut through twisting, turning roads or race tracks with alarming precision and poise. And its braking capabilities are, generally speaking, well-matched to its top-speed and acceleration abilities.

Unfortunately, like most production cars, the Camaro is somewhat of a "Jack of all trades, but a master of none." In other words: It does everything well, but it isn't truly exceptional at anything. But, of course, you already know this, and that's probably why you're reading this book now—you want to improve those aspects of the car that are most important to you.

Aftermarket performance parts plus race-proven modifications and tuning methods have given the Camaro owner an abundance of ways to enhance every aspect of his or her F-body, including not only its acceleration, handling, and braking, but its appearance, its ride comfort, its safety, its security, and even its convenience.

Modification Guidelines

There are at least two problems you need to be keenly aware of, as you embark on your project of modifying your Camaro. First, modifications are usually trade-offs; and, second, modifications should complement one another.

Though the subject is open for debate, it is generally understood and accepted that any modification you make typically improves one aspect of performance, but sacrifices another. Everything boils down to a trade-off. For example, if you increase engine power, the engine

Championship-winning race teams know you've got to pay attention to all the details when building a high-performance car, especially those that relate to safety!

likely burns more gasoline, plus the car probably will develop traction problems. So, even though your engine may make 50 more horsepower, your quarter-mile drag strip elapsed times may actually get slower, because the cars tires are likely spinning off the line. The same holds true for handling: If you tune the car to ride comfortably on the street, its on-track cornering ability will almost always hampered. Likewise, braking upgrades are double-edged swords: Softer compound brake pads often work better for the street, since they don't require much heat to grab the rotors well. If you try to race with them, you'll likely melt them, causing them to glaze over and

thus lengthen stopping distances. So, the modifications you make should balance these trade-offs. Fortunately, this often requires only that you think realistically about what you need your car to do for you: If it spends 90 percent of its time on the street, being used as a weekday commuter car, then don't set it up for the race track, or you won't like driving it day in and day out. And it might even be dangerous.

Parts Must Function in Harmony

Making sure that the parts you install or the modifications that you make all complement each other is a much harder problem to solve, simply because there are so

many options available to you. Unless you have access to sophisticated testing equipment and a nearly unlimited budget that would allow you to purchase every part and test it in conjunction with every other part, there are few ways of ensuring that the parts you install really do work better together than any other possible combination.

To better your odds of avoiding those sorts of problems—as well as to ensure safety—you should always take the time to preplan what upgrades you make, and in what order. Often, this starts with asking yourself a simple question of: "What do I want my Camaro to do when I'm done?"

Because no two Camaro drivers are quite the same, no two answers to that simple question can be quite the same. Some owners prefer a car that provides a stunning visual impact that really draws a crowd on cruise night. Others want cornering and braking perfection at all costs. Still others are concerned solely with straight-line drag race-style acceleration. And some may want bits of each, or some completely different outcome.

What *you* want, specifically, really doesn't matter. What does matter is how you achieve the desired results. Planning your upgrades beforehand can save you time and money, as well as maximize the performance of your Camaro.

Devising the Build-Up Plan

Surprisingly, though, the planning stage doesn't always have to be your burden. Aftermarket performance parts companies are always planning upgrades, and since most companies offer a catalog full of different parts, they generally spend a great deal of time thinking about—and testing—the manner in which their parts interact with each other. And while some enthusiasts scoff at the notion of getting a bunch of related parts from a single company, the truth of the matter is, by going the "single-vendor solution" route, you're pretty much assured that everything, will work well together. Whereas, if you buy Part A from Company A and Part B from Company B, either might work fine on their own, but combined they could

If you don't work safely, you might not live to enjoy the fruits of your labor. So, whenever you're working under your Camaro, make sure you use a sturdy jack on solid ground and that you support the car on suitable jackstands.

pose problems—from installation, to performance, to maintenance, longevity or repairs.

Parts Kit Options

Even better than just buying a bunch of parts from one vendor, though, is the notion of performance parts "kits" that contain a variety of parts that are specifically designed to work together, and may not even be offered separately. Often, these kits, such as Holley's "System-Max" line, are tested on engine and/or chassis dynamometers to verify that each part of the kit improves performance when they're all installed together. Put bluntly, buying "kits" takes all the guesswork out of parts selection: The companies have already tested the parts together and know that they complement each other.

Another big advantage to parts kits is that the companies can often give you an estimate of just how much of an improvement the kit rewards you with, versus the stock components. So you won't have to say, "Well, I think it added about 20 horsepower." Instead, you can say, "Yeah, the kit adds 35 horsepower!" With individual parts, it's harder for manufacturers to provide an accurate performance increase estimate, since they have no idea what effect the rest of the related parts have on the final performance.

A Build-Up with Safety In Mind

Whether your favorite professional driver competes in NASCAR, NHRA, or SCCA competition, you can bet one thing is for sure: He (or she) knows the value of a safe race car—they depend on them each and every time they take to the track.

But while those race machines may be purpose-built to withstand crashes at insane speeds, stock Camaros were engineered for significantly slower speeds—speeds that you're likely to exceed, due to the modifications you're planning.

Whenever you start talking about faster speeds, there are two given truths that you should keep in mind: Things happen much faster at high speeds, and things happen with more force at high speeds. For

these reasons, you need to be sure that your car reacts the instant you turn the steering wheel, shift a gear, hit the brakes, or jump on the gas. Any delays could cost you a race, or possibly your life.

Getting Off to A Good Start

Avoiding problems actually starts with making sure the car is in tip-top shape. You should make sure the front-end components are tight and well-greased. You need to make sure that your wheel bearings are in good condition and well-greased. And the "fan" belts must be in good condition. And your Camaro's vital

It's a good idea to chock the wheels, too, to prevent the car from rolling accidentally.

Shop Safety

Whether your ultimate goal is a killer Camaro for the street or an untouchable one for the track, every step of your build-up should have one thing in common: Safety.

As every mechanic and race car crafter knows, safety often starts with how and where you work on your cars. The ideal setting would be a large, well-lit shop with a concrete floor, proper fire extinguishers, a hose, and just about every tool imaginable, including air compressors, a vehicle lift system, a chassis dyno, and much, much more. But don't feel bad if your shop doesn't have half that stuff—few shops do, even the professional ones.

Still, some tools are absolutely necessary. For instance, we've all heard the horror stories of jacks that suddenly collapsed, crushing whoever was working under the car because they didn't have the car securely supported on jackstands. If you aren't careful, you could be the example others point to in the future, saying, "See what can happen if you're stupid." Besides, how much of an idiot do you think you would feel like if you were hospitalized for weeks, costing thousands of dollars, all because you were too cheap to get a $20 set of jackstands or some similar safety equipment. Of course, the same warning goes for safety-wear. Those tales of blindness caused by chemicals that splashed into someone's eyes, amputated fingers, crushed toes, and, yes, even plain, old bashed knuckles are all based in fact. No injury is fun, and preventing them requires the proper tools, so get them!

But the tools alone won't do the job. You've also got to work smartly,

you've got to have the know-how to use each tool in the proper manner. For jacks and jackstands, that means working on solid, level ground—and preferably with a partner around just in case. When working with torches or with flammable substances around sources of high heat—such as exhaust systems, brake rotors or drums, or even electrical wires—you should always have both a proper fire extinguisher and a hose close at hand.

And as far as tools go, take the extra moment and spend the extra few dollars to get the right tool for the job; screwdrivers are for turning screws, not prying components apart or together. Using the right tool makes the job go a lot easier, plus it minimizes your chance of injuring yourself or someone else—and it can make the difference between installing a new part or destroying it in the process.

Of course, it also helps to know how certain items come apart and go back together, and it's hard to beat a shop manual for that kind of insight. Likewise, it's worthwhile to pick up books that cover the specific area of the car you are working on, such as books on tuning and rebuilding fuel injection systems, or bodywork and paint guides. Reference books can be absolutely invaluable tools—maybe the most useful tool in your garage—so make sure you use them, and save yourself some hassles.

So, basically, "shop safety" boils down to common sense. And when you're working on cars, a little common sense can literally save your life. So, play it smart and work carefully.

A sturdy jack, like this three-ton unit from Sears, is a lot easier and safer to work with than narrow jacks that can easily tip over when extended. A non-slip jack pad, like this one from the Eastwood Company, not only helps prevent accidents but also keeps your Camaro's undercarriage looking like new.

fluids—its engine oil, coolant, brake fluid, transmission fluid, differential fluid, and even the fuel—must be in good shape. Obviously, if certain parts are going to be replaced shortly, you may wish to forego replacing them now. But never leave any questionable part on the car if it can, in any way, affect safety. This is especially true of your steering and braking systems, both of which are critical to your safety.

Once your car is "up to snuff," you can start planning your modifications. While you can think project-by-project, it's best to develop a comprehensive plan that strives to attain a specific set of goals. Don't just

think: "I want to go faster." Instead, think: "I want my trap speed to increase by 10 miles per hour" or "I want to cut five seconds off my lap times." Be specific, because that's the only way you can determine whether you're attaining your goals.

You also need to plan your entire car to function as an integrated system. If you're planning to increase engine output to 450 horsepower, the stock F-body transmission and rearend won't be up to the task of channeling that power to the ground. And what good is 450 horsepower if a weak link in the drivetrain keeps you from tapping all 450 horses?

Planning a Smart Upgrade Schedule

When you get down to working on your F-body, you are going to find that there are two ways of doing things: The right way, and the way everyone actually does them. Priority should be given to making the car structurally stronger, to improving the brake system and to other similar tasks that ensure your safety. You never want to take chances on things that affect safety equipment! Unfortunately, such systems are rarely glamorous. New subframe connectors might do wonders for your Camaro's structural rigidity, but it's hard to say just how much they improve your car's performance. So, while your head may know it's smarter to spend your first couple hundred bucks on subframe connectors, your heart really yearns for more of a thrill ride.

Keeping all that in mind, a smart "schedule" of upgrades would start with strengthening the chassis, then proceed to beefing up the brakes, next to working on refining the suspension and steering systems, then to fortifying the drivetrain, and finally, to building up the engine. Ancillary upgrades, such as body parts and interior make-overs that don't directly affect performance, can be done pretty much whenever they're desired, or as your finances allow.

Of course, for a variety of reasons—not the least of which boils down to your finances, available time, or even just your particular desires—you might be working in

Selecting a Car For Your Build-Up

If you haven't already got a Camaro, you owe it to yourself to consider just what you want in it for before you dash out and plunk down a wad of cash or sign your life away.

If you're planning on using your Camaro for serious competition use, the best models are the hardtop coupes, because T-tops and convertibles suffer from substantially weaker chassis structures. Any model works well on the street, so it becomes a matter of preference then. It should be noted that the 1992 Camaros have stronger structures thanks to adhesives applied at panel seams, in addition to welding. Fourth-generation cars utilize the same technology to produce a strong, rattle- and squeak-free structure under a variety of driving conditions.

In terms of engines, the LT1 and LT4 (which was installed in a handful of 1997 SLP Camaro SS models) provide awesome performance, plus they have an already generous supply of aftermarket power parts available to further increase output, reliability, or economy.

The LS1 engine is an outstanding engine and is sure to be embraced by the aftermarket, though at the time this book was published, upgrades for it were extremely limited.

The older LB9 and B2L TPI engines are excellent as well, though they are becoming dated quickly, and the more recent parts developments are being developed for the LT1/LT4 and LS1 engines first. If you're interested in or already own a third-generation Camaro, the B2L 350 is a better engine, only because of its larger displacement, which makes more power more easily

than the short-cubed 305 LB9 engine. But remember that the T5 transmission was only available with the LB9, because it couldn't handle the B2L's power in stock form, let alone with numerous performance modifications.

Chassis systems differed little within each of the two generations that this book covers (the 1982–1992 "third-generation" models and the 1993-and-newer "fourth-generation" Camaros), but there are subtle differences, especially for vehicles equipped with certain options. Of the third-generation cars, you should look at the 1988–1992 cars, because their front suspension allowed slightly more caster adjustment than early models. Cars with four-wheel disc brakes are preferable to those with rear drums, because brake upgrades are much more numerous for disc systems, plus they perform better under a wider variety of conditions. For third-generation cars, the ultimate factory brake system is the 1LE system, but beyond that the standard Z28 system provided adequate performance in stock form and can be upgraded easily. Fourth-generation cars received substantially better brakes in 1998 with massive, thick, vented rotors and heavy-duty calipers similar to those used on the 180-mile-per-hour fifth-generation Corvette, making them the clear choice brakes-wise.

Naturally, later models of each generation tend to have numerous minor improvements that make them preferable to earlier models, although most such improvements can be retrofitted onto the earlier models.

Measuring Build-Up Results

Some people can afford to just spend a fortune on performance parts, bolt them on, then hope they provide the expected performance boost. The rest of us have to choose our upgrades carefully to both fit our budgets and, hopefully, address our worst problems first. Then we need to squeeze every mile per hour we can out of that upgrade, to make sure we get the most for our money.

If you're lucky, you might randomly purchase the exact right parts at the exact right time, but the odds aren't in your favor. A more proven method is to assess your car's current performance carefully to determine its weak spots, then, after you take steps to correct the flaw, test your performance again to gauge your fix's effectiveness.

While there are many methods available to do just that. One of the most cost-effective and convenient ways is to use a performance computer, such as the Vericom VC2000.

The VC2000 uses an accelerometer to measure acceleration forces. It then computes distance and speed through time-based calculations. The result is a variety of data that you can use to help you assess your Camaro's current performance and to tune it for maximum performance.

A single run with the VC2000 provides an elapsed time (from an internal clock), speed, g-forces, and distance traveled. An optional engine RPM sensor makes it possible to then calculate rear wheel torque and horsepower, too. And you can make runs to a particular distance (a quarter-mile, for example); runs to a specific speed (0–60 miles per hour, for instance); and even runs that don't start until a user-defined speed or g-force (which is helpful for avoiding traction problems that might otherwise invalidate test data).

We used a Vericom VC2000 system whenever possible to assess the gains (or losses) we experienced from upgrades, and found the results to be highly accurate when compared to traditional data acquisition methods (dragstrip Chrondek timing, dynamometers, etc.). (However, you should not attempt to directly compare data from the VC2000 to data gained through other methods, because there are some variances due to the different

Performance computers like the Vericom VC2000 are excellent tools for measuring any improvements you make, plus they can be invaluable for determining what changes should be made.

methods of data acquisition.)

An additional option available on VC2000 systems adds the ability to capture data and export it to a desktop or laptop personal computer, giving you the ability to chart performance runs for a graphical representation of the run, which can make it a lot easier to see where your car's performance is stumbling during a run.

some completely different order. If you have an "order" at all.

But given that safety should be paramount, we've arranged this book to present the most cautious and safe progression of projects, in hopes that you are inspired to follow a similar sequence. Of course, each chapter has been produced in such a manner that each can simply be looked at as a stand-alone segment, which allows you to jump "willy nilly" from chapter to chapter, in whatever order you choose, without feeling lost.

But don't blame us if your new gazillion-horsepower engine pretzelizes your F-body's chassis because you chose to put off buying subframe connectors until later.

Protect Parts *Before* Installing Them

It's far easier and quicker to preserve a particular component before it deteriorates than it is to restore it after. Your first step of any project includes taking the few moments to properly preserve each component that you install. More than likely, preservation warrants several light coats of paint. Several companies offer a full line of restoration supplies, including numerous paints that mimic the look of real, bare, "as-cast." By painting and preserving parts now, they will stay in terrific shape for years to come.

If you could look through your Camaro's body panels, you would find its structure. Composed of subframe rails, the floorpan, the cowl and windshield frame, the rocker panel sections, and other parts, the structure is the foundation of your Camaro. For the most part, it's solely responsible for whether the car feels solid and stable. *Chevrolet photo*

CHAPTER THREE

CHASSIS STRUCTURE

All 1982–1998 Camaros feature a unibody chassis that utilizes the body as an integral component of the car's overall structure; they don't use a separate frame. Unibody construction is a mixed bag of goods. Perhaps the most favorable aspect of unibody construction is that it allows General Motors to construct Camaros inexpensively, which keeps the cars affordable. Unfortunately, unibody construction isn't generally considered to provide the strongest chassis structures; in the case of the Camaro, the chassis structure flexes, twists, and bends when stressed.

The most visible example of how a Camaro's structure distorts occurs when turning from a flat road surface into a driveway that has a sharp incline. As the inside front wheel first starts to climb the incline, you can literally see, feel, and hear the car twist.

Third-generation (1982–1992) cars have been widely criticized for their weak chassis structures that permit substantial body twist and flex. And while the fourth-generation (1993–1998) cars are significantly

stronger (thanks largely to stiffer rocker panel sections and a reinforced firewall/cowl area), they, too, can still benefit from a stronger structure.

Z28 models are more likely to suffer structure flex than are softer-sprung base coupe models, since the coupe's springs can absorb more of the suspension input, unlike the Z's springs, which transmit more of the force to the structure.

T-top models, with their massive cut-outs for the roof panels, are noticeably weaker than hardtop models, but convertibles are by far the worst Camaros, structurally. Lacking the rigidity of a metal roof and "B" pillars (the "posts" behind the side windows that support the roof), the existing structure has nowhere to "channel" the forces imposed by the suspension input. Chevrolet attempted to compensate for the loss of the roof by adding special "X" bracing beneath the cars. Though the fix did improve the convertible's structural integrity, the topless models were still significantly more flimsy than their fixed-roof counterparts.

Weak Structures Hinder Performance

Without a solid, stable chassis structure, the suspension system can't predictably control wheel movements. Suspension inputs such as bumps, weight transfer resulting from rapid acceleration or deceleration, or throwing the car into a corner may distort the chassis structure rather than compress the spring or shock. This is the result of the structure being weaker than the springs.

Because the structure bends, but eventually returns to its original shape (except in extreme cases when structure damage occurs), racers and suspension engineers often consider a car's chassis structure to be like a "fifth spring." As the structure bends, it stores potential energy, which is converted into kinetic energy when it springs back to its original shape.

A weak structure presents two immediate performance problems: First, it bends, so you don't really know how the suspension is going to end up behaving; second, it springs back from its bent shape at some point, again upsetting the suspension setup.

Suspension engineers (or you) can compensate for some structure flex, but such a suspension setup compromises performance. Instead of just tuning the suspension system to deal with a given input, you have to program the suspension to absorb more of the force from the input (which generally means softening the suspension to a point that performance is diminished). The other option is to build a suspension system that reacts not to the input itself, but to the structure's reaction to the input—sort of "second-guessing" what the suspension needs to do. But how can you reliably predict how the structure reacts to inputs, when the structure's reaction varies from one bump or corner to the next, as well as with the speed at which the input is encountered? And what about when the structure "springs" back to its original shape? Your suspension system has to be set up to deal with that event, too.

But your weak structural problems won't end there. In fact, that's just the beginning, because flexing structure occurs as part of a vicious

Here's a better look at the floorpan and subframe rails of a third-generation model's unibody assembly. Because the front and rear subframes aren't directly connected to each other, but instead rely upon the thin floorpan (as well as other areas of the body assembly) to tie them together, the overall assembly isn't rigid enough for serious high-performance use. Fourth-generation models are nearly identical in construction.

cycle. Each time the structure flexes, it becomes slightly weaker, so it's less able to resist flexing the next time it encounters a similar input. Before long, the structure has lost its rigidity and flexes, bends, and twists in response to even modest forces.

All this twisting also takes its toll on other portions of the car,

especially the doors and rear hatch. It's not uncommon for a Camaro with high miles to be so weak that its doors won't easily open, nor close without the end of the door literally being lifted to align the latch with the door striker (don't confuse this symptom of a weak structure with worn-out door hinges, however,

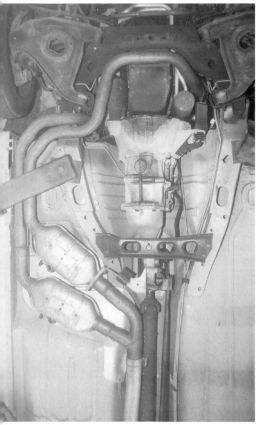

Here's a closer look at the front subframe rails of the third-generation structure. Note that they not only don't run full length back to mate with the rear rails, but they also have to rely upon only a small stamped-steel cross-member to tie each to the other to resist twisting forces. By comparison, the 1997 Corvette uses a thick steel plate roughly 30 inches long that's secured by 36 bolts to keep one side of the floorpan anchored to the other!

which are also common, but more easily and inexpensively fixed).

Even if your Camaro's doors don't noticeably droop while the car's on all fours, its structure may already be weakening. You can quickly check it by jacking either or both ends of the car and seeing how the doors operate then. Its likely they will be at least slightly harder to open and close, and don't be alarmed if that's the case with your car. Discovering only minimal flex is like catching the problem early, and at least you're aware of it so that you can then begin to take steps to strengthen the structure before things get too weak.

While the fourth-generation Camaro is *nearly* identical to the third-generation underneath, engineers beefed up the size of the front subframe rails considerably.

Strengthening the Structure

When it comes to strengthening 1982–1998 Camaros, there are essentially three weak spots and a number of available methods of correcting those deficiencies.

The production "F-body" chassis structure's three main weaknesses involve its front end, its floorpan, and the surface against which the steering box mounts. The front end twists when one side is loaded (i.e., stressed) more heavily than the other. Depending on the severity of the forces acting on the front end, the entire front end can actually bend upwards at the firewall/cowl area.

Contributing to the front end problems is the fact that the floorpan section between the front and rear frame rails can't sufficiently resist twisting and bending forces.

Finally, the steering box mounting surface flexes in response to the torque of the steering box, especially at lower speeds, and when the box is turned to the full-lock position, which causes the box to strain and pull against its mounts, possibly leading to cracks or weak spots.

Fortunately—or rather through good re-engineering—curing these ailments can be fairly straightforward and easy. If you plan to retain the car's stock structure, but want to enhance it, then you can simply

install braces in key locations to significantly stiffen the car's structure in those areas.

On the other hand, if you're planning on competing at a professional level in either SCCA road racing or drag racing competition, you need to invest in a tube chassis, if only because sanctioning bodies for Pro events require chassis structures to be built according to very specific rules for safety reasons. In this case, all you're really retaining of a Camaro is a handful of body panels—if that.

As with most changes you are likely considering, each chassis "upgrade" has its own particular advantages and disadvantages, and what's right for one person or situation isn't necessarily right for everyone nor every situation. In the end, you have to choose carefully and wisely.

Tube Frames

If you are interested in building a race-only machine that you hope to compete professionally with (as in, for money), and the rules allow it, you would be wise to look into a custom-built tube frame, similar to those used in SCCA Trans-Am or NASCAR Winston Cup racing. These aren't for street use, and they aren't cheap. They also mean that the rest of this book isn't going to be as applicable to your situation (except for the theories behind *how* you should select parts), since a custom-built frame isn't likely to retain much of the production suspension, brake, steering, exhaust, engine, drivetrain, or any other parts.

Still, if you're going racing in a class that permits (or requires) a tube chassis, they're about the strongest things going—and they're infinitely more safe than a production car, should you happen to smack into a wall or another car. Just ask any professional driver who's done it.

Bolt-On Chassis Braces

For street use, or in race classes that require a production chassis structure, a few carefully selected and properly installed structural braces are all you need to suitably fortify the production Camaro structure. But not all braces are created equally, so it pays to shop around and to know what makes one brace better than another.

Strut Tower Braces

When you turn a corner in any car, the vehicle's weight attempts to transfer to the outer front corner of the car, which helps to firmly plant that tire against the pavement. At the same time, the inner front corner of the car becomes unloaded. In an ideal setup, these dynamics would simply cause the vehicle to "gyrate" around a single point located somewhere near the middle of the car; it would roll toward the side, then pitch forward somewhat. The problem for Camaros is that when the weight transfers to the right front, that corner actually bends upwards, rather than just compressing the front spring. Thus, the front end actually pivots on several axis: It not only rotates toward the side, around a centerline down the long axis of the car, but the front end on that side bends upward at the base of the windshield, while the other side remains basically correct. A turn in the opposite direction would have the opposite effect.

The way to combat this front end flex is to tie the front end flex points together with a strut tower brace—a device constructed of one or more steel tubes that span from one side's strut tower to the other side's tower. This greatly enhances the ability for the front end to resist twisting forces, because the heavily loaded side can "push" against the unloaded side, dividing the total force of the load between the two sides.

Of course, merely spanning from one side to the other really only cures part of the problem. While cornering, a tower-to-tower brace lessens the tendency of the outside wheel's corner to bend upward, since the force resulting from the weight transfer to the outside corner would also have to move the inside corner at the same time. That's a significant improvement—and a noticeable one. Unfortunately, simple tower-to-tower braces do little to prevent bending at the cowl (windshield base).

A better solution is a brace that not only ties the strut towers to each other, but also ties the braces into the firewall/cowl area. By triangulating the front end, movement of the right front corner is suppressed by not only the tower-to-tower cross brace, but by the tower-to-cowl brace. And since the opposite (left-hand) strut tower is also tied to the cowl with a brace, that tower is better able to withstand flexing forces, too. In this way, only the most severe forces (accidents) cause the front end to flex.

It's also important to consider the construction of the brace itself. Braces that feature any kind of pivot points, such as Heim joints, or use bolts to connect two or more pieces together, are less capable of preventing movement than one-piece braces.

Subframe Connectors

The Camaro's floorpan is weak when subjected to torsional (twisting) or bending (front-to-rear) forces because of the basic limitations of the unibody chassis structure design. Without sturdy steel frame rails, unibody cars rely heavily on thin sheet metal floorpans, rocker panels, and even the car's roof to prevent bending and twisting. But these portions of the car aren't capable of fully counteracting the forces encountered when cornering, accelerating, or decelerating hard—especially in convertible and T-top models, or models with sunroofs or moonroofs.

To understand how the chassis twists and flexes, it's sometimes helpful to picture a plastic ice-cube tray: When grasping each end of the tray, it's easy to rotate your hands in opposite directions (one toward you, one away) and cause the tray to twist. You can also bend each end toward

Another problem for third- and fourth-generation Camaros is a structurally weak front end, which this strut tower brace can cure. Many strut tower braces consist of only a single bar running from one shock/strut tower to the other. This third-generation Camaro brace from HP Motorsports not only ties the towers together but also secures them to the cowl, which results in a far stronger front structure that is much more resistant to bending and twisting forces. *HP Motorsports photo*

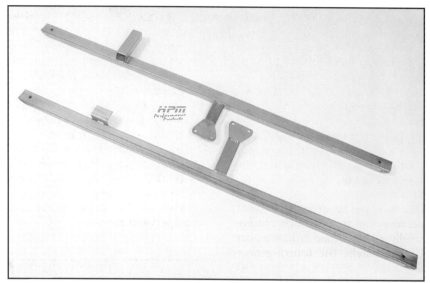

One of the most important structural enhancements you can make is to install subframe connectors, like these from HP Motorsports. These pieces tie the front and rear subframe rails together, plus anchor to the floorpan for further stiffening. *HP Motorsports photo*

RK Sport's "Double Diamond" subframe connectors feature a rather unique design that secures them to several points, including the front and rear subframes, the floorpan, and the rocker sections, resulting in a tremendously stronger structure. *RK Sport photo*

the other, causing the middle to sag or rise. That's exactly how your Camaro reacts to loads placed on the chassis structure when you drive.

By installing steel frame sections that tie the right front subframe to the right rear subframe, and the left front to the left rear, the chassis is much more resistant to bending and twisting. Some subframe connectors go even further and actually connect each side, often with an X-style brace, for even greater resistance to twisting forces.

But not all subframe connectors are created equally. In fact, subframe connector designs vary widely. The most basic design differences center on whether the connectors bolt in or need to be welded in place.

Bolt-in subframe connectors are easier for the do-it-yourselfer to install at home. However, they are inferior to weld-in connectors because of the surface area against which they connect. To help understand this, you have to think about how subframe connectors physically connect to the subframe sections, and specifically how much metal they come in contact with. If the subframe rails have 3/8-inch holes drilled through them through which the subframe connector bolts must pass, then the circumference of each hole is just 1.1775 inches. Since the

bolt passes through both sides of the subframe rail, the total surface area (the area the bolt contacts or connects with) is 2.355 inches per bolt, or 4.71 inches per subframe rail end, since most bolt-in subframe connectors use two bolts per end. In other words, all the bending and twisting forces get focused and channeled to less than five inches of metal. Naturally, those forces eventually pound out the holes, making it egg- or oval-shaped, which both decreases the contact area significantly, and allows for free play, which negates the point of having subframe connectors installed in the first place.

Welding, on the other hand, allows you to lay a bead along a full 10 to 12 inches per subframe rail. Obviously, even just 10 inches is far more capable of withstanding a given load than is an area less than half that size. Plus, assuming the weld was done properly, it won't loosen, so the subframe connectors continue to do their job for the life of the car, with no slack, no slop, and no problems. Of course, most bolt-in connectors can be strengthened by welding, too.

Another differentiation point for subframe connectors is the material from which they're made. Most bars are made of square steel tubing. Square steel tubing is reasonably strong, but that's not why companies use it. Square steel tubing is less expensive, and it's easy to work with, which minimizes manufacturing costs. And while it's better to have subframe connectors made of square steel tubing than no subframe connectors at all, you need only look as far as your favorite race car—drag car, stock car, Trans-Am car, or Indy Car—to see that professional chassis builders rely on seamless round steel tubing. The reason is simple: It's stronger. Whereas square steel tubing has distinct "corners" that can act as stress risers (points at which stress forces converge), round tubes have no such points, so they're less likely to bend under stress.

Lastly is the issue of quality design work: How well the subframe connectors fit, and how much modification work is required for installation. High-quality subframe connectors shouldn't require modifications to either the connectors or the vehicle, yet should provide ample clearance between themselves and any vehicle components. Given that General Motors has had to change equipment installed on Camaros over the years, however, it's virtually impossible for a single connector to fit all the vehicles of a given design (such as all 1982–92 "third-generation" F-bodies). Still, many companies opt to do just that, requiring the customer to modify his or her vehicle to accommodate their subframe connector. It's an economics issue, in reality—it costs the company more money to create different subframe connectors for cars equipped with different equipment—but customers see it as a quality issue: The part they buy doesn't fit without modifications. The best companies have different designs to accommodate the different vehicle configurations, and their customers are more pleased because installation goes more smoothly.

Steering Box Brace

A lesser-known chassis weakness of third-generation Camaros is one that could actually have quite serious consequences: Flexing of the steering box mounting surface, which could lead to erratic steering response, or even outright steering failure.

The problem stems from high forces transmitted from the steering box to the chassis, especially under low-speed cornering, such as when maneuvering around a shopping mall parking lot. Fat performance tires present a great deal of resistance at low speeds, which imparts considerable stress into the steering system, and ultimately attempts to rip the steering box from its mounting surface—especially during "full-lock" turns, where steering torque is greatest. Over time, these forces weaken the chassis surface around the steering box and can result in torn metal.

Whether the chassis is weakened or torn at the steering box, the result is the same—steering actions are delayed while the chassis flexes, leading to unresponsive and erratic steering. Ironically, though the damage stems from low-speed steering, the resulting problem is far more serious at high speeds than at low ones.

It is possible to repair the damaged area, though the best solution is to avoid the problem in the first place by installing a brace that reinforces the steering box mounting area. Cars that have already suffered damage can have the area repaired by either grafting in replacement metal, or by reinforcing the weakened metal. In either case, the area should be reinforced with a suitable brace afterward to prevent future damage.

Incidentally, fourth-generation cars don't need a steering box brace, because the steering rack mounts solidly to the front cross-member. Unfortunately, the fourth-generation cars are more susceptible to other steering-related problems, which are covered in more detail in chapter 5, "Suspension and Steering".

Roll Cages

Depending on your perspective, roll cages are either structural aids or interior modifications. In actuality, they're both. From a structural standpoint, they tie various points of the chassis together, preventing bending and twisting, much the same as subframe connectors do. From an interior standpoint, roll cages have a certain aesthetic attraction—they show your competitors that you're serious about racing—but they also tend to impede ingress and egress to and from the car's interior (especially the back seat), thanks to all the tubes.

The effectiveness of a roll cage varies with its particular design, primarily with the number of attachment points. The simplest roll cage designs are so-called "four-point" cages, because they have a hoop that installs between the front and rear seats and spans from side-to-side (one attachment "point" on each side). Two braces, one on each side, run from the hoop rearward and connect to the chassis in the rear storage compartment.

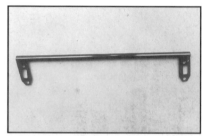

Third-generation Camaros suffer from a weak steering box mounting surface. When subjected to high stress, especially from low-speed, full-lock turns such as you might encounter during parking lot maneuvers, the steering box can literally rip apart the sheet metal to which it is attached. This simple bolt-in brace from Global West Suspension significantly strengthens the steering box area.

Here, the steering brace is installed between the front subframe rails and the antiroll bar, and blends in almost invisibly.

Depending on what class you race in or how fast your car is, you may be required to install a roll cage, such as this one from RK Sport. Roll cages provide somewhat similar functions as subframe connectors, except that the roll cage mounts only to the body structure in several places. Note the removable cross bar, which makes it possible to use the back seat, as well as recline the front seats. *RK Sport photo*

Better roll cages have six attachment points—they add two forward braces, one per side, that connect the vertical hoop tubing to the floorpan near the front of the doors. Some cages include a single crossbrace between the hoop's vertical supports, or even an "X" brace between the vertical supports to resist twisting.

From there you start getting into competition-only cages with 8, 10, or even more attachment points that can leave your interior with tubes running this way and that way, severely limiting interior movement.

For street cars, a four-point hoop, without crossbracing is the most convenient, since it still permits use of the back seat. Six-point cages offer greater strength, but do limit access to the rear seats, and make entry into even the front seats difficult. Still, if you only plan on using the front seats and don't mind the inconvenience, they're the way to go. Anything more than a six-point cage is usually too restrictive (and overkill) for a street car, but is definitely worthwhile for a car that spends a good deal of time on the race track at high speeds.

Roll cages come in bolt-in and weld-in varieties, and, for the same

reasons as subframe connectors, weld-in units are preferable, since they provide a stronger overall structure. Although bolt-in cages are a significant improvement over no cage at all, the cage can be removed if you find it too intrusive. Some race classes also specify one type of cage or the other—how many tubes, and whether it's a bolt-in or weld-in type—so be sure to consult the appropriate rule books if you're planning on doing any racing.

Beyond the structural and safety functions, some roll bars provide additional features. For instance, some feature attachment points for five-point safety belts, and others even have mounts for video cameras (multiple mounts, in some cases) in case you want to videotape your racing to either see what you're doing right or wrong, or just for fun.

Finding the Right Chassis Setup

Given that there are only a handful of chassis upgrades for street-bound Camaros, there's really no reason—beyond your personal finances or racing class limitations—that you can't equip yours with all the

appropriate upgrades for your particular chosen field of performance.

But that raises the question of just what's appropriate for the different performance venues—high-performance street driving, drag racing, autocrossing, or road racing. While each can benefit from one or more of the various structural upgrades, few require all of them. And don't forget that certain racing classes, notably stock-type classes, prohibit the use of some equipment. Always check the rules before you make any additions.

High-Performance Street Driving

Realistically, third- and especially fourth-generation Camaro coupes are more than adequately designed for street use—even so-called high-performance street use. Convertibles and T-top cars, however, are another matter; their structures are noticeably weaker and can greatly benefit from subframe connectors. For coupes, the connectors provide benefits, though you're not likely to feel a dramatic improvement.

Likewise, strut tower braces aren't really necessary, either. And certainly roll cages are overkill. The one device that has specific merit, but virtually no noticeable benefits in terms of performance, is the steering box mounting surface reinforcement brace. In short, if you're looking for a good "bang for the buck" upgrade, you should spend your money on other aspects of the car, and come back to the structural upgrades later, when further power, handling, or braking upgrades would benefit from them.

Drag Racing

Whether you make only occasional forays to the drag strip, or it's actually become your home away from home, you've probably already learned that the limitations of your F-car aren't related to structure as much as they are to power and traction.

While it's still important for the vehicle to be reasonably sturdy, structurally, it's not absolutely vital that it be rock-solid—at least, not at the speeds you're likely to run. Again, as with street use, your car will be lengths ahead by focusing on the powertrain and suspension.

One notable exception, however, is a roll cage. Installing a roll cage strengthens the chassis somewhat, especially a cage with six or more chassis attachment points, but the real reason we recommend one is the safety factor—it should protect you if you ever flip your car on its roof.

Autocrossing

The funny thing about autocrossing is that despite running the courses at speeds slower than encountered in most school zones, it is one of the most demanding forms of motorsports for a car, Camaros included. All that weaving in and out of the cones on an autocross course puts a Camaro's chassis structure to the test—one your Camaro is likely to fail, unless you've made some changes.

The most immediate upgrade worth making, if rules permit it, is to install a strut tower brace. Even on cars with stock suspension setups, you'll experience better, more precise handling because the chassis won't be acting like a fifth spring, winding up on the entry into a corner then—*boing!*—snapping back suddenly, resulting in erratic, hard-to-predict handling. Instead, you are rewarded with more consistent runs.

While you're fiddling around at the front of the car, you should spend the 10 minutes required to install a steering box mounting brace, because autocross conditions—relatively low speeds with frequent, demanding turns—produce the severe forces that can weaken and damage the steering box mounting surface. Not only is it likely that the steering box mounting surface flexes, but given the almost constant steering motions, the odds are much higher that flexing will lead to a crack and utter steering failure.

Following the strut tower and steering box mounting braces, owners of third-generation (1982–1992) cars should find their cars respond well to the addition of subframe connectors. If you like the idea of adding a roll cage, that is probably best left until last.

Fourth-generation (1993–up) cars, on the other hand, can do the opposite—add the roll cage, then the subframe connectors—because of the fourth-generation Camaro's modestly but measurably stiffer chassis structure.

Road Racing

Unlike the other activities you can use your Camaro for, road racing presents constant challenges because of the sustained high speeds at which you must compete. Since everything happens quicker when you're going faster, it's more important than ever that the car respond instantly to your commands, and handle precisely, if you're going to avoid trouble. And if you do get into trouble, you want a sturdy car around you, to protect you.

Rules vary from year to year, class to class, and sanctioning body to sanctioning body, but most allow the types of typical add-ons we've discussed. And while you can always do the upgrades one at a time, it's best to just jump right in and add everything at once, including the strut tower brace, the subframe connectors, and the roll cage (preferably a six-point or better). The one item that's not as critical is the steering box mounting brace for 1982–1992 cars, given that most road racing steering actions take place at high speeds, which minimizes the loads placed on the box. But as the steering box brace is an inexpensive add-on, and does improve steering response, there's really no point in skipping it.

Brakes can never be good enough, at least in the mind of many racers. While the stock Camaro binders are reasonably effective, there are numerous upgrades available that greatly improve their performance, which can help you improve your performance out on the track.

BRAKES

If there's one aspect of your car that just isn't worth *any* shortcuts, it's the brake system. Brakes are your safety net—if you haven't got brakes, you don't have a chance of stopping after getting into trouble. And whether you're able to "bail yourself out" may depend on what brake equipment you've upgraded to.

It shouldn't surprise you that brake system components aren't all created equally. Standard factory-installed brake systems on most third-and fourth-generation Camaros were designed to match the performance of the car's other production-stock systems (i.e., the unmodified engine, unaltered suspension, etc.). The brakes are designed to provide more than sufficient stopping force for the speeds encountered with only stock hardware. Mind you, the factory-installed brakes won't necessarily keep you from crashing—they're designed to be safe anywhere within and slightly beyond the car's production-stock performance capabilities.

While GM designs its brake systems to have a certain margin of safety that allows them to handle some power and handling improvements over the stock equipment, if you have changed more than only the most basic parts, it's quite possible you have exceeded that margin.

For example, if your engine modifications have primarily been limited to minor "bolt-ons" like a new adjustable fuel pressure regulator, a free-flowing air filter, and other minor modifications, you haven't really boosted power by much, so the factory brakes should still provide ample stopping power. But if you've added headers, a camshaft, and maybe an induction system with larger intake ports or runners—or serious items like nitrous oxide, a supercharger, or a turbo—then you need to carefully consider whether your stock brakes are overworked.

Likewise, if you've modified the suspension so that it allows you to carry more speed around a track, demands on your brakes increase, since they work harder to slow the car down for the entry into a corner, or to avoid crashing into some obstacle . . . like the slower cars of your competitors.

But looking at your car's performance hardware alone can't be your only basis for brake system upgrades. Much more importantly, you need to consider the environment in which the car operates and the conditions it experiences. High-performance street drivers won't need anywhere near the modifications that a high-speed road racer requires.

Of course, even before you begin to try to figure out your braking needs, you need to have a good understanding of braking system

fundamentals, so that you can pin-point your car's weak points and determine what you need to do to improve them.

Brake System Basics

Brake systems exist for one purpose only: to slow down a vehicle. Despite this single, seemingly simple goal, and the rather simple components involved in a typical brake system, understanding them baffles and mystifies many people. Fortunately, brake systems don't have to be a mental challenge. If you keep a few simple principles in mind, and think things through carefully, you should be able to design a high-performance braking system for your Camaro.

The first thing to keep in mind about brake systems is that they're really just energy converters. How do we know this? Well, the laws of physics tell us that energy can neither be lost nor gained, only converted. In car terms, a moving car has a whole bunch of kinetic energy (we usually think of it as momentum). We need to get rid of that kinetic energy, and to do that we know that energy has to be converted to something else. One of the easiest things to convert it to is heat (thermal energy), which brakes do by generating friction. So, your brakes literally "burn off" speed. The more friction your brakes can create, the more heat they can create. But consider yourself warned: More heat is only a good thing if your brake system and its many components can properly withstand that heat.

Second, you need to realize that the quickest way to stop a car (in all but a few circumstances) is to have each wheel reach and maintain its maximum traction threshold, because that's the point at which its tire is developing maximum friction against the road surface. Interestingly enough, this doesn't mean you want to "lock up" the wheels, because when the wheels are locked up, the tire actually slips along atop debris ripped from both the tire and the road surface. This is the very same reason that stopping on snow is so difficult—your tires have only minimal traction, since there's nothing "fixed" against which to

Standard Camaro brakes were dramatically beefed-up for the 1998 models. Most components are the same design as the outstanding 1997 Corvette braking hardware. Note the large rotor and large aluminum caliper that provide the stopping forces. Owners of 1993–1996 models can upgrade to this impressive system, or, like owners of 1982–1992 cars, they can upgrade their brakes with high-performance aftermarket components.

From the side, the 1998 equipment hardly looks different from the older parts.

"push." There are a few exceptions to this "don't skid" rule, such as trying to stop in deep sand. But in almost every situation, your Camaro stops quicker and far more controllably if the wheels do not lock up.

Wheel lock-up is related to the brake fluid pressure within the system. Too much pressure causes the pads to seize the rotor, stopping it and the wheel from spinning altogether, so the tire skids. This condition is especially prevalent on the rear wheels, since weight transfers from the rear of the car to the front during braking maneuvers, thus unloading or making the back end very light. With minimal weight to keep the rear tires pressed against the road surface, it takes very little pressure to make them lock up and skid. General Motors installs a brake fluid pressure regulator

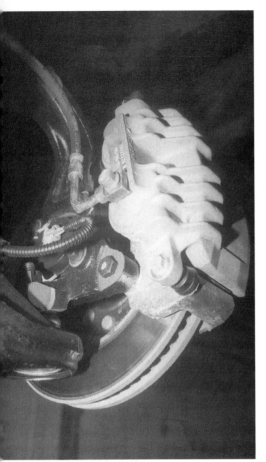

ABS systems utilize wheel speed sensors to monitor revolutions of the wheel, when it senses one wheel is stopped, but the others are continuing to rotate, the ABS computer concludes that wheel is skidding, so it causes the ABS control unit to reduce brake pressure to that wheel, allowing it to spin.

between the master cylinder and the calipers to reduce brake pressure to the rear calipers, in hopes of preventing them from locking-up the wheels, which could cause a driver to lose control and crash.

Anti-lock brakes, which are standard on the 1993 and newer fourth-generation Camaros, also rely on pressure reduction to prevent skidding, though their controls are more sophisticated. (See "How Anti-Lock Brakes Work.")

How Brakes Work

Your Camaro's brake system is actually remarkably simple, and when everything is kept in proper condition, it's rock-solid reliable and performs well. Like most brake systems since the middle of the twentieth century, Camaro brakes depend upon hydraulic pressure to force the brake pads against the rotor.

Everything starts—or, rather, stops—when you step on the brake pedal. The pedal arm pushes a plunger into the master cylinder, creating pressure in the system by pushing against the brake fluid in the brake lines. Since fluids don't compress, pushing on the fluid has the same effect as pushing on a steel rod. If you push one end, the other end moves the same amount of fluid at the other end of the brake lines, and pushes against the back of the caliper pistons. This forces them and the pads against the rotor, creating friction that slows the car. A drum brake system operates the same way, but instead of a caliper, you have a wheel cylinder that spreads the brakes shoes until they contact the inner surface of the brake drum.

That's a somewhat simplified braking system. In the real world, several factors influence how effectively pressure is transmitted from your foot to the rotors. First of all, there's the pressure regulator, mentioned earlier, which reduces pressure to the rear calipers, to minimize the chance that they'll cause the rear wheels to lock up.

You also have to realize that any air in the brake fluid *is* compressible, which means that pushing on the fluid at one end of a brake line does not necessarily move the fluid at the other end of the line an equal amount. This is often why you may experience a "soft" or "spongy" brake pedal. And old brake fluid always has some air in it.

There's also the fact that rubber flexible brake hoses can expand when subjected to brake pressure. So, even though the fluid within the hoses doesn't compress, the volume of the hose increases, allowing more fluid to enter the hose than is forced to exit it.

There is also a minute amount of caliper "deflection" or deformation that occurs as the result of pressure within the caliper that normally tries to force the pistons out of their bores, but since the pads prevent that, the pressure "backs up" and causes the caliper body to deflect away from the pistons. This deformation causes a delay in braking action.

And, most notably in high-performance and racing use, brake pads actually give off a gas as they wear against the rotor, which can actually cause the pad to "lift" off the rotor surface and glide on a cushion of the gases, thereby reducing friction.

Finally, there could be any number of problems with the system caused by damaged components, such as warped rotors, pinched brake lines, leaking hoses, or other problems. Any of these conditions obviously results in diminished brake system performance.

Fixing Warped Rotors

Does your brake pedal pulsate when you step on it to apply the brakes? If so, one or more of your brake rotors are warped (or a drum is out-of-round). There are basically two ways to fix this problem: the Right Way, and the Wrong Way.

The Wrong Way is what most people—including almost every brake shop in the country—do: "turning" or grinding the rotors, until they're once again true. The problem with the Wrong Way is that turning the rotors removes material from the rotor, and that means there's less material to absorb and dissipate heat. And given that 99 times out of 100, the rotors warped because they overheated in the first place, your now-thinner rotors are far more likely to warp again—and soon. On top of that, by turning your rotors you've increased the chances of a catastrophic rotor failure, since the thin rotor could potentially overheat severely enough to crack and separate.

The Right Way to cure the warped rotor problem, is simple: Replace them. Sure it's expensive, but when driving your car at breakneck speeds, you want to be able to stop. Besides, you're going to have to replace the rotors sooner or later. You're only preventing the inevitable and saving yourself a "turning fee" in the process.

The Friction Factor in Brake Performance

It's the rubbing of the pad against the rotor (or the shoes against the drum) that creates the friction that generates heat. And as we covered at the start of this chapter, the more heat the brakes can generate, the more speed (energy) can be converted into heat, so the more stopping power you'll have.

Naturally, several factors influence how much friction your brake system can generate. Brake fluid pressure, piston size, rotor size, and the composition and size of the pad's friction material all have a role in how effectively the calipers can latch onto the rotors.

Under normal driving conditions, light effort on the brake pedal creates only low pressure within the brake lines, causing the caliper pistons to only lightly push the pads against the rotors. Higher braking effort, such as when you jump on the brake pedal during a panic stop, creates high brake pressure that pushes the pad much more firmly against the rotor, creating more friction.

Caliper Pistons

The size (diameter) of the pistons inside the calipers also has a lot to do with the clamping force of the brakes. Smaller pistons produce less force, at a given pressure, than do larger pistons. So, if your calipers have relatively large pistons, more friction is generated than calipers equipped with smaller pistons. Larger pistons are also better able to cope with heat than smaller pistons, though they pay a penalty in terms of weight. Stainless steel is the usual choice for pistons used in performance calipers, though some race-only systems may use lighter, more exotic metals.

Brake Rotors

Rotor size is vitally important to performance brake systems. All other things being equal (which, of course, they never really are), a larger rotor makes for a better braking system, because it provides more "swept area"—the amount of area that passes between the brake pads during one complete revolution of the rotor. Swept area is important because even

though heat is needed in a brake system, too much heat can literally cause the surface of the pads to melt, which minimizes friction. Bigger rotors prevent this because they have more area over which friction-generated heat can dissipate; plus, a given point on the large rotor's face spends more time in cool air, out from under the pad, than a similar point on a small rotor. Thus, large rotors are much more capable of shedding heat, than are small rotors.

Brake Pad Material

But dollar-for-dollar, the most important part of the friction equation is the brake pad itself, specifically the size and composition of its friction material. To help you think of how pads function, it helps to compare them to tires. The size of the pad matters for the same reason that a wider tire provides more cornering traction; just like a wider tire puts more rubber on the road, a larger pad puts more material in contact with the rotor when the brakes are activated, so more friction can be generated. That's fairly straight forward. Size also matters because a larger pad has more surface area over which to dissipate heat. In other words, if a specific amount of heat is generated during braking, a small pad has to focus all that heat into a concentrated area, whereas a larger pad can spread that heat out across a larger area.

Pad compound plays a role the same way tire compound is important to traction. Just as a soft-compound tire lets the tire conform to—and grab onto—every nook and cranny in a road surface (compared to a hard compound, which grabs only the top of the road surface), a soft-compound brake pad is able to generate considerable friction. Unfortunately, soft-compound brake pads, like those found on most generic passenger cars, generate so much friction and heat so quickly that they overheat easily, greatly reducing their ability to grab the rotor. Still, soft-compound brake pads are fine if you do only slow, around-town, stop-and-go driving.

Harder-compound brake pads aren't as able to grab the rotor, initially, but they do a better job of dealing with heat. Quite simply, they don't absorb as much, and since they

The real difference can be clearly seen here: The 1998 rotor is substantially thicker, with larger vanes, which help the rotor dissipate heat exceptionally well.

don't grab quite as well, they aren't generating as much heat in the first place. In fact, hard racing-type brake pads really aren't necessarily the hot setup for street driving, since they actually don't begin to work well until they are thoroughly heated up. Street driving rarely involves braking situations that would build anywhere near the required heat for the race-type pads to warm up. Hard-compound pads also wear longer than soft-compound pads, since they don't shred themselves in the process of generating friction.

Beyond heat management, pad compound material makes a difference for the simple fact that some materials have a higher friction coefficient than others. For example, rubber builds more friction than plastic. In the case of pads, the friction material is made up of several different compounds, which often include some metals (semi- and full-metallic pads, for example), along with other elements. More recently, carbon-metallic pads have proven to be the hot setup for race cars, because they not only generate a lot of friction, but they're able to withstand and dissipate heat exceptionally well.

Brake Parts Must Work in Harmony

Combining all these different factors to develop the "perfect" braking system, isn't easy. In fact, it's nearly impossible, because braking requirements change, based on a number of factors, including the track design, the weather, driving style, the vehicle's setup, vehicle weight, and more.

Racers compensate for this by customizing their car's brake system to suit the particular demands of the day. For instance, despite the extreme speeds NASCAR stock car racers achieve at superspeedways like the 2.5-mile Daytona International Speedway or the 2.66-mile Talladega Speedway, the drivers rarely need to use the brakes because of the steep, high-banked turns. In fact, unless they're avoiding an accident, the most use the brakes get during a race are when the drivers are coming in for pit stops. With those braking requirements in mind, teams tend to try to minimize weight, so they typically run smaller calipers, fewer cooling ducts, smaller and thinner rotors, and softer pad compounds.

However, as drivers of SCCA Trans-Am Camaros know, road racing is an entirely different matter. They use their brakes heavily and frequently, so they use large, wide rotor; large calipers with multiple large pistons; large, hard-compound pads; and several cooling air ducts per rotor and caliper—sometimes as many as four hoses per wheel: two to cool the caliper and two to cool the rotor.

Brake System Components

A brake system is made up of many separate parts. Understanding how each one functions, how it interacts with any other parts, and any factors that may influence its operation is crucial if you hope to determine the best combination for your needs.

Brake Fluid

Brake fluid is the blood of the brake system, and without it, you simply don't have brakes. The fluid itself is what transmits your foot action to the calipers or wheel cylinders and causes them to clamp down on the rotor or expand against the drum. And short of finding a puddle of brake fluid in the driveway, few people give much thought to their brake fluid. But they—and you—should.

Perhaps the reason we spend so little time thinking about brake fluid is that it does its job so well that we rarely have a reason to think about it. Or so it would seem. The truth of the matter, though, is that from the moment you tear open the safety seal on a bottle of brake fluid, that fluid becomes contaminated with moisture, which affects how well brake fluid can do its job.

The degree to which moisture in the brake system affects its operation depends somewhat on which type of fluid you have. DOT-3 and DOT-4

Proper Brake Bias

Cars need to have different brake line pressures for the front brakes than for the rear brakes, because the rear end of the car becomes very light while braking, as weight transfers to the front of the car. If front and rear hydraulic pressures were equal, the rear brakes would lock up at almost the same instant that you step on the brakes. The factory handles this problem by installing a brake proportioning (or bias) valve between the master cylinder and the calipers. Factory proportioning valves split the brake system into two circuits: the front brakes and the rear brakes. The rear brake circuit reduces brake pressure to prevent lock-up under most circumstances. As you make changes to your brake system—different pad compounds, larger rotors, even wider, stickier tires—friction properties of the brakes and/or wheels and tires are affected. Thus, front/rear brake bias is affected, and thus the line pressures may need to be increased or, more than likely, reduced. That's where adjustable proportioning valves come into play.

An adjustable brake proportioning valve has a knob that can be turned to modulate the line pressure to a specific wheel or wheels, depending on how it is plumbed into the brake system. Professional race cars might use an adjustable proportioning valve for each wheel so that a driver can optimize breaking pressures to minimize the chances of lock-up. Such a setup is a valuable tool for tuning a car to a particular track. On the street, a single adjustable valve in place of the factory valve (thus creating a front channel and a rear channel) is usually more than

sufficient, and significantly cuts down on the headaches of tuning the system.

The ideal brake proportioning would result in all of the wheels locking up at the same time. Obviously, however, given how weight shifts on a vehicle in turns, versus straight-line deceleration, pressures need to be different for each wheel under the different circumstances.

Since all 1993-and-newer Camaros and Firebirds feature anti-lock braking systems, you might question whether an adjustable proportioning valve is necessary. After all, ABS is supposed to prevent wheel lock-up, right? Well, technically, no. ABS actually responds to wheel lock-up, then instantaneously reduces pressure to that wheel, then reapplies pressure, and repeats the process until all the wheels are decelerating at approximately the same rate. The imperative part of this to keep in mind is that your wheels *do* lock up with ABS; ABS just limits them to locking for a very brief period of time. Because of this, it's important that each wheel decelerate at nearly the same rate without ABS, to minimize intrusion of the anti-lock system, which greatly affects both stopping distance and feedback to the driver of just what each wheel is doing while braking.

Now, having said all that, it's only fair to point out that the trouble and expense of installing an adjustable proportioning valve on cars equipped with ABS just isn't worth it for street use because the anti-lock system delivers virtually the same benefits, with no hassle whatsoever. Still, for racing, adjustable proportioning valves are valuable tuning tools.

The adjustable proportioning valve can be mounted inside the passenger compartment, within easy reach of the driver during a race. The driver can turn the adjusting knob to increase or decrease pressure to a specific wheel or set of wheels, depending on how the brake system is configured.

fluids can absorb moisture, mixing it with the brake fluid, whereas silicone-based DOT-5 fluid can not absorb moisture, which leads it to form droplets of water. Now, as we covered earlier, fluids—even water—are not compressible, so the problem with water in the lines isn't actually the water itself, but rather what happens to the water when it is subjected to heat.

When the brakes are applied, the pads contact the rotor, generating heat. Most of that heat is absorbed by the rotor, then dissipated into the air. But some of that heat is absorbed by the pads, then transferred to the caliper pistons, and then to the fluid. Brake fluid is designed to take a lot of heat before it begins to boil—Department of Transportation regulations require it to have a minimum wet (saturated with water) boiling point of 284 degrees Fahrenheit. The problem with water in the lines, though, is that water boils at 212 degrees. And when water boils, it gives off steam, which is mostly just air. And air is very compressible! So, with steam (air) in the lines, when you step on the brake pedal, some of that pedal travel is being used up merely compressing the air, rather than forcing the pads against the rotors. Since DOT-5 fluid essentially lets water "puddle up" within the lines, it is much less tolerant of heat, because the water boils easier. This is why DOT-5 fluid should never be used for racing, where your brakes are quite likely to get hot enough to cause the water in the lines to boil.

Steam in the lines creates a second, more minor problem in your brake system. As the water in the lines is converted to steam, the steam actually expands, which does move some fluid within the system, and can actually force the pistons against the pads, causing the pads to drag on the rotor. Aside from potentially slowing the vehicle, the constant contact of the pads against the rotor prevents the brake system from properly cooling, which could lead to parts failure.

DOT-3 and DOT-4 fluids disperse the water and actually mix it with the brake fluid, which lowers the brake fluid's boiling point (never below the DOT's mandated minimum of 284 degrees, however), but raises the water's boiling point. You might want to think of it as you do coolant/antifreeze, which does much the same thing for the water in your cooling system (lowers its freezing point and raises its boiling point).

You should also be aware that while DOT-3 and DOT-4 fluids can be readily mixed together in the same brake system, DOT-5 fluid cannot be mixed with either of them. In the end, there's really very little reason to want to run DOT-5 fluid.

The effects of moisture in the brake lines are obviously something you should try to avoid. It would be only natural to conclude that you can prevent moisture from entering the system by ensuring the system was "airtight." However, the harsh reality of the situation is that you can't prevent moisture from getting into the system. Sure, you need to make sure all the hoses and lines are in good condition, without any leaks, and that all the hose connections and piston seals are sealing the system properly, but even if the system were completely closed up and impenetrable, moisture would still collect in the lines because of condensation that would form as the brake lines cooled down after being warm or hot from use.

Because you can't keep moisture out of the system, you need to make sure that you change your brake fluid frequently. Road racers should change their fluid before every race, because their brakes are a vital piece of safety equipment, given the high speeds of road racing. Autocrossers work their brakes pretty hard, so they should plan on changing their fluid at least once a month. Drag racers and street drivers, even casual commuters, should plan on changing their brake fluid at least once a year, preferably more often.

If you keep your brake fluid changed regularly, it remains mostly moisture-free. Without moisture in the system, the boiling point of the fluid remains high—as high as 570-degrees-Fahrenheit "dry" boiling point for some high-performance fluids. This means that you can work your brakes a lot harder without having to fear the pedal getting soft or that you won't have brakes when you most need them.

So, by changing your fluid frequently, your brakes have a higher tolerance for heat and a lower risk of failure, both of which add up to a possibly significant advantage over competitors who don't prepare their brakes so fastidiously. But, of course, the only real reason you should need to maintain your brake system properly is the simple fact that one day your life might depend on it.

It's a good idea to inspect your old pads periodically to determine whether they are wearing evenly. Uneven wear typically indicates the calipers are sticking on their guide pins, so you may need to clean and deburr the guide pins and possibly smear a dab of anti-seize compound on them during reassembly.

Pads and Shoes

Years ago, brake pads were brake pads, and shoes were shoes. There wasn't much thought given to their design, their construction, or their function, so long as they worked. Now, of course, we know better.

The most dramatic advance we've seen in brake pads centers on the actual friction material that comes in contact with the rotor when the brakes are applied. New compounds manage heat better, yet provide more friction, too. And with a wide variety of pad materials available, there's no excuse for not optimizing your brakes for your particular driving environment—including each specific track or course on which you may compete.

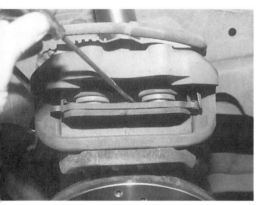

Then, you can turn your attention to replacing the brake pads. Start by removing the old pads from caliper. Ours were easily pried out, but other caliper designs require different methods of removal.

Our stock pads had a paper-like backing material to keep them quiet, but our new pads did not. In the interest of sanity, we carefully removed the old backing material and placed it on the new backing plates.

The science of choosing brake system compounds is basically the inverse of how you choose tire compounds. While harder tire compounds provide better tire life on the street, they slip too much on the track to be of much use. Soft-compound racing tires, on the other hand, would be chewed up and wasted in too few miles of street driving to be worth the expense. Brake compounds are just the opposite . . . sort of.

In street applications, the brakes aren't used too frequently, and when they are, they're generally used to gradually slow the car from a relatively slow speed. This means that the brake systems don't build much heat, and whatever heat they do build generally has plenty of time to dissipate before the brakes are used again. In such cases, you need pads that work well when cold, so that they grab the rotor (or drum) hard on the first stop of the morning.

Naturally, racing situations are different, though. In those cases, the brakes will be used hard, which means they'll quickly build lots of heat, and they'll be used frequently, which gives them little time to cool off. Under these circumstances, you need pad compounds that won't "glaze over" due to the tremendous heat. Harder compounds provide that heat resistance, but they do so with a penalty: They provide much less friction when cold. But as the pads heat up, they soften somewhat, allowing them to provide more friction than would hot soft-compound pads subjected to the same conditions.

The problem with soft-compound "street" pads is that, when subjected to racing-style conditions, the heat causes them to partially melt, resulting in a "glaze" on their friction surface, which prevents them from grabbing at all. In a way, soft-compound brake pads behave a lot like sticks of butter: When they're cold, they stay together well, but when they get hot, they basically melt and slip and slide across the face of the rotor, providing greatly diminished friction.

Race pads have the opposite problem. They're so hard that at low temperatures, they won't grab. And unless you use your brakes a lot, they won't build enough heat to work well on the street.

For street/high-performance use, the ideal pad is somewhere in between street pads and race pads. They'll be made of a compound that provides reasonable grip when cold, so that you're not a danger to others when you're making your morning commute. But they'll also withstand heat reasonably well, so that they don't glaze over during occasional "spirited" dashes through your favorite set of back roads.

In the old days, street pads were generally made of only "organic" compounds. High-performance pads were usually of a "semi-metallic" construction, and racing-style pads were "full-metallic" pads. Today, however, the choices are much less clear.

Today, pads with different percentages of metallic "substrates" provide different stopping characteristics and yet would all be considered "semi-metallic" pads. And more and more production street cars are leaving the factory with semi-metallic pads, due to increasing vehicle weights and decreasing brake component sizes, which both result in increased system heat.

For performance and racing situations, braking specialty shops offer several levels of pad compounds, giving you the ability to choose the right compound for your mix of street and track driving. One of the most recent developments has been the use of "carbon-metallic" pads, which offer much less susceptibility to heat with much-improved friction, a seemingly "best of both worlds" solution.

Beyond just the pad material, brake pad designs also influence braking performance. Standard, low-performance brake pads generally feature a friction material riveted or bonded (glued) to a steel backing plate. In the case of bonded pads, the friction material is often just one large slab of material. And while it may seem that the larger surface area of such a pad would be a good thing, the problem isn't entirely unlike that of using treadless racing tires on the street: They actually slip more because of debris. When the pads contact the rotors, pad material is worn from the pad, and metal is even worn from the rotor. You are more familiar with this debris as brake dust that shows up on your wheels, turning them a dingy grayish color. While most of that dust lands on your wheels or drifts off on the air rushing by, some of that dust gets in between the pad and the rotor, and with flat pads, there's no way to get rid of the dust, so the pad skids along on top of the dust, minimizing its contact with the rotor, and thus minimizing braking system performance.

A further complication arises due to the fact that brake pads give off gases as they heat up. A quick analogy here is the old air-hockey game that floats a puck above the table surface on a cushion of air. Or you might choose to think of a Hovercraft, which also floats on air. The gases released from the pads push them away from the rotor surface, and friction is minimized.

Performance brake pads are usually riveted or bonded to the backing plates, but they often feature some form of cleaning groove through which brake dust and gases can be ushered away, thus allowing the pad to fully contact the rotor and develop much more friction.

In extreme cases, often for racing purposes only, pads may actually feature special heat-blocking backing plates to minimize heat transfer to the caliper, and thus to the brake fluid.

Braided Hoses versus Rubber

Because Camaros have suspension systems that allow the wheels to move up and down, the brakes can't have hard brake lines run all the way to the calipers from the master cylinder. So, a flexible hose is used to connect the caliper to the hard chassis-mounted brake lines. On stock production vehicles, special high-pressure rubber hoses are used, primarily because they are cost-effective and they work well for 95 percent of Camaro buyers. However, for high-performance use, rubber hoses are too weak, so you need a stronger hose, which means switching to Teflon-lined braided brake hose.

Braided brake hoses add a margin of safety, and they improve brake feel and action. The safety upgrades come thanks to the increased strength of braided lines: They're not as likely to expand under hard use (high pressures in the line) as are

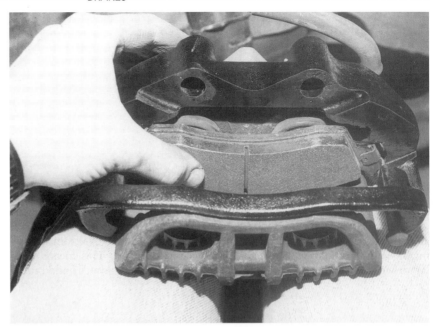

Installing the Stillen Metal Matrix pads into the cleaned caliper was literally a snap. Our only hitch was that we had to enlarge the knock-outs in the pad ears to provide sufficient clearance for the guide pins.

How Anti-lock Brakes Work

With standard (non-ABS) systems, the only factors that influence brake pressure are your foot and the fact that the system is "closed," preventing all the fluid from gushing out whenever you step on the brake. So, brake pressure is basically directly proportional to how hard you step on the pedal.

ABS systems, however, are a bit more complicated. Between the master cylinder and the individual calipers (or wheel cylinders on drum brake-equipped cars) is the "black box" that performs the magic of rapidly decreasing and reapplying pressure through the use of a small piston within a cylinder. An electric motor drives a piston within the cylinder, changing the volume of the particular channel to which the cylinder is connected. As the volume of the channel increases, line pressure decreases; as the volume decreases, pressure increases. If this sounds familiar, it should; it's the same as stepping on the brake pedal then releasing it. Only the ABS system can do it about 100 times a second.

What triggers all this pressure modulation activity are the wheel speed sensors. Input data from a sensor on each front wheel, plus one sensor for the two rear wheels, are compared. If the data match (some wheel-to-wheel variance is expected, to account for cornering), then the system doesn't engage. But when it senses one wheel's speed drops to or near zero, while the other's are all speeding along, it knows that one wheel is skidding, so the ABS pressure modulation hardware is activated until the stopped wheel's speed again corresponds to those of the other wheels.

Interestingly enough, the Camaro's acceleration slip regulation traction control system works basically opposite of the ABS system: ASR first reads the expected vehicle speed from the transmission's speed sensor, then it checks whether the front wheels are spinning, whether the brakes are applied, and what the throttle activity is (both position and any change). If the computer reads that the potential speed (at the transmission tailshaft) is high, but the front wheel speed indicates the vehicle is moving slower, and the brakes aren't applied, the ASR system causes the rear brakes to apply, engine output to be reduced by altering timing and fuel delivery, and throttle pressure to be reduced by the activation of a "throttle relaxer" motor, all of which end up reducing rear wheel speed until the parameters match up.

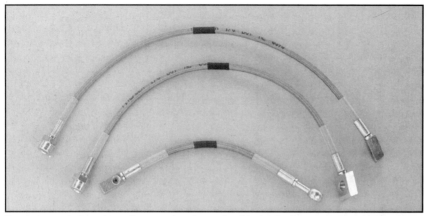

Because car's have suspension, they have flexible brake hoses to channel brake fluid to the calipers. But stock rubber brake hoses can expand under pressure, which adversely affects operation of the calipers. Braided steel brake hoses, like those available from Russell or Earl's, don't stretch like rubber hoses. Braided lines maintain consistent fluid pressure on the caliper greatly improving the feel and performance of your brakes.

flexible, stock-type rubber hoses. That's especially important in racing situations, where high line pressures mercilessly stress brake hoses, stop after stop.

The improved feel and more predictable braking action come as the result of the stronger construction of braided lines. There's no pressure loss or braking delay from hoses expanding when pressure is applied. With rubber hoses, when you apply a great deal of pressure to the brake pedal, such as during a panic stop, pressure in the brake lines causes the flexible rubber hoses to expand like a balloon, absorbing some of the pressure. Actually, the hose's volume increases when the hose expands, which requires more pedal travel to pump more fluid into the hose to fill it. When the hoses reach their maximum amount of expansion, one of two things happens: The hose breaks, or brake pressure builds as the hoses resist further expansion, thus stabilizing pressure. If the hose fails, there's not much you can do except aim for something cheap, and preferably soft.

Hopefully the hose won't break, though. Assuming they don't fail, however, the hoses attempt to contract back to their original size. As they contract, it creates additional pressure in the system, forcing some fluid back toward the master cylinder, but some also goes toward the caliper pistons, causing the pads to press more firmly against the rotor, possibly enough to cause the brakes to lock up. At low speeds, this might not prove to be much of a problem, but at high racing speeds, this can be deadly, because your brakes won't grab when you expect them to, because of the expansion, then may suddenly lock up when the hoses try to contract.

You might think that the ABS-equipped fourth-generation (1993+) cars wouldn't suffer the same skidding consequences as third-generation (1982–1992) cars, and they won't. But that doesn't mean expanding rubber brake hoses won't cause problems. Remember that ABS is a reactive system—it waits for a wheel to lock up before engaging. So, when the hose has expanded and begins to contract back to its normal size, the wheel may still lock up, however briefly. Then the ABS kicks in to reduce fluid pressure to that wheel, so braking efficiency is artificially lowered beneath the maximum friction threshold. And ABS does nothing to alleviate the problem of a spongy pedal resulting from the initial expansion of the brake hoses, so the end result is that braking action is still highly unpredictable, though the chance of crashing is much lower.

If you agree that braided hoses make sense for stock-type applications, then it probably won't surprise you that they make even more sense for cars that have modified brakes or wheel and tire combinations.

The simplest example of how modifications can place higher demands on your brake hoses is to consider what happens when you install wider and/or stickier tires. Wider tires increase the tire's contact patch with the road surface, while stickier, soft-compound race tires provide better grip by maximizing

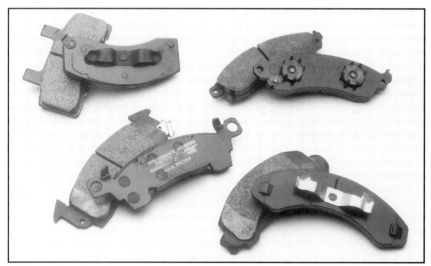

Perhaps the most important component of your brakes are the brake pads, since they're the devices responsible for actually grabbing the rotor to slow the car down. While you might think you would want soft brake pads to improve braking, as you do with tires, the opposite is actually true. Soft pads generate too much heat too quickly and will melt, essentially leaving you without any brakes. Currently, Performance Friction's line of carbon metallic pads provide the ultimate in stopping power.

the tire's contact with the road surface by conforming better to each nook and cranny, as well as through higher-friction compounds. In either case, the maximum traction threshold for the tire is raised, requiring more effort to make it skid. That means your brakes are able to make use of additional brake pressure (you can stand on the pedal harder) before the brakes lock up. That additional pressure may be enough to cause stock hoses to fail, especially if they're older hoses or have some minute defect.

Expansion of the brake hoses works both ways, too. Just as the hoses expand when you increase pressure by stepping on the brake pedal, they can also expand (minutely) when the rotor may instantaneously lock up during hard braking maneuvers. For example, if a wheel is slipping on a wet or sandy surface, the driver gets "feedback" in the form of pulses resulting from brake pressure surges that are generated by the tire gripping and slipping when it goes from a good, dry traction surface to a wet or sandy one. That feedback can tell the driver what to do in terms of steering, throttle, and braking actions to avoid spinning out. But with a system that uses rubber hoses, those pressure surges would be masked, or at least dampened, when the hoses expand, so the driver is effectively "flying blind," and thus much more likely to have an accident.

Lastly, braided lines are much less likely to puncture if they come in contact with some sort of debris, such as pieces of body sheet metal torn from a racing competitor's car during a race, or even from a piece of broken exhaust pipe or wayward retread carcass on the street.

It should be noted that braided brake hoses, because they don't stretch like rubber hoses, tend to fail spectacularly when they fail. Rather than develop a tiny hole when subjected to pressure, as a rubber hose typically would, they just blow out. For this reason, few braided brake hoses are DOT-approved for street use, though there are street-legal hoses available for both third- and fourth-generation Camaros, depending on the specific brake system configuration.

This is a comparison of a stock 1LE solid-faced rotor to a cross-drilled Stillen replacement unit. Though the pair look virtually identical, the cross-drilled rotors dissipate heat quicker, preventing brake fade under severe conditions. Whenever you upgrade components, make sure you compare parts to verify that they are, indeed, interchangeable.

Most rotors available are slotted or finned. Both the stock 1LE rotor (left) and the replacement cross-drilled Stillen rotors had the air cooling fins.

Rotors

Solid vs. vented. Solid-faced vs. slotted (grooved) vs. cross-drilled. One-piece or multipiece. Iron or aluminum. Large diameter or small. There are lots of options when it comes to choosing brake rotors. And, next to the pads, they are considered to be the second most important part of the brake system. Some would even say they're *the* most important part of the brake system, since they are subjected to the most heat.

When thinking about brake rotors, it's often helpful to think about bicycle hand brakes. Since the brake rotor on most bicycles is the wheel's rim, it's easy to understand how the brake caliper slows the wheel's rotation: The caliper is directly grabbing the wheel.

In a car, the rotors and wheels are separate parts, but they are connected by the hub and wheel studs, to which both the rotor and the wheel mount. Since the brake rotor and the wheel

Straight cross-drilling results in a significant number of stress risers along the sharp edges of the holes. Stillen avoids this problem by chamfering the holes, except those between the rotor faces.

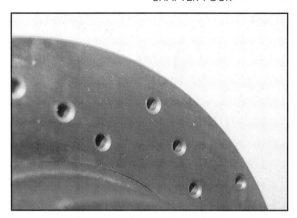

Whenever you change rotors, you should always install new wheel bearings. When packing bearings, it's preferable to use synthetic grease, such as Mobil 1, because it withstands heat and prevents wear better than conventional grease. The packed inner bearing gets set into our Stillen rotor. It's a good idea to change bearings at least every two years or so, or more often if you race.

You'll also need to install new bearing seals, to prevent contaminants from destroying the new bearing.

are effectively connected together, by slowing the rotor, you are slowing the hub and thus the wheel.

In addition to serving as the means to slow the wheel, a rotor also serves as a giant heat sink. It absorbs the bulk of the heat that results when the pad contacts the rotor. Then it tries to dissipate that heat into the air that flows through and around the rotor. It's this second duty, heat management, that must be carefully considered when you try to select the right rotors for your Camaro. If your rotors don't shed enough heat, they could fracture and come apart.

The first thing to consider when selecting rotors is whether they are solid or vented rotors. Solid rotors are simple and inexpensive; they're merely large round discs. Vented rotors, however, are more like two discs that sandwich an array of fins that radiate from the center of the rotor out toward its edge. Between the fins are air gaps, through which air can circulate. The whole point of vented rotors is that they increase surface area, which allows them to better shed heat.

Not all vented rotors are the same, though. Normal vented rotors have straight fins, or vanes, while high-performance or racing vented rotors may feature curved fins that add even more surface area, but must be run in a specific rotational direction to be effective. The bulk of the rotors available for Camaros, though, are of the straight-fin, vented variety.

Vented rotors are considered highly preferable to solid rotors, because solid rotors simply aren't able to dissipate heat well enough. Nearly every professional motorsports team relies on vented brake rotors, because under grueling racing conditions, solid rotors would become so hot that the tiniest flaw would likely become a crack, which would ultimately break, causing the rotor to come apart. Even if the solid rotor doesn't break up, it would likely remain so hot that the pads would begin to melt, thereby hampering the brake's ability to slow the car.

In recent years, engineers have attempted to find ways to improve the effectiveness of vented rotors.

Applying the same sort of logic that makes vented rotors superior to solid ones, engineers and race teams have tried "cross-drilling" the rotors—drilling small holes through the rotor's surfaces to provide even more surface area to aid cooling. Cross-drilled rotors also provide the gases and brake dust emitted from the brake pads with a means of escaping from under the pad, plus they lighten the rotor. While cross-drilling has proven effective in cooling the rotors and thus allowing the brakes to operate at a cooler temperature for better friction and increased pad life, cross-drilling isn't without its drawbacks. Specifically, cross-drilled rotors are more prone to cracking than are solid-faced vented rotors.

The reason cross-drilled rotors crack is because the edges of the drilled holes have sharp edges that act as "stress risers," or convergence points for stresses within the rotors. Some companies alleviate this problem to some degree by chamfering the edges of the drilled holes on the rotor faces. However, since the holes also have sharp edges in the vented midsection of the rotors where chamfering bits can't be used, there's no way to eliminate all the stress risers. Realistically, chamfering the exposed edges of the drilled holes cuts in half a rotor's chances of failing.

Slotted rotors were designed in response to the problem encountered with cross-drilled rotors. Rather than drill completely through the face of the rotor, which creates the stress risers in the unreachable vented midsection of the rotor, slotted rotors have grooves machined into their surfaces that extend only partway through the rotor's surface. The grooves can also be chamfered, leaving no sharp edges, thus no stress-risers from which cracks can easily develop. The grooves still provide additional surface area for cooling purposes, and the gases and brake dust still have a way to escape from under the pad.

Proponents of slotted, or grooved, rotors point out that machined grooves in the friction surfaces of the rotors provide the added surface area of cross-drilling, without the inherent crack-prone stress risers. The machined grooves don't penetrate

The caliper controls the movements of the pads. Good calipers, like this PBR unit that's part of the third-generation Camaro's 1LE hardware and is also used in many aftermarket performance brake system kits, features smooth, reliable braking action under all conditions—hot or cold, wet or dry.

through to the interior of the rotor, where they can't be machined.

However, slotted rotors aren't without potential faults, either. Because the rotors are so thin at the grooves, heat tends to weaken the metal there, which can potentially lead to cracking.

But despite what appears to be a theoretical benefit, you only need to look as far as your favorite professional NASCAR, SCCA, IRL, or CART racing team's brake rotors to find out the best setup. Nearly all of them use solid-faced vented rotors, foregoing the possibility of additional cooling and cleaning capacity for the extra strength and durability that the solid-faced rotors enjoy over their modified counterparts.

Note, however, that the vented rotors used by pro motorsports teams have wide vent gaps between the inside and outside rotor faces, which allow for wider fins with more surface area for better cooling. Street cars don't often have the same luxury, since wider rotors require wider calipers (or thinner pads, which means shorter pad life). While cross-drilled or slotted rotors may not be

the hot full-race setup, they do provide added cooling, cleaning, and anti-gassing advantages for street and street-stock racing uses, where they often experience much less heat than do the brakes on pro race cars.

Another thing that's instantly apparent with racing rotors is their size. They're large, to provide more "swept area." Large rotors have more material that can absorb heat. Large-diameter rotors also have more surface area than a small rotor, plus the outer edge of the caliper travels through more air during one complete revolution than does the outer edge of a small-diameter rotor. If you picture a specific point on the face of a rotor near the rotor's outer edge, that point travels around in a circle as the rotor spins. The larger the rotor, the further that point can be from the rotor's centerpoint; thus, the larger the circumference of the circular path the point follows, the longer the point has to cool down before it is subjected to heat and friction created by the brake pad again. Since the rotor has longer to dissipate heat, it dissipates more heat than a smaller diameter rotor, so it

One way you can usually prevent sticking or binding calipers is to keep your brakes clean. Dust and debris can accumulate and prevent the calipers from smoothly sliding on their guide pins.

runs cooler. And if the rotor runs cooler, it can absorb more heat during each pass than a small rotor. As the rotor absorbs more heat, less heat is transferred to the pad, caliper, and fluid, so the entire brake system runs cooler.

Drawing again from our bike wheel analogy, we can easily understand how a larger rotor (like the bike's wheel) provides more leverage, to make braking easier. Despite the miniscule bicycle brake pads, the brakes provide exceptional stopping force. A larger automotive brake rotor provides the same mechanical advantage.

Rotor designs also differ in terms of how many components they consist of, as well as what material they are made of.

Production rotors are one-piece machined, cast-iron units. As such, they're both heavier and more time-consuming to change when they need replacement. Multipiece rotors typically consist of a "hat" that gets fastened to the hub, then a separate "bolt-on" rotor disc. The hats are often made of lighter-weight aluminum, while the rotor disc is generally still machined, cast iron because of its ability to handle high temperatures. Aluminum rotors aren't widely available and should be avoided because it is relatively easy to heat them to their melting point!

Calipers

Calipers do the job of actually clamping the brake pads against the rotor. The clamping action is provided by pressure that enters the caliper through the brake line (or hose, in the front), which presses against the back of the caliper's piston, forcing it out of its bore. As the piston move out of its bore, it pushes the brake pad against the surface of the rotor. The more pressure on the back of the piston, the more force the pad contacts the rotor with.

Third- and fourth-generation Camaros use calipers with only a single piston, located on the in-board side of the caliper. On such systems, the caliper is designed to "float" back and forth (inside to outside) on guide pins. As the fluid pressure pushes the inner pad against the rotor, the pad can't move any farther, so the pressure backs up and pushes the in-board side of the caliper away from the rotor, sliding along the guide pins. As the in-board side of the caliper slides away from the caliper (toward the center of the vehicle), the out-board side of the caliper is pulled against the rotor. Since there's a pad mounted to the inside of the out-board side of the caliper, both pads are now in contact with the rotor, providing even clamping force as long as the guide pins allow the caliper to slide freely.

More sophisticated systems, such as those intended for serious road racing, may feature multiple pistons, with one or more in each side of the caliper. If a caliper features pistons on each side of the caliper, the caliper is typically rigidly mounted on a bracket.

Most production Camaro brake calipers are made of cast iron, resulting in strong calipers that are also inexpensive to manufacture. However, cast iron is also heavy, and it does not dissipate heat well. The weight is detrimental to suspension action, because it increases unsprung weight (weight that does not move up or down, relative to the ground), which slows suspension reaction to road inputs.

When Chevy engineers introduced the secretive RPO 1LE road racing package for Camaros in 1989, the system featured finned, cast-aluminum PBR brake calipers, which were similar to those used on the Corvette at the time. The aluminum was both lighter and better at shedding heat, and the fins further aided heat dissipation. Over the next several years, the 1LE's rear calipers were used on the SEO (Special Equipment Option) B4C "Police Package" Camaros, as well as Camaros equipped with RPO R6P and four-wheel disc brakes. The 1998 Camaro is the first Camaro to feature four-wheel, aluminum brake calipers as standard equipment. These calipers are the same design as those used on the 1997 Corvette, though without the "CORVETTE" lettering and black finish.

Race-only aftermarket calipers are typically made of either cast or machined billet aluminum.

While weight of the caliper does ultimately affect its action, the biggest determining factor is the size of the piston or pistons that the brake fluid acts upon. A larger piston produces more friction in response to a given pressure than a smaller piston subjected to the same pressure, and larger pistons do a better job of dissipating heat, since they have more surface area. So, larger pistons are generally preferable.

Caliper pistons are typically made of either aluminum (stock) or stainless steel. Again, stainless steel is better able to handle high temperatures, plus it does not corrode as easily as aluminum, nor does it expand and contract as much as aluminum when subjected to temperature extremes, which allows for better seal designs and better piston action.

If your brakes are subjected to extreme heat, such as might result from a short, turn-filled race course that features long runs, your calipers may need auxiliary shielding from the heat. Many aftermarket calipers have additional heat shields available as an option, or for installation later.

It's also worth noting that if you upgrade your brakes with larger rotors and different calipers, you have to ensure adequate clearance between the caliper and the vehicle's wheel. If clearance is less than roughly one half inch, you should consider larger wheels in order to realize the full performance potential of your new brake system.

Drum Brakes

We haven't spent much time discussing the rear drum brakes that were standard equipment on third- and fourth-generation Camaros for many, many years. These systems are quite reliable and actually perform quite well both on the street and on most types of race tracks. However, because drum brakes trap a good deal of heat inside the drum, and given their complexity, drum brakes are not good choices for road racing cars.

There are far fewer performance upgrade parts for drum brakes than for disc brakes. In fact, the only items you're likely to be able to locate are replacement brake shoes with different compound friction materials. General Motors had used iron-lined aluminum brake drums on its B- and G-body cars (Caprice/Impala and Monte Carlo) during the 1980s, and it's possible that these drums could be adapted to the Camaro, though those drums are difficult to find and hardly worth the trouble, given their minimal performance improvements.

Instead, stock cast-iron drums can be modified to improve brake performance. The face of the drums (the wheel mounting surface) can be drilled outside of the hub's contact area to improve cooling. Likewise, the drum brake backing plates can be drilled for the same reason. There are a few warnings about drilling

In the case of drum brakes, few upgrades are available. Performance brake shoes can make a difference, but for true high-performance use, you should consider upgrading to rear disc brakes.

Left
Racers typically utilize multiple adjustable proportioning valves that they can use to tune braking performance to suit the demands of a particular track or track conditions.

drums and backing plates that deserve mention. First, anytime you remove material from the drums or backing plates, you are weakening those components, possibly enough to cause failure. If you don't know what you're doing, these are modifications that are best left to professionals. Second, the holes subject the brakes to more water and debris, which may affect braking action in unforeseeable ways, and complete brake failure is possible. So, think twice about making such modifications. A third option for dealing with drum brakes is simply replacing them with either factory or aftermarket disc

brakes. Switching to discs may just be an expensive exercise that gives you little added performance in return, since the rear brakes actually contribute so little to braking under most conditions.

Adjustable Brake Proportioning Valves

Production Camaros feature a brake pressure "proportioning valve" that reduces brake pressure to the rear brakes by introducing a restriction to the flow of the brake fluid. The goal is to prevent the rear wheels from locking up and possibly causing an uncontrollable spin. The problem is

that the stock proportioning valve can't take into account any changes in the vehicle's setup or condition.

This can be important, because if you change your Camaro's rear tires to wider or stickier tires, the rear brakes require more pressure to induce lock-up than they would with only the stock tires. But with a factory proportioning valve, the pressure can't be increased, so braking efficiency is compromised. The tires won't reach their maximum traction threshold; thus, maximum braking force won't be achieved.

Racers correct for this limitation and allow themselves to tune the car's brake system based on the demands of the specific track by installing one or more adjustable brake pressure proportioning valves.

While the factory proportioning valve only reduces pressure to the pair of rear wheels, racers—like those in the SCCA Trans-Am series—may have a separate adjustable proportioning valve for each wheel, which would allow them to reduce brake pressure to any wheel that may tend to lock-up, based on any number of conditions related to suspension setup, track configuration, driver style, and more.

On the street, a single adjustable proportioning valve (to affect only the rear brakes) is all that is necessary or recommended. The range of driving conditions is so broad that further adjustment (for side-to-side or corner-to-corner balance, for example) actually limits braking action more than it improves it.

Cooling Ducts

As we've discussed many times, a good brake system has to manage heat well. In order to convert a lot of momentum to heat, the brake hardware needs to be able to generate a lot of heat. But unless the brakes shed heat well, they'll quickly reach their maximum temperature and won't be able to absorb any additional heat, plus they'll be more likely to "fade" as certain parts overheat.

Fortunately, a quick, effective, and inexpensive means of improving your brake system's heat-dissipation abilities is to install brake cooling ducts. Road racers have long known about the advantages

The master cylinder, with the brake fluid reservoir atop it and the proportioning valve below, generates pressure in the brake lines in response to input from the brake pedal. The proportioning valve reduces pressure to the rear wheels (in production applications) in order to prevent the rear wheels from locking up before the fronts, which could cause the car to skid out of control.

of running hoses from the front of the car toward the brake components; often you can run hoses from either the grille or beneath the chin spoiler with good results. The Trans-Am Camaros of the 1960s even used brake cooling ducts, and the same simple technology works equally well today. General Motors engineers found that by incorporating 3-inch brake cooling ducts into the 1997 Corvette, pad life was increased by more than 33 percent, and braking performance was measurably improved during racing-type use.

By ducting cool air through a hose aimed at the center (hub) of the brake rotor, you assure that the brake rotor has a continual supply of cool air that can absorb heat from the entire rotor. By directing that cool air into the hub of the rotor, the heat is ushered outward, away from the rotor and hub, preventing wheel bearing problems.

A second duct, if desired, can be plumbed to flow air across the brake caliper, to help keep the pads, caliper, and fluid cooler.

Because brake cooling ducts really only carry cool air, they can be made of nearly anything. One of the simplest materials for do-it-yourselfers to get their hands on is expandable heating duct tubing, such as that available from home improvement stores.

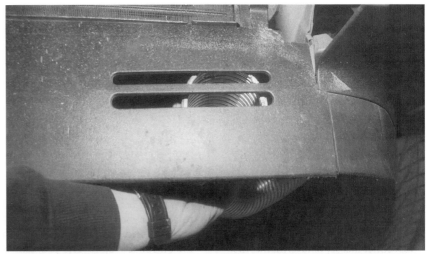

If you race your Camaro regularly, you may wish to consider installing brake cooling ducts, which you can make from flexible heating ductwork available from most home supply stores. In the front, you can have the ducts draw air from behind the air dam (cutting slits in the dam as needed to allow air to flow through to the ducts). Ducts for the back brakes can simply scoop air from under the car or from beneath the rocker panels.

A 3-inch hose can easily be run from the front fascia or air dam of the Camaro, up under the front end and aimed at the center of the rotors, and secured to the chassis with simple "zip" ties or wire.

Note that brake cooling ducts are generally overkill for the street and drag racing, because in those situations, brake systems rarely reach high enough temperatures for long enough periods of time to require cooling.

If you choose to install brake duct hoses, however, bear in mind that you may need to revise your brake pad selection, because of the reduction in the operating temperature of your brakes.

Line Locks

Drag racers know the value of a good line lock system, which keeps the front brakes locked but allows the rear wheels to spin freely for a good

Suspension and Tire Influences on Your Brakes

We've all heard the old "leg bone's connected to the hip bone" song that describes how your body's skeletal system is interconnected. Well, your Camaro's chassis systems—the brakes, suspension, steering, powertrain, etc.—are all inextricably linked to one another. Any change to one system causes the other systems to change, too.

When it comes to your brake system, the system that affects its performance the most is the suspension, and specifically your tires. If you upgrade your tires to wider or stickier performance tires, you're increasing their friction with the ground, which means your brakes need higher brake fluid line pressure to induce lock-up. You gain the extra pressure simply by stepping on the brake harder, but note that pressure

requirements may not increase equally for the front and rear brakes, thus potentially creating an imbalance in front/rear brake bias.

Changes that affect weight transfer also impact your brake system's performance. Stiffer springs and/or stiffer shocks minimize weight transfer during braking, which keep the rear tires more firmly planted on the ground, thus providing the tires with more traction than stock. The increased traction prevents the rear brakes from locking up unless additional pressure is applied, compared to stock conditions. The opposite is true of changes that promote weight transfer. Softer springs and shocks allow more weight to transfer quicker than stock, thus "unloading" the rear wheels more quickly, decreasing traction, and

allowing the rear brakes to lock up at a lower brake pressure. The same holds true for replacement torque arms, which can also affect weight transfer during braking events.

Understand also that when braking while cornering, you must consider whether the wheel to the inside of the corner can lock up as it is "unweighted" in the corner. Again, stiffer springs minimize weight transfer, so the braking pressure required to induce lock-up for each wheel remains essentially the same. Large-diameter stabilizer bars and stiff shock dampers have similar effects, while small bars and soft shocks and springs increase the likelihood that one wheel or another locks up prematurely.

prestaging burnout. Several manufacturers offer kits that you simply plumb into the front brake line, then activate with a small electrical button-type switch that you usually attach to the shifter inside the car.

The way a line lock kit works is that after you step on the brake pedal, you engage the line lock by pressing the switch button, which activates a servo motor that prevents the line pressure to the front wheels from dropping when you take your foot off the brake pedal.

Line locks can actually be quite dangerous for the street, so if you decide to install one, it's a good idea to either make the switch easily removable, by installing it with a quick-disconnect electrical connector. Or you may elect to disable the system by cutting the power to it.

Fluid Recirculators

Fluid recirculators are trick parts that you're not likely to need for a stock-based Camaro, nor are they likely to be legal equipment in most classes, but they do bear mentioning, if only to explain how technology has addressed the problem of boiling fluid.

With a fluid recirculator, every time you step on the brake pedal, a small amount of fluid is forced through each brake caliper and out into a fluid return line that leads to the master cylinder. By giving fluid a way out of the "dead end" caliper, cooler fluid is allowed to enter in its place, which boosts braking performance.

Top-Quality Stock Braking Equipment

When it comes to brake systems, third- and fourth-generation Camaros have some pretty decent hardware—at the very least, the stock equipment provides a sound foundation on which to make some improvements.

All models, from 1982 on up, feature front disc brakes, while most of the performance models—the Z28s, IROC-Zs, plus some V-6 models—typically came factory-equipped with rear disc brakes, too. And, for those buyers who feel the "regular" four-wheel disc system doesn't provide quite enough whoa-power, there's RPO 1LE, which outfits Camaros with a top-notch braking system. GM offers the system to help the F-bodies dominate in showroom stock road racing, such as the Firestone Firehawk and IMSA World Challenge series. Third-generation

1LE cars share virtually no brake parts with their lesser brethren—they have larger rotors at all four corners, Corvette-like aluminum PBR pad-guided calipers, heavier-duty wheel bearings and a specific proportioning valve that preserves the front-to-rear brake pressure balance, and attempts to minimize premature lock-up of any particular wheel before the others.

When the fourth-generation F-bodies hit the streets in 1993, Z28s did so with four-wheel disc brakes that offered a "swept area" (total area of each rotor contacted by the brake pads during a complete revolution) nearly equal to that of the third-generation 1LE systems. The V-6 models shared the beefy front discs, though they continued to sport drums out back. All of the new models featured a Delco anti-lock braking system that provided drivers with surefooted stops in dry, wet, or otherwise slippery conditions. V-6 models later got an all-disc option; then in 1997, the four-corner disc brakes became standard equipment on the V-6 cars, too. Further improvements came with the 1998 models, which all received highly fortified standard four-wheel disc brakes with larger, thicker, vented brake rotors; new aluminum calipers based on the new fifth-generation Corvette units; and a new Bosch-designed four-wheel anti-lock system to complement their new front fascias and power-packed LS1 engines on the performance versions.

Consider yourself fortunate if you've got four-wheel discs under your F-body. But if you've got a disc/drum setup, don't despair—it's actually more than adequate for even high-performance street vehicles. You might be skeptical of that last statement, and that's completely understandable, given how much of the world has been brainwashed into believing that drum brakes are hideously inadequate. But despite what many auto makers and even aftermarket brake parts companies tell you, most cars really don't need rear disc brakes. The front brakes provide most of your car's stopping power, while the rear brakes pitch in only about 20 to 25 percent of the car's total braking ability. The reason

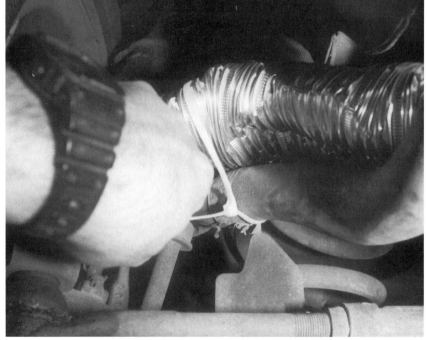

Make sure you secure the ducts to the chassis to prevent them from interfering with any engine or chassis components.

is straightforward and simple: As the car slows, its weight is transferred forward, effectively unloading weight from the rear wheels, making them prone to skidding, so rear brake pressure has to be considerably lower than front brake pressure. This condition is especially true with street cars suspended by relatively soft springs and shocks, which allow for even greater weight transfer. Furthermore, given that braking on the street rarely causes sustained high temperatures, drum brakes typically have ample time to cool down between stops.

But if you don't have to worry about drum brakes, what do you have to worry about? Well, in a word, plenty.

Your Camaro's brake system is composed of a myriad of parts that must all work in harmony if you're going to stop efficiently and effectively. Aside from the most obvious part, the brake pedal, you've got the master cylinder, which usually has a power brake booster attached to it; the proportioning valve; the steel brake lines; flexible brake hoses; the calipers (or wheel cylinders for drum brake systems); the pads or shoes; the rotors or drums; and on 1993-and-newer cars, there's the ABS hardware. And let's not forget that several different component designs were used throughout the years for each of these parts, as GM made changes from year to year.

Regardless of whatever braking equipment your Camaro or Firebird came with from the factory, though, there's always room for improvement. But, as with most aspects of your build-up, you first need to consider the application of your car, such as high-performance street driving, drag racing, autocrossing, road racing—or maybe a mix of some or all of these. The specific demands of the driving environment dictate what modifications and upgrades are necessary or desired.

High-Performance Street Driving

Street driving makes relatively modest demands on a braking system: Even highway speeds (assuming, of course, that you obey the law) are much lower than those encountered during most forms of

For best results, aim each duct's outlet toward the center of the rotor, so that the cool air rushes in, then flows out through the fins, cooling the rotor as it goes.

competition, plus stops are far less frequent and can often be accomplished with far less pedal pressure, since prudent street driving dictates gradual stops.

Given those conditions, street-bound braking systems benefit from mild upgrades to specific areas that improve all-around braking. The most dramatic improvement is felt with new brake pads (or shoes, for drum-equipped cars), which also turn out to be a cost-effective upgrade. Fresh fluid, which should be changed every year, is also a must for proper operation. And while you're changing the fluid, swap out those sad and sorry flexible rubber hoses for braided lines—or at least for new rubber ones, if yours are as much as three years old.

If your rotors are warped (the pedal pulses when you apply the brakes), you should consider replacing them with cross-drilled or slotted versions, or at least new stock replacements if you're on a budget. Don't waste your time or money "turning"

your old rotors, though, because that's only a temporary fix—and not a very good one. Your turned rotors will warp again, and they'll warp sooner and more severely, because they'll have less material through which to disperse and dissipate heat.

Drag Racing

Because of the high speeds attained while drag racing, and the fact that most drag strips have a limited length of shut-down space, good brakes are vitally important. However, despite those high speeds and the rather short time and space in which stops must occur, drag racing still places only moderate demands on a vehicle's braking system, at least for a stock-class vehicle. There are two good reasons for this: First is the fact that brakes are only used once per run; second is the fact that racers typically have a lengthy trip back to the pits, which is generally long enough that enough air flows over the brake components to cool them off. And if it wasn't a long enough trip, the car generally has at least a moderately long wait before it has to make another run, thus ensuring that the brakes are cool before needed again.

The fact that brake pads and rotors are cold before each run doesn't measurably affect braking action, since they heat up so quickly once the brakes are applied, thanks to the combination of high speeds and high pedal pressure.

As with any other application, any drag car should start out with fresh fluid and braided flex hoses. Semi-metallic pads are generally necessary, given the heat that is produced, but stock rotors can be used, because they usually have plenty of time after the run to dissipate the heat built up during the run.

Autocrossing

Despite brief runs, autocrossing can be quite punishing on brakes. Because you're running against the clock, you compress a lot of action into a very short time: You accelerate as quickly as possible from gate to gate, then get on the brakes hard to slow down in a hurry in order to make it through the turn, before jumping back on the gas to sprint to the next gate. It's not unusual to do this 30 or 40 times in a run, resulting in brakes that get mighty hot. And since you won't be sustaining any moderate-to-high speeds, airflow to the brakes is poor, leaving them little chance of shedding that heat. As if that weren't bad enough, most autocrossers shamefully finish their run and immediately park their car to wait for their next run, thereby depriving not only their brakes of much-needed cooling airflow, but

the engine, the tires, the transmission, the rear end, and virtually every other part, too. You should *always* give the car a chance to cool down by casually driving around for a few minutes.

That kind of abuse can be adequately dealt with, however, if you prepare your brake system for it. Start by changing the fluid and upgrading to braided steel flex lines. The new fluid rids the system of any moisture that would otherwise make the pedal mushy. The braided lines provide a more accurate pedal feel and make the brakes respond more quickly to your actions. That fluid needs to be changed more often, too. Plan on changing it at least every half-dozen races (events, not runs). More frequently would be better, but few people have the time or money for that if you're autocrossing as a hobby. If you're racing to make money, though, you would be wise to change the fluid prior to every race.

Of course, new fluid is just good maintenance, and braided lines are only for accuracy. Neither of these things makes your brakes better able to deal with the punishment. For that, you need to look at your pads and your rotors. The heat build-up dictates semi-metallic pads. Stops are more repeatable and predictable, and you won't go through pads as quickly, either.

If you've got the money, cross-drilled or slotted (grooved) rotors shed heat better than stock solid or solid-faced vented rotors for the street. If you're going racing professionally, though, stick with solid-faced vented rotors for their greater strength, but try to get the widest

rotors possible to improve airflow through the vents.

Again, upgrading to the proper pads greatly improves performance and reliability.

Road Racing

The harshest conditions for brake systems are encountered during road racing, which features not only high speeds, but frequent, high-g periods of deceleration to crawling speeds. Under these conditions, brakes build tremendous heat, stop after stop, so the pads must work well when hot, and every component must shed heat rapidly. Even that generally isn't enough, however. In most cases, some form of cooling system—usually simple ducts that direct cool air toward the brakes—is needed to keep temperatures within acceptable ranges. On professional race cars, teams might employ heat-damping shields and even fluid recirculators that purge calipers of heated fluid and replenish them with cooler fluid that expands less, thus preventing a mushy pedal and poor-acting brakes.

For stock-based road racing efforts, you want to change to cross-drilled or slotted rotors, for their cooling abilities, lighter weight, and better cleaning and anti-gassing capabilities.

Pad selection varies from track to track, but carbon-metallic pads are generally considered the best pads that not a lot of money can buy.

Braided brake hoses are a must for any halfway serious race car, as is changing the fluid before every race. And if you want that extra little something, an adjustable proportioning valve to tweak rear line pressure is the ticket.

SUSPENSION AND STEERING

From the moment the third-generation Camaro debuted, it was viewed as a large step forward in Camaro performance. While the previous-generation Camaro had grown larger and heavier through the years, the new 1982 Camaro was smaller, lighter, and sleeker. Many enthusiasts even considered the 1982 third-generation Camaro to be a modern rendition of the original 1967 Camaro, not only because the two were nearly the same size and weight, but also because the cars performed similarly in terms of straight-line performance.

Thankfully, however, when talk turned to the subject of turning corners, the new third-generation car was considered the hands-down favorite. In fact, the 1982 Camaro was considered by many to be the best-handling Camaro ever, to that time. With its modified MacPherson strut front suspension and Salisbury-type live rear axle, the GM engineers did an amazing job selecting spring rates, shock valving, anti-roll bar diameters, and other components to arrive at a setup that provided a relatively comfortable ride on the street, with commendable handling when pushed through the corners.

Just a few short years after the introduction of the 1982 model, the engineers were able to refine the Z28's suspension setup to the point where *Car and Driver* magazine selected it as the best-handling American production car—even besting its big brother, the Corvette.

Never satisfied, though, engineers continually tweaked suspension settings to provide the base models with a pleasurable yet sporty ride, and the Z28 models with slot car-like prowess. But for racing, even the Z28's stiff suspension wasn't enough to make the car competitive, so, as part of the 1989-and-later 1LE performance package, the engineers cooked up a thoroughly heavy-duty suspension combination that featured unforgivingly stiff springs; large-diameter, high-pressure shock absorbers and front strut cartridges; extra-large-diameter stabilizer (anti-roll) bars; and a healthy dose of polyurethane bushings. The result was a car that few buyers would be happy with on the street, thanks to its pounding ride (hence the reason GM went out of its way to keep the option's availability hush-hush). But on the track, those springs, shocks, and other equipment gave the car the ability to slice through corners—and the competition—at insane speeds.

But as well as the third-generation's front suspension worked, the modified MacPherson strut system had distinct limitations. So, when the time came to design the fourth-generation Camaro, engineers allocated considerable time and expense to developing a no-compromise front suspension system. It could be tuned to provide an unquestionably comfortable ride for the base V-6 "secretary special" models, or take-no-prisoners performance setups for the Z28 and 1LE models. The SLA (Short/Long Arm) system that resulted achieved everything the engineers had hoped for and more, and the Camaro moved into a new realm of performance.

The Basic Suspension Designs

Third- and fourth-generation Camaro suspension systems are good; the GM engineers that designed them did a terrific job, and those that followed—the engineers that upgraded and updated the systems throughout the years—were nothing short of brilliant. But despite their best efforts, the stock suspension systems aren't without their own particular faults. When you consider the constraints placed on engineers by GM, it's little surprise: Camaros are used for a variety of uses, most of which are mundane in nature. These cars must be able to perform each job admirably, or the owner is unhappy, and GM potentially loses a customer for life.

So the chassis engineers had to again resort to making the Camaro appeal to the broad market, while knowingly sacrificing some performance, in terms of both at-the-limits stability and overall comfort.

Before we get into specifically addressing some steps you can take to modify your Camaro's suspension to better suit your tastes, it's often beneficial to become familiar with the system designs themselves.

1982–1992 Front Suspension

First- and second-generation Camaros had used a combination of a long and a short control arm on each side of the front end, with a coil spring and shock absorber in between to control oscillations. Unfortunately, GM didn't know nearly as much about suspension

system design when engineers drew up the early Camaro front end. As a result, the system's geometry, the angles at which it operates, performed poorly for anything but straight-line cruising.

The third-generation Camaro front suspension system was radically different. Though the system still utilized a long, lower control arm, it no longer had an upper arm. Nor did it utilize a traditional shock absorber. Instead, the new Camaro used a modified design of the MacPherson strut front suspension. Most MacPherson strut designs employ a coil spring that mounts around the top of the strut cartridge, which is essentially just a shock constructed of heavier-duty materials. The strut itself handled not only the job of dampening spring movements, but also served as the replacement for the upper control arm. The top of the strut was firmly secured to the strut tower (inner fender) of the car, and controlled the caster and camber of the front wheel. In the Camaro's modified form, the coil spring remained in its traditional location, sandwiched between the lower control arm and the frame rail, rather than around the strut.

One of the main advantages of the MacPherson strut design is its simplicity. The other is its cost, which is related to the design's simplicity. By eliminating the upper control arm, GM was able to cut down on the number of necessary parts, plus reduce assembly time.

Unfortunately, the MacPherson strut design (even the Camaro's modified version) has some distinct limitations in terms of performance capabilities. The Number One problem is one of geometry. Because the top of the strut is firmly mounted in place, geometry changes considerably between different points on the suspension's arc of travel. Ultimately, the change affects tire contact with the ground.

Additionally, the struts are not as convenient to change as traditional shocks, which makes a suspension tuner's job more difficult. In fact, the strut serves as the top mount for the front suspension system. Any change to the strut disturbs the front wheel alignment, requiring realignment to prevent chewing up tires.

Another problem is the range of camber and caster adjustment available on third-generation Camaros. When set at rest, camber is adjusted quite precisely. Changes in suspension geometry throughout the suspension travel adversely affect camber. As the suspension compresses and rebounds, traction is impaired.

Finally, third-generation Camaro steering equipment was actually little-different from the system used on the original 1967 models. Third-generation cars have a recirculating ball steering box along with a complicated system of steering linkage to transmit the rotational movement of the steering wheel into a directional movement of the front wheels. The steering box itself worked well, but wear was often a problem. The box's internals would become sloppy with age, making it imprecise. The network of linkage only worsened the situation. At each connection, the system utilized yet another flexible joint to allow for front wheel movement (both steering and suspension movements). Each of these joints decreased steering accuracy and introduced another potential trouble spot for future wear problems.

Here's a peek at the underside of a stock third-generation Camaro's front suspension system. Note the large, stamped-steel control arms (also known as "A-arms" because of their shape). A network of steering linkage turns the wheels, while coil springs, modified MacPherson strut shock dampers, and a beefy stabilizer bar work together to control wheel movements over bumps and around corners.

1993–1998
Front Suspension

Virtually all of the third-generation Camaro's front suspension ailments were eliminated when Chevrolet switched (back) to a combination of short and long suspension control arms, with more traditional shocks and springs.

Unlike older (first- and second-generation) Camaro control arms, the new arms are not considered A-arms, because their shape does not resemble the letter. Rather than have both of the arm's mounting bushings on relatively equal pivot planes, as were those of most older GM A-arm designs, the new Camaro's stamped-steel lower control arm design utilizes a single pivot that is in-line with the shock and wheel center, which improves reaction to lateral cornering loads and allows the use of harder bushing materials without diminishing ride quality. A second bushing is mounted rearward of the first, in a vertical orientation, and only influences fore-aft alignment of the arm, especially in response to "impacts" with bumps and obstacles that would otherwise try to bend the arm rearward. This second bushing can be quite soft to absorb impact forces, without negatively affecting performance through corners.

The shorter, stamped-steel upper A-arm is mounted to a lengthy "gooseneck" steering knuckle to reduce suspension loads. Use of an upper arm again allows the steering knuckle to swing a gentler arc, thus minimizing camber changes to the wheel and tire at different suspension travel heights. A ball-joint permits the knuckle to pivot as the arm moves.

A coil-over shock absorber minimizes the size of the system and makes upgrades much easier, since changing the shock or spring doesn't necessitate re-aligning the front end. Again, a stabilizer bar assists the springs in controlling body roll.

Rack-and-pinion steering gear is used for better steering response, better "feel" of what the tires are doing, plus reduced complexity and size.

In terms of design problems, the fourth-generation suspension system really doesn't have any significant shortcomings—at least none that won't be addressed by different

The fourth-generation Camaros feature a much-improved front suspension system. This photo shows the unique shape of the boxed, stamped-steel lower control arms that mount coil-over-type shock and spring assemblies. Rather than relying on a strut to both dampen spring oscillations and serve as the top suspension mount, the fourth-gen cars have an upper A-arm that maintains wheel geometry far better than the strut ever could. A simple rack-and-pinion steering system provides improved steering feel and response.

shocks, springs, bushings, or other simple component changes. The steering system is also remarkably better than that of the third generation, though the fourth-generation design is more prone to experiencing bump-steer (unwanted steering inputs as a result of compressed or extended suspension).

Rear Suspension: The Common Denominator

Both the third- and fourth-generation cars utilize the same rear suspension system. Between the two eras, only the shocks and springs are different, and their differences are minimal at best, relating only to subtle changes in the shape of the floorpan that affect mounting each component.

The fact that both generations share the same live rear axle design is both good and bad. In the cars' favor is the fact that, with nearly two decade's worth of refinement since the system was originally designed, the Camaro's rear end is controlled so well that few live-axle cars can match its ride and handling.

Still, GM's own engineers are intimately familiar with the limitations of the live axle's suspension

requirements. In fact, they have had an independent rear suspension (IRS) like the Corvette's on their Camaro "wish list" for many years, and they've even gone so far as to build several prototypes or concept cars to evaluate the production feasibility of such a system. But, in the end, despite whatever performance advantages such a system might provide, neither the design budget nor the typical Camaro buyer's finances would handle the added cost of an IRS.

Given that we're more or less stuck with the production rear suspension (unless you're crafting a true race car, which likely has a racing-only suspension system), your best alternative is to assess what undesirable effects the suspension is introducing into your driving, then come up with a treatment program that addresses those shortcomings.

The most common problem with the Camaro rear suspension system is unwanted movement of the rear end, which is typically caused by its flimsy locating members (the lower control arms, torque arm, and Panhard rod or track bar) and the bushings used to "cushion" those items' connections to the body and rear axle assembly. The bushings themselves are an important barrier that prevents vibrations and "road noise" from disturbing you in the passenger compartment.

The problem, though, is that as the rubber bushings compress to absorb vibrations and violent movements of the rear axle assembly, their "crushed size" affects the rear axle assembly's orientation under the car.

And since several bushings may crush (i.e., compress) at the same, the placement of the rear end could be significantly compromised, because the compression of all bushings could "add up" at the rear end; for example, if the front (body) bushing for a lower control arm compresses forward 1 millimeter, and the rear (axle) bushing on the same control arm compresses forward one millimeter, as well, the rear axle housing actually moves forward 2 millimeters on that side. While 2 millimeters may not sound like much, it affects suspension geometry, wheelbase, pinion angle, and other factors. And such movement doesn't produce beneficial, desirable results.

Another problem that few people seem to give much thought is that the rear ends are located laterally (side to side) under the car by a Panhard rod (also called a track bar), which connects to the rear axle housing at one end, and to the body structure at the

Improving Control with Braced Suspension Parts

When faced with the need to upgrade your Camaro's suspension components, it's all too easy to feel that the only worthwhile steps to take involve buying new aftermarket performance parts to replace the weak factory pieces. Sure, some of the aftermarket parts available offer features that would be difficult—if not impossible—to add to factory parts, but the truth of the matter is that you can upgrade the factory components, if you have the skills and equipment to do so, and come away from the job quite satisfied with the performance and even more satisfied with the cost.

Of particular note are the rear lower control arms and the Panhard rod, which in stock form are merely stamped-steel parts. With a MIG, TIG, or gas welder and some heavy-gauge sheet stock, you can box the control arms and the Panhard rod, substantially increasing their resistance to bending, twisting and flexing. The same technique can beef up the front lower control arms and the stock torque arm.

In addition, if you are adept at fabricating parts, you could homebrew your own subframe connectors, a driveshaft safety loop, strut tower braces, and other parts.

Rear suspension systems for third- and fourth-generation Camaros are virtually identical and share almost all parts, from the rear axle assemblies to the control arms, Panhard rod, shock absorbers, and other parts. Unfortunately, the Camaro rear suspension is also the car's Achilles heel, so it often requires (and deserves) the most attention when upgrading for better performance.

other. If you picture the arc swung by the Panhard rod, it becomes obvious that the rear axle does move side to side, depending on how much the suspension compresses, or how much the suspension is "lowered." While there's nothing that can be done to prevent rear axle assembly "displacement" due to suspension action, you can correct its displacement due to lowering the suspension.

A third problem has to do with the stock torque arm's effect on suspension geometry. The stock torque arm is used to prevent the rear axle assembly from rotating around its axles. It does this on stock vehicles by "connecting" the front portion of the differential case to the transmission's tailhousing with a rubber-bushed mount. It's imperative that the torque arm be able to swing in an arc, as the rear suspension compresses and extends, but the stock system allows too much flex, so the rear axle assembly can excessively rotate, leading to pinion-angle problems, which can dramatically hamper performance.

Wheels

Since 1982, the Camaro has been equipped at the factory with 14-, 15-, 16- and 17-inch wheels, and a number of different tire sizes, tread patterns, and sidewall designs have been used. Your options only expand when you consider installing aftermarket wheels and tires on your Camaro.

The factory wheels are either stamped steel or cast aluminum, depending on size and design.

Performance Parts on the Cheap: Salvage Yard Production Parts

If you're like most amateur racers, you don't have much of a budget to spend on racing parts. And it can be pretty frustrating to feel like your racing is suffering just because you've got to keep food on the table. But, as the saying goes, there's more than one way to skin a cat.

Rather than maxing out your credit cards or depleting your life savings for a handful of aftermarket suspension parts, you could spend a mere fraction of that amount at the local salvage yard and come away with a truckload of various factory springs, anti-sway bars, shocks, and extra control arms and other parts.

Why would you want to do such a thing? Well, if you scavenge parts from a variety of differently equipped Camaros and/or Firebirds (remember, they're the same car, but each GM division was free to calibrate them differently), you have a whole heap of parts with which to experiment, and hopefully you'll find a combination that brings a smile to your own face, and a frown to your competitors' faces.

You better your odds of succeeding if you make sure you get parts from cars with different engines and/or option packages. Since springs for cars equipped with inline four-cylinder engines are "softer" than are those for V-6 models, which are likewise softer than V-8 springs, you may be able to select springs that allow you to dial-in better weight transfer, or minimize it. You also need to consider that Z28 springs were heavier than base V-8

Camaro springs. And convertible springs were generally different, too. And 1LE springs again added another possibility (though these are rare finds at salvage yards, they are available over-the-counter from your local GM dealer's parts department). Some models, like 1996-and-up V-6 cars, could be ordered with ride and handling packages that featured revised spring and shock rates for "sportier" handling.

Likewise, antiroll bars used on different models were of different sizes. Trial-and-error testing may yield an almost ideal balance of ride and handling. In fact, in some cases, it may actually be preferable to use a factory antiroll bar instead of an aftermarket bar, since most factory bars are lighter-weight hollow tubes, while most aftermarket bars are considerably heavier solid bars.

Pulling all these old parts off salvage yard wrecks, then trying them on your car, may seem like a lot of work, but it can actually be fun, and the price should be right. In terms of what parts fit what cars, remember that parts from one generation car should freely and easily transfer to another car of the same generation (i.e., parts from a 1982–1992 car should fit any 1982–1992 car, and parts from a 1993-and-newer model should fit any 1993-and-newer). In terms of the rear suspension systems, parts should even swap from third-generation to fourth and vice versa, with the exception of the shocks (due to changes to the floorpan, which serves as the shocks' upper attachment point).

Though not often thought of as parts of the suspension system, your Camaro's wheels and tires are truthfully the system's most important elements, because they are the final word in traction needed for your Camaro's performance ABCs—Accelerating, Braking, and Cornering. Late-model Z28 and IROC Camaros have used Goodyear rubber exclusively to provide a well-rounded handling package. Beginning with the Eagle GTs on the 1982 Z28s through the Eagle VR "Gatorbacks" used on IROCs and Z28s until 1992, and again with the Eagle GS-Cs available on fourth-generation Z28s, the Goodyear Eagles have proven to be outstanding street tires and, in soft-compound form, have had tremendous success on race tracks.

They're good wheels that look right at home on your Camaro, but they can be improved upon.

Steel wheels are inexpensive, but they're not very strong, and they're heavy. When subjected to high cornering forces, the wheels can actually bend, which affects handling—especially when they "spring" back to their original true, round form. Aluminum wheels, on the other hand, are lightweight, so they help reduce unsprung mass, which translates into quicker suspension system action. Despite their light weight, aluminum wheels are stronger than steel wheels, especially forged aluminum wheels.

Upgrading to larger-diameter wheels quickens steering response, while wider wheels allows you to mount wider tires, which helps traction. A "Plus 1" upgrade would entail going up an inch in wheel diameter, and correspondingly reducing the tire's aspect ratio. For instance, a change from 16-inch wheels with 50-series tires to 17-inch wheels with 40-series tires is a Plus 1 change. If you went to 18-inch wheels and 30- or 35-series tires, that would be a Plus 2 change (from a 16-inch wheel/50-series combination).

The only real drawback to the "Plus" system, aside from the expense of new wheels and tires, is that as the wheel diameter increases and the sidewall of the tire decreases, you feel more road imperfections. Steering feedback increases, possibly to the point of being an annoyance for everyday driving. Your suspension settings affect how much "road noise" you feel with each wheel and tire combination: A softer suspension, especially one still equipped with rubber bushings, is more tolerant of a short sidewall tire than a large-diameter wheel and a stiff suspension equipped with polyurethane bushings.

When choosing wheel sizes, you also need to concern yourself with the wheel's "backspacing," the distance from the back of the wheel's mounting surface to the bead lip. Camaros have a lot of backspacing, but you can only have so much before the wheel and tire would contact suspension or body parts. Fortunately, most wheel manufacturers can tell you whether a particular wheel works on your Camaro. If you choose to ignore their recommendations and go for a wider wheel, you must carefully measure to make sure the wheel won't hamper steering or suspension movement.

Other wheel considerations to think about while shopping around are the wheel's impact on brake cooling, appearance, how much maintenance is required, and the type of surface finish. A solid wheel poses a serious impediment to the flow of cool air to the brake components. If you're drag racing, this isn't a serious problem since your brakes are used only periodically, but if you're street driving, autocrossing, or road racing, you want a nice, open-style wheel. A traditional "five-spoke" design with large open areas between the spokes allows air to flow freely to the caliper and rotor, significantly lowering their operating temperatures.

Appearances are personal matters, so you've naturally got to decide what you like the looks of. Of course, few people can afford to order wheels, bolt them on, then decide whether or not they like them. There are a couple methods that you can use to get some idea of whether you like a particular wheel on your car.

The first is to see the wheels on someone else's Camaro, such as at a car show. Color differences aside, if the wheels look good (to you) on another Camaro, they probably will look good on yours. But if you can't find another Camaro with the wheels you're interested in, you might try to find a friend with a computer and a photograph scanner. Have your friend scan in a picture of your Camaro that shows the side (profile) of the car. Then have him (or her) scan in photos of the wheels you like, then place those wheels on the picture of your car. It's a great way to quickly get an idea how things will look.

The Tire Rack, a tire and wheel dealer, has taken this last idea and taken all the work out of it for you, providing a free, virtual wheel showroom available at their Internet World Wide Web site. With Tire Rack's system (a downloadable version is available), you simply click on the car you want to work with, choose a color, then the system presents the applicable wheel choices, and you can click on any or all of them to see what they look like on the car.

This may sound like a petty point to bring up, but cleaning wheels can be a pain in the neck (and back, and arms, and . . .). Complex wheel designs, like basket-weave patterns or ones with numerous drilled

The fun part of choosing wheels is picking the style you want. The hard part is making sure the larger wheels you want fit your car. You need to measure the inside diameter of the tire to ensure it clears your brake hardware and steering linkage. This is especially important for cars with aftermarket brake calipers, which are notorious for requiring larger-than-stock wheels.

holes, simulated rivets, or whatever, can be tiresome and difficult to clean. Simple designs with only a few large spokes, or even solid wheels, are the easiest to clean. Typically, the harder a wheel is to clean, the less you want to clean it, so it looks grungy. This makes your car look grungy, and inevitably owners are unhappy with the wheels, and maybe even the entire car.

The finish applied to a wheel has a lot to do with the wheel's appearance and the maintenance you need to do. Most aluminum wheels are treated to some form of clear-coat protective finish to help preserve the wheel. These sort of finishes usually keep the wheels looking good for several years, but be aware that some coatings can become easily scratched, chipped, "fogged," or may flake off, which can make the wheels look uglier than if they had no protective finish at all.

Tires

Tires are another complicated issue to deal with, because there are so many tire manufacturers making so many different tire lines, in so many different sizes for many different driving conditions that the combinations are practically overwhelming.

About the only thing easy to decide on about your next set of tires is the size of wheel they fit—if you've got 17-inch wheels, you need 17-inch tires. From there, things get noticeably tougher.

Tire Sizes

The width, aspect ratio, and speed rating are three common factors you need to consider. Stock Z28s have used 245/50ZR-16 tires for years. The "245" is the width, in millimeters. The "50" is the aspect ratio—the sidewall's height given as a percentage of the tread's width. The "Z" is the speed rating for a tire that's built to withstand sustained speeds over 149 miles per hour. The "R" tells us it's a radial tire, and the "16" tells us the wheel diameter it fits.

Wide tires can actually have a detrimental effect on handling. Pavement with ruts gives fits to drivers of cars with wide tires, because the car wants to "wander" or even "dart" back and forth across the road. The

problem generally boils down to the wide tires being too wide to fit completely within the rut (as do the narrow tires on most vehicles), so the wide tires constantly climb in and out of the ruts, pulling the car this way and that way as they do. The problem is often noticeable with tires of just 245 millimeters tread width, and tends to get worse with wider tires.

However, if you can live with such a condition, or if you're lucky enough to live someplace where rutted roads aren't too common, then wider tires allow you to put more rubber in contact with the road surface, thus providing more traction for accelerating, braking, and turning. The widest tire that fits inside third- and fourth-generation Camaros without much effort or concern is a 275/40-17 unit. Wider than that and you need to be careful with wheel selection and clearances. Some owners of fourth-generation Camaros have managed to outfit their cars with massive 315/35-17 rear tires, but clearances were extremely tight.

Tire Ratings

Beyond the usual dimensions, there are other numbers on a tire worth looking at. The government requires tire manufacturers to grade each tire design's performance, with

respect to treadwear, traction, and temperature. Treadwear ratings are given numerically, with higher numbers representing longer tread life (thus, a harder rubber compound). A typical high-performance tire has a treadwear rating of approximately 220, and with casual, prudent driving, should last roughly 20,000 miles (there's no direct correlation between treadwear ratings and expected mileage, because driving conditions and styles vary so widely). Traction and temperature are each rated with an "A," "B," or "C" grade, with "A" being excellent, and "C" being acceptable. "B" is normal for a passenger car tire, while high-performance tires should always be "A"-rated. Likewise, an "A" temperature rating means the tire handles heat very well, while a "C" rating is acceptable.

Inflation pressures are another item to inspect. Most passenger car tires are designed for a maximum of 32–35 pounds of air per square inch, but many high-performance tires are designed to handle as much as 44–50 pounds per square inch. More pressure stiffens the tire, helping it steer more easily and react more quickly to steering inputs. But high tire pressures also degrade ride comfort. In most cases, 32 pounds of pressure is more than adequate for street dri-

Another vital measurement is the backspacing—the distance from the rear of the wheel's mounting surface to its bead. Use of a straight-edge and tape measure make quick work of taking the measurement, then you have to compare that measurement to any obstacles on your car that might interfere with the wheel fitting.

ving, but competition use may require the tuning flexibility afforded by higher pressure ratings, in order to properly set up your suspension system. Note that over-inflating a tire (which doesn't necessarily mean exceeding the maximum pressure for which the tire is rated) causes it to wear unevenly, typically using up the center of the tread quickly.

Tread Designs

Depending on the driving conditions, tread design has the biggest effect on traction, even more than tread compound, which is covered following this discussion on tread design. The tread design determines just how much rubber actually contacts the road under any circumstance: dry, wet, sandy, or snowy.

For race cars, the ultimate tread design is a simple, "treadless" slick, because it puts the most rubber on the ground. But slicks are only good if the road surface is clean and dry. Without a tread to displace the sand, water, or snow, the tire rides atop anything on the road, so traction is severely limited. On water, this con-

dition is known as *hydroplaning*. It's sort of like trying to walk on marbles: Instead of your feet moving you forward, they end up sending the marbles backward, behind you.

For the street, the Department of Transportation (D.O.T.) requires tires to have a minimum of 3/32 inch of tread, to ensure at least some (albeit minimal) water displacement for driving in the rain or on wet roads.

So, while any tread is better than none (for street driving), some tread patterns are better than others. Again, for wet-weather driving, you want large channels between tread blocks that allow water to quickly and easily flow out from under the tire. Some tread designs even aid the process by directing the water out.

Goodyear's Eagle "Gatorback," which was standard equipment for many years on third-generation Z28s and IROC-Zs with 16-inch wheels, was such a tire, and its tread design was based on Formula 1 racing rain tires. The Eagle GS-C, which was standard equipment on 1993–1998 Z28s, improved on the Gatorback tread thanks to the inclusion of a

large "aquachannel" and an asymmetrical tread pattern (the tread blocks were different across the face of the tire, from inside to outside). Goodyear's Eagle F-1, which was introduced on the 1997 Corvette, utilizes a second aquachannel and an enhanced tread pattern to yield still better wet-weather traction. Other manufacturers have similar developments and designs.

Crucial to tread design is the tread compound—the actual rubber from which the tread is formed. Tread compounds can be quite different. For instance, an eraser and a sneaker tread are both made of rubber, but if you drag them across a course surface the eraser leaves shreds of itself behind, while the sneaker does not. That's because the eraser's rubber compound is much softer. Tires can be the same way.

Soft tread compounds provide more traction, because they conform better to the road surface on which they roll—they reach into every nook and cranny and grab hold. Harder compound tires, on the other hand, ride along only gripping the top of the road surface. If you've ever dug your feet into the ground to get a little more traction while pushing something, you're familiar with why soft compound tires provide more grip for your car.

The problem with soft-compound tires is that, like the eraser, they shred off bits of rubber as they grip the road, so they don't last very long.

Regular street tires are fairly hard so that they provide a long tread life. In fact, it's not uncommon for passenger car tires to last 50,000 miles or more, because their tread compounds are quite hard. But performance tires typically only last 20,000–25,000 miles because their tread compounds are much softer. Tread life is indicated on the sidewall of the tire with a numeric rating under or following the word "Wear"; the higher the number, the longer the tread life. A Goodyear Eagle GS-C has a treadwear rating of 220, and typically lasts up to 25,000 miles.

By comparison, a racing version of the GS-C, the GS-CS (the extra "S" is for "Soft"), has a treadwear rating of 50, and wouldn't last more than a few hundred miles on the street!

It used to be tough to choose wheels for your car because you didn't know what they would look like until you bolted them to the car. But by then you had already spent the money, so even if they were butt-ugly you were stuck with them. But the Tire Rack has a great solution to this age-old problem: its interactive wheel guide, available for free through the company's World Wide Web site (visit http://www.tirerack.com). Just by clicking on a wheel style (only styles that fit your car are shown), you'll get to see what the wheels look like.

Specialty Tires

Beyond the numerous street tires available are a number of "specialty" tires. So-called specialty tires may be for street use, or they may be for competition use only, or they may even be for use on both the street and the race track. The important part of a specialty tire is that its design is in some way optimized to perform better in certain situations or conditions than typical street tires.

A simple example of a specialty tire is a mud and snow tire. Camaros are notoriously poor drivers in snowy, winter conditions, but mud and snow tires help.

Some, like Goodyear's Extended Mobility Tires (EMTs for short), which are available in Eagle GS-C and F-1 tread designs, are for the street and provide an exceptional feature: The ability to be used at highway speeds for up to 200 miles without any air in them! So-called "run-flat" tires are a great convenience on the street, because you needn't worry about getting a flat tire while on a trip, or if it's raining. You simply keep driving to the nearest service center and have the tire repaired (or replaced, depending on the severity of the damage). Another advantage is that you can reclaim some lost storage space that would normally be taken up by a spare tire and jacking equipment (since you would never need them).

The catch to run-flat tires is that because the tires won't ever look flat, and they don't feel flat when you're driving, you need a means of monitoring the tire pressures while you're driving. If a tire is at zero pounds of air pressure, and you're going faster than 55 miles per hour, or you've been driving several hundred miles, you could be risking a serious accident. While the Corvette has had an optional tire pressure sensing system since 1994, the Camaro has never had one from the factory (though it is expected to become available). However, by the time you read this, systems similar to the Corvette's should be available from aftermarket sources.

Another type of specialty tire is the soft-compound racing version of regular street performance tires, such as the aforementioned GS-CS version of the Goodyear Eagle GS-C.

Such tires are available because many race-sanctioning bodies, including most notably the Sports Car Club of America (SCCA), require competitors to run D.O.T.-approved tires in many classes. So, tire manufacturers use an existing tire design but use a softer rubber compound to improve traction significantly.

Most soft-compound tires, such as BF Goodrich's R-1 competition tires are available only with minimal tread depth, as well, to further increase traction and performance by minimizing tread "squirm" (the effect of standard-height tread blocks twisting and flexing while driving). These soft-compound tires are generally for either autocross or road race use, and, in fact, some manufacturers offer different compounds for each.

For drag racing purposes, several manufacturers, including Goodyear, Firestone, and Mickey Thompson, produce bias-ply drag tires that have soft sidewalls, a soft rubber

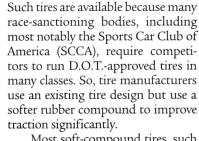

A common size for Z28 tires: P245/50ZR-16. The P tells us the tire uses the metric system. The 245 is the tire's tread width in millimeters. The 50 defines the aspect ratio of the sidewall height to the tread's width, given as a percentage. The Z is the speed rating (sustained speeds of 149+ mph). The R stands for Radial construction. Finally, the 16 tells us the tire requires a 16-inch-diameter wheel.

Goodyear's newest street Eagle—the F-1 GS—was introduced on the 1997 Corvette in EMT (Extended Mobility Tire, a.k.a. "run-flat") form and is available in sizes commonly used on Camaros. The F-1 was designed to provide exceptional wet and dry traction, plus a quiet, comfortable ride. It represents a remarkable improvement over the GS-C, which, itself, was much better than the Gatorback and its predecessor, the Eagle GT. *Goodyear Tire & Rubber Company photo*

Three more critical specifications you'll find on a tire's sidewall are its treadwear, traction, and temperature ratings. This tire has a relatively soft "220" treadwear rating, which helps it achieve an "A" traction rating (other ratings are "B" and "C," in descending order). Finally, the temperature rating tells us how well the tire stands up to heat generated while driving; this tire got an "A" here, too.

A final critical spec is the maximum inflation pressure, which for this tire is 44 psi. While you should never exceed the maximum pressure (because you risk a serious and dangerous tire failure if you do), you probably won't want to run your tires that high anyway. On the street, 44 psi would be quite hard and uncomfortable. On the track, it may actually limit traction as much as underinflation.

compound, and either a slick tread or a minimal tread pattern. These tires, however, are for competition use only; they are not D.O.T.-approved because of their soft sidewalls that can cause erratic and possibly dangerous tire movements in reaction to bumps or sudden maneuvers. It's also important to understand that bias-ply and radial tires should never be "mixed and matched," such as running bias-ply tires on the rear of a car that has radials up front, because the two types of tires behave so differently.

Tire Speed Ratings

Rating	Max. Sustained Speed (miles per hour)
Q	99
R	106
S	112
T	118
U	124
H	130
V	over 130
V*	149
Z	over 149

with 3-character Service Description after tire size designation (e.g., P225/60R-15 93V)

At the time this publication was produced, BF Goodrich was the only tire manufacturer offering a D.O.T.-approved drag racing radial tire. Because it's D.O.T.-approved, it's legal for car owners to drive on them to get to their local drag strip, which is a big concern for many people who can't afford a trailer on which to haul their car to the track. Even more important, though, is the fact that the tire is of radial construction. This makes it safe and practical for people to use in conjunction with regular street radial tires, which are far, far more common today than bias-ply tires. The catch to the BFG Drag Radial is that the radial construction results in a stronger sidewall that does not flex, so the drag radial requires a much different suspension setup to properly "hook up." Naturally, as a D.O.T.-approved tire, the BFG Drag Radial does have a minimal tread pattern, to make it safe for use on wet roads, though the soft tread compound won't last terribly long if you drive it on the street often.

Recommended Suspension Setups

The particular suspension "set-up"—the components you run and how you tune and adjust them—to use on your Camaro depends on how and where the car is used, as well as your own driving preferences. While it's impossible to describe an ideal setup for anyone, each of the four typical applications your Camaro can face—high-performance street use, drag racing, autocrossing, or road racing—have general requirements that make certain suspension setups more effective than others.

The idea of installing upgrade "kits" has been promoted elsewhere in this book, and it's no less applicable here. Suspension component manufacturers often develop packages of shocks, springs, stabilizer bars, and bushings that are designed to complement one another and should provide satisfactory results. Of course, sometimes you have to buy some parts from one manufacturer and other parts from another manufacturer. When you do, make sure you get recommendations from, say, the shock manufacturers, as to what spring rates work well with the shocks you're getting. Randomly buying parts likely results in a costly, unimpressive suspension system, but a little forethought and asking a few simple questions may be all that's needed to put together a thoroughly satisfying suspension setup.

High-Performance Street Use

Because public streets are rarely as well-maintained as race tracks, you want to maintain some compliance in the system to deal with minor road imperfections—cracked pavement, potholes, small rocks, etc. Stock rubber bushings are best for this job. Polyurethane bushings improve the accuracy of your suspension system, but you're likely to be rewarded with squeaks and creeks, plus a significantly harsher ride. The exception is stabilizer bar bushings; polyurethane stabilizer bar mounting bushings help eliminate some body roll while cornering, but they are barely noticeable compared to rubber bushings on the street. Solid bushings and Heim joints should never be used on the street on control arms or shock absorbers.

Aside from shock, spring, and stabilizer bar upgrades, there are few changes that can be made, or are worth making, to the front suspension for street use. The rear suspension, however, can be greatly improved by eliminating its many weak connecting members (control arms, Panhard rod, torque arm) and introducing some adjustability into the system.

In terms of best-bang-for-the-buck, a replacement torque arm with a provision for adjusting pinion angle should be Number One on the list. It provides an immediate, easily noticeable improvement in how the car launches and pulls away from corners. The rear end housing, for once, won't be working against you. It will work for you, and help you plant the tires better for more traction!

Following that would be replacement or strengthening of control arms and Panhard rod, to minimize unwanted rear axle housing movement. And if you're switching to wider or larger-diameter wheels with accompanying over size tires, you should invest in an adjustable Panhard rod, which lets

you get your rear back in line with the rest of the car. This goes for lowering the car, too, which also offsets the rear axle assembly to the left without an adjustable Panhard rod.

Spring, shock damper, and stabilizer bar selection depends a great deal on driver preference and the particular demands placed on your Camaro. In most cases, replacement springs only make the ride more uncomfortable, while providing little, if any, performance improvement for street use. And aside from appearances, there is really no measurable advantage to lowering a third- or fourth-generation Camaro. In fact, because the car tends to ground-out more often when lowered, a strong argument could be made for leaving ride height, and the springs you run under your Camaro, alone.

Shocks, on the other hand, can be upgraded quite effectively. Of the three types (hydraulic twin tube,

gas-charged hydraulic twin tube, and high-pressure gas-charged hydraulic monotube), the gas-charged twin tubes typically provide a more compliant, comfortable ride; monotubes, because of their large pistons, react quickly and noticeably to even the slightest inputs, but that generally makes for a more responsive, performance-oriented feel.

Ideally, you should consider adjustable shocks that allow you to dial in more or less compression and rebound damping to tune the ride to the needs of the moment— keep the shocks set soft for street driving, then at the races, crank them up for a firmer, higher-performance ride. Some shocks are rebound-adjustable only, while only a few offer adjustments for both

Suspension Lowering Considerations

Dropping your Camaro into the weeds may give it what you consider to be a cool look, and it may even provide some additional handling benefits, but there are right ways and wrong ways to go about reducing the ride height.

In the old days, it was common to lower ride height by simply cutting sections of spring off the coil springs, thereby shortening the spring. But that causes several problems. For instance, some F-bodies came from the factory with "progressive-rate" springs, meaning that the first inch or so of compression occurred at a specific spring rate (expressed in pounds per inch), after which the springs generally require a higher pressure to compress further. But by cutting sections of a coil off, you may be altering how the spring reacts to inputs, which means you affect spring action, which means ride and handling are affected.

The very methods of cutting coils also causes problems. Both a torch and a grinder wheel can generate enough heat to fatigue the spring, thereby weakening it. Again, ride and handling are affected.

Lowering the car also changes the suspension and steering geometry. In the front end, a lowered ride height results in what is known as

"bumpsteer," a condition that arises from the difference between the arc swung by the tie rod end and the arc swung by the steering knuckle. The factory suspension heights keep both arcs nearly equal, except at extreme suspension travel. But lowering the suspension means the steering knuckle operates within the upper "extreme" range more often, so the length of the tie rod is effectively shortened, and when the vehicle hits a bump, causing the suspension to compress, the wheels actually turn inward toward the center of the vehicle slightly.

Aftermarket companies offer kits to correct the situation by repositioning the tie rods to realign them with the arc swung by the steering knuckle to which they attach, but the best and easiest way to correct the problem is to avoid it altogether. Besides, lowering your Camaro only causes it to ground-out on even more speed bumps, entrance ramps, and other obstacles.

The rear suspension is also affected by lowering, because the arc of the Panhard rod forces the rearend to become misaligned. Furthermore, lowering upsets pinion angle. An adjustable Panhard rod is the only way to correct the misalignment, while an adjustable torque arm corrects the poor pinion angle.

For years, drag racing a Camaro has presented a problem: drag slicks use a bias-ply construction method, while street tires are radials. Drag tires have soft sidewalls that just don't like to put up with any cornering forces, so drag tires—even grooved ones—had to be carried to the track and mounted on the car there. Thankfully, BF Goodrich has come to our rescue with its Comp T/A Drag Radial. It's a drag tire, but it's also a D.O.T.-approved tire that you can drive on to the track. And its radial construction gives the tire a stiffer sidewall that actually makes street driving a safe, sane thing to do with the Drag Radial. Of course, it provides tremendous traction at the strip.

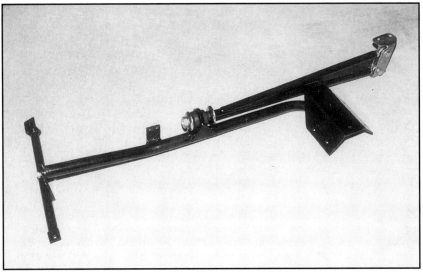

One of the best things you can do for your Camaro's rear suspension is replace its flimsy torque arm with an adjustable aftermarket torque arm, like this one, from Global West Suspension. The replacement arm changes the way the rear suspension works, and actually helps plant the rear tires more firmly under acceleration for better traction off the line or out of a corner.

rebound *and* compression strokes. A nice option for fourth-generation Camaro owners is the availability of a remotely adjustable shock set that allows you to alter your Camaro's shock damping right from the cockpit simply by pushing a button.

Stabilizer bars, too, can produce a significant change in handling attitude, though you should keep in mind that a stiffer stabilizer bar (usually larger diameter) tends to make your car feel as if it has higher-rate springs; thus, ride comfort may be compromised. As mentioned above, changing to polyurethane stabilizer bar mounting bushings yields a cost-effective and noticeable improvement that won't disturb the ride much, if any.

Finally, your wheel and tire combinations may come down to more of an aesthetic choice than anything

Alignment Settings/Tips

All of the best shocks, springs, stabilizer bars, and performance tires won't make your car feel good driving down the road if the front end alignment isn't optimized for the kind of driving that you do.

The three settings that determine overall front end alignment for each wheel are Toe, Caster, and Camber.

Toe expresses the direction of the front of the front wheels. It is expressed as "toe-in" if the wheels point inward, toward the center of the car. Conversely, it is called "toe-out" if the tires point away from the center of the car. Toe is generally what people are referring to when they say their car needs an alignment because it is "pulling" to one side or the other. If one wheel is adjusted with more toe-in than the other, the effect is similar to turning the steering wheel (i.e., both wheels are, more or less, pointed in the same direction, but not straight ahead), and either the front or rear edges of individual tread blocks display feathered edges. Toe is often set differently for the front wheels to counter the tendency for "crowned"

roads (where the center of the road is raised higher than the sides to promote water runoff) to cause the car to turn off the road.

Caster is the angle of the wheel's steering axis, described as viewed from the side of the vehicle, and generally affects the overall stability of the car and the steering wheel's tendency to self-center (i.e., return to straight-ahead from a turn). If the top of the steering axis tilts rearward, the wheel has positive caster, but if it tilts forward, it has negative caster. Positive caster makes the car much more stable at high speed, but increases steering effort, while negative camber has the opposite effect.

Finally, *camber* describes the tilt of the top of the front wheels, as viewed from ahead of or behind the wheels. If the top of the wheels tilt inward, toward the center of the vehicle, the wheel has *negative* camber, whereas positive camber would be tilting the top of the wheel outward, away from the center of the car. Camber directly affects the tire's contact patch by altering what part of

the tread, and how much of it, from side to side contacts the ground. For autocross and road-racing competition, a certain degree of negative camber is preferred because it maximizes tire contact during hard cornering, when the angle of the vehicle (and thus the angle of the wheel) would normally tend to lift the inside of the tire and roll the tire onto its outer sidewall. Improper camber settings wear the inside (too much negative camber) or outside (too much positive camber) of the tread abnormally. Camber settings have a lot to do with whether a car oversteers (the back end tends to swing around) or understeers (the front end keeps going straight) through corners.

Global West Suspension provided the following starting points, based on its extensive experience racing and driving Camaros in high-performance street situations. As always, exact settings may vary due to driver preferences, track layout and conditions, and specific vehicle equipment, so adjust settings as necessary for your particular situation.

	Caster			Camber			Toe (total)
	L	(deg.)	R	L	(deg.)	R	(in.)
HP Street	5P		5-1/2P	1N		1N	3/32
Drag Racing	4P		4P	0		0	1/32
Autocross Racing	6P		6P	1-1/2N		1-1/2N	1/16-1/8 (out)
Road Racing	6P		6P	1-1/2N		1-1/2N	1/16

Legend: N = Negative, P = Positive

else, but there are a few things worth considering. In terms of wheels, the widest wheel that fits practically is a 9-incher. Wider wheels can fit but start to compromise clearances, steering, bearing loads, and other factors. As far as diameter goes, 16- and 17-inch wheels fit nicely and look good, and some 18-inch or larger wheels may be appealing to you. In order to maintain the overall tire diameter, as you move to larger-diameter wheels, you need to reduce the tire's aspect ratio to ensure that your speedometer remains properly calibrated (which can affect performance of other systems). For instance, a 16-inch wheel and 50-series tire are standard Z28 equipment; 17-inch wheels are optional with 40-series rubber; and 18-inch wheels would need 35-series tires to stay in the circumference ballpark. But the larger the wheel diameter and the smaller the tire's aspect ratio, the more ride comfort is reduced, because the combination amplifies anomalies in the pavement. The upside of large-diameter wheels and short-sidewall tires, though, is greatly enhanced steering response.

The other dimension you're likely interested in is tire width. While it's tempting to want to stick to the widest tires that fit under your Camaro, that isn't always the smartest thing to do. If your part of the world is subject to "ruts" in the pavement—spots where the volume of traffic has caused the pavement to compress—you're probably already familiar with darty steering. This is caused by your Camaro's wide tires constantly climbing into and out of those ruts made by narrower tires. Going to wider tires only increases the problem.

A last note on tires for street use is the availability of Goodyear's "run-flat" Extended Mobility Tires. Designed with extra-stiff sidewalls, these tires actually let you drive up to 200 miles at highway speeds (55 miles per hour) with *zero* pounds of air pressure! Unlike some other "run-flat" types of tires, these tires do not require special wheels interlocking beads; the EMTs work on standard wheels. And because they've been used by Corvettes for some time, the EMTs are available in a number of popular sizes for Camaros.

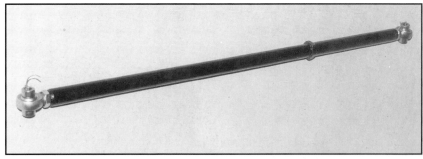

The stock Panhard rod (also called a "track bar") is responsible for the rear axle assembly's side-to-side alignment under your Camaro. But the stock Panhard rod is made of weak stamped steel, isn't adjustable and is expected to somehow compensate for production tolerances that often result in the rearend being misaligned. In short, the production Panhard rod isn't up to the job its asked to perform. Furthermore, lowering your Camaro further disrupts rear axle assembly alignment, worsening the problem. An adjustable Panhard rod, like this tubular steel unit from Global West Suspension can correct for these deficiencies and keeps the rear axle assembly properly positioned through even the most severe corners.

The catch is that because of their extra-stiff sidewalls, EMTs *never* look or feel like their air pressure is low, even when they have none, so you need an air pressure monitoring system that can alert you to a loss of pressure so that you can get the tire repaired or replaced before it becomes dangerous to drive on. The folks at Schrader (the valve people) have developed a system (based on the 1997 Corvette's pressure monitoring system) that should be available by the time you read this, and your local Goodyear dealer should be able to find out about it for you. While it's technically possible to use Goodyear's EMT tires without the pressure monitoring system, it's not recommended because even if you're absolutely *religious* about checking tire pressure with a hand-held gauge, you can't possibly account for problems you may experience while you're driving the car. If you were cruising along at 70 miles per hour and the tire was out of air, it would quickly overheat and destroy itself, making an accident quite likely—one that could injure or kill you or someone else.

Drag Racing

In drag racing, the name of the game is planting those back tires as firmly as possible against the ground. You can get your Camaro to help you do that through a number of upgrades and modifications.

Up front, you need to start by removing the stabilizer bar, or at least disconnecting it from the lower control arms when racing (and reconnecting it for street driving), otherwise it may limit weight transfer. Removing the bar altogether reduces vehicle weight somewhat, and may be worthwhile, too, since shaving pounds can help you go quicker and faster.

You also need to change the front shocks and springs. Since gas-charged shocks effectively increase spring rates (by further damping the spring oscillations), you want to stick to straight hydraulic-only shocks. Softer front spring help unload the front suspension at the launch and promote weight transfer to the rear wheels, which helps to plant them better. Specific aftermarket parts are available for this, including adjustable drag shocks that provide a great deal of tuning flexibility for particular track conditions. If you're on a budget, you might try utilizing a set of production shocks and springs intended for a V-6 model, though the performance won't be as impressive as with purpose-built drag shocks and springs.

The rear suspension is greatly improved by the installation of an adjustable torque arm that lets you set the pinion angle to account for track conditions.

Another nice addition to the rear suspension is a set of adjustable lower control arm mounts. Global West Suspension's "VariTrac" mount kit gets welded to the rear axle housing's lower control arm mounts and adds an additional two sets of mounting holes, which allows you to change the rear suspension's geometry to better suit your driving needs.

Shocks and springs also need to be changed to work in concert with the front units; typically most drag shocks and springs are sold in sets of four each, since mismatching can create deadly handling problems. Again, installing softer V-6 springs and shocks on a V-8 car achieves some of the same advantages if you can't afford to purchase the aftermarket items, but don't expect to beat a similar car that does have the aftermarket pieces under it.

The rear stabilizer bar may or may not prove helpful, depending on your particular car's powertrain, track conditions, and even your

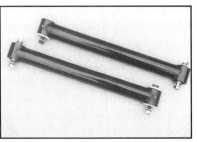

Like the Panhard rod and production torque arm, the factory rear control arms are made of flimsy stamped steel that bends and distorts when subjected to heavy acceleration, braking or cornering forces. Replacement control arms, like this Global West Suspension units, are much stronger and help keep the rear axle assembly properly located.

Del-A-Lum bushings (lower), from Global West Suspension, provide the benefits of polyurethane bushings—minimized play—without the restrictive binding problem. The bushings are also greasable to minimize noise.

driving style. Try it (cautiously!) with and without the bar and let the time slips dictate what you should do.

Upgrading the control arms and Panhard rod to heavier-duty pieces can provide some piece of mind, but you can achieve virtually the same benefits at a fraction of the cost simply by boxing the "open" side of the stock items by welding on some steel plates.

Bushings do deserve some attention, too. Soft, stock, rubber bushings can permit too much axle housing movement, but polyurethane bushings may bind up, which can cause other problems. Heim joints and solid bushings eliminate the slop and are a good route to go if the car is solely used for on-track drag racing. A final option, Del-A-Lum bushings, are a good choice for dual-purpose street/strip use because they aren't as unforgiving as solid bushings, but they won't bind like polyurethane bushings.

Wheel selection for drag racing is fairly straightforward: They need to be light-weight, yet strong enough to withstand the forces encountered at the track. Steel wheels are fine, but aluminum is usually lighter weight.

With tires, choices open up a bit more. Rules dictate the maximum tire width you can run, so always consult the rule books to see what your chosen class permits. Then you need to decide between a traditional bias-ply slick and the DOT-approved BF Goodrich Drag Radial, which has a minimal tread. Slicks, because they have such weak sidewalls, are never to be used on the street; plus, mixing bias-ply slicks with radials is a known recipe for disaster. It's just not a wise thing to do.

Autocrossing

Autocrossing demands that the suspension respond immediately and act precisely, otherwise you can quickly become out-of-shape, possibly enough to clip a cone, miss a gate, or even run right off course. But the suspension also has to behave well under hard braking and acceleration, too. In essence, autocrossing just magnifies what a car experiences on the street by several times, so the suspension has to provide a good balance of cornering and straight-line performance. The one area that may

be permitted to suffer is ride comfort, unless the car is still going to be street-driven during the week.

It should be noted that SCCA Solo racing rules are very specific about what modifications are permitted within the many racing classes. Make sure you consult the rule book before you make any changes, if you're hoping to remain within a particular class.

The key concern in autocrossing is that the car must be nimble, ready and able to change direction in an instant—it must be absolutely agile, cat-like. In order to achieve that agility, the car needs an exceptional grip on the ground, and therein lies the trick: balancing the positive and negative effects of weight transfer, both side-to-side and end-to-end. Too much weight transfer side-to-side and the inside tires lose their grip on the ground. Too little body roll and the outside tires won't be planted firmly enough, and the car won't want to steer—it will push going into a corner and get loose when power is re-applied.

The same holds true for end-to-end (fore-aft) weight transfer under braking and acceleration. If the front end doesn't get weighted heavily enough (i.e., enough weight isn't transferred from the rear end forward), the front tires won't be planted firmly enough to prevent understeer (the tendency of the car to continue going straight while the front tires are trying to turn it). Similarly, if too much weight transfers forward, the rear end becomes too light and the car oversteers (the rear end swings around).

The biggest gain you will notice comes from mounting up a set of super-sticky autocross competition tires, like BF Goodrich's R-1 or Goodyear's Eagle GS-CS. These tires provide gobs more grip than comparatively hard street tires, maximizing traction and allowing you to notice which parts of your Camaro's suspension are working well and which aren't.

Increasing traction at the front end places even greater loads on the already overstressed tie rod adjustment sleeves, so it's wise to replace the flimsy stock sleeves with heavy-duty aftermarket units. It's an easy, inexpensive swap that could just keep your front tires from facing each other at an inopportune time.

The next worthwhile step to make is an inexpensive one: a performance front end alignment. Your vehicle's specific suspension setup, the particular course layout, and even your driving preferences determine the ideal alignment specs, but the following recommendations should serve as good starting points. The first change involves increasing positive caster (the rearward tilt of the steering axis) to between 5 and 7 degrees. Pre-1987 third-generation cars max out at approximately 4 degrees positive camber, so take as much as you can get with them. Camber (the inward or outward tilt of the wheels) should ideally be set to approximately 1/2 to 1-1/2 degrees negative (inward) camber, although 1982–1987 cars only allow camber to go as far as 1/2 degree positive (out- ward), without modifications. Finally, toe should be set to approximately 1/32-1/8 inch *out* in order to remove play from the system and provide more responsive steering.

At the track, you need to adjust tire pressures to maximize each tire's contact patch. Check out the sidebar, "Maximum Tire Traction, Maximum Tire Life" for more info on how to properly check and set tire pressures.

Maximum Tire Traction, Maximum Tire Life

Let's face it: Performance tires are expensive. Unless you've got deep pockets that are lined with more than just lint (like mine), then it's in your own best interest to maximize your tire's tread life. It just so happens that most things necessary to make a tire last a good long life, also improve traction under most normal driving conditions.

The most important steps you can take to get the most from your tires are to keep the tire pressure properly adjusted, to rotate the tires periodically to even-out wear, to keep them properly balanced, and to keep the front end properly aligned.

Tire Pressures - Elsewhere in this chapter there's information on how to properly adjust tire air pressures for racing use, with the goal being to maximize traction. But on the street, those higher-than-usual pressures aren't going to provide satisfactory ride comfort or tread wear (they, however, help you get better fuel mileage by reducing rolling resistance). Over-inflated tires cause the middle of the tire's tread to balloon outward, thus it contacts the road much more than the sides of the tread, leading to accelerated wear of the center tread section. And since the tires feel rock-hard, unless you've got very supple springs and shocks, you feel every pebble and crack in the pavement.

Under-inflated tires can be just as problematic, though. Instead of ballooning the center of the tread outward, on an under-inflated tire the center tread section collapses inward, causing the tread's outer edges to carry most of the vehicle weight, thus causing them to wear more rapidly than usual. The sidewalls also heat up much more than usual and can cause internal damage to belts and cords in the tire. Rolling resistance is increased, so fuel mileage declines, and handling suffers because the tire squirms under the wheel, resisting steering inputs, rolling under while cornering and other problems. The only possible benefit of under-inflated tires is that they are softer, so they can improve ride comfort, but that's hardly worth the price of a new set of tires. (Besides, if ultimate ride comfort is your goal, you should have bought a used Cadillac.)

The goal, then, is to find a happy medium. Reading tire temperatures isn't accurate for street use, since any given stretch of road may cause one side of a tire or the other to build more heat. So, the best method is to simply monitor tire wear. For street driving, and depending on the particular tire, Camaros generally provide an acceptable balance of ride comfort, tread life, and handling with roughly 30–32 psi in the rear tires and 32–36 psi in the front tires.

Tire Rotations - Rotating tires from one corner of the vehicle to another gives each tire a chance to experience a variety of road and handling conditions. A good example would be moving the rear tires forward to subject them to steering forces that they wouldn't experience on the rear of the car.

Unfortunately, rotating wheels and tires can be difficult on most Camaros, given clearance differences between the front and rear wheelwells. And if you happen to have different-size wheels and/or tires on the front of your Camaro than on the back, you won't be able to rotate the tires. And you won't be able to swap tires from side to side if they are directional, unless you pay to have the tires dismounted from the wheels then remounted facing the opposite direction.

Still, if your particular wheel and tire combination allow periodic tire rotations (every 6,000 miles)—even if it's only front to rear, then back again the next time—you should rotate them religiously. You will be amazed how much longer the tires lasts, and how evenly they wear. As an example, despite enthusiastic street driving, I've personally run two sets of Goodyear Eagles (first VR "Gatorbacks," then GS-Cs) for more than 26,000 miles each with even wear, while most Camaro drivers I've spoken with complain that their tires had to be replaced after 18,000–20,000 miles due to cupping and uneven wear. When asked if they rotated their tires, nearly all sheepishly admitted they hadn't.

Tire Balance - When you were younger, you probably played on one of those little flying saucers at the playground that spun around in a circle. You'd run along beside it, getting it to spin faster and faster, then jump on, only to have to struggle to stay on, because centrifugal force was trying to toss you off onto your rump. Well, your wheel and tire combination is just like that flying saucer at the playground. As the tire rotates, it tries to throw that imbalance off the tire, which causes the tires to grow in that spot. Simultaneously, it causes a point 180-degrees away to be pulled inward, so the tire wears rapidly at the imbalance and hardly at all on the other "side" of the tire. But by adding weight 180-degrees from the imbalance, you can cancel out the imbalance, and restore the wheel's smooth rotation, so the tire spins round again and wears evenly.

Alignment - Alignments are covered elsewhere in this chapter, so we won't get into it here. However, to sum it up: Improper toe settings causes the tread blocks to feather their front or rear edges, while improper camber settings wear one side of the tire tread more than the other. Unusual caster settings don't result in abnormal tire wear.

With tire contact and steering action well in tune, you can begin turning your attention to the actual suspension shortcomings of your Camaro, and, arguably, there's no greater shortcoming than the rear suspension. A good first improvement for the rear suspension is to replace all four shocks with adjustable units, such as those from Koni, which allows you to control weight transfer fore and aft, as well as side-to-side, plus tune the handling for particular course designs. Double-adjustable shocks provide the best tuning opportunities, so splurge if you can afford it.

Your next moves should aim at removing slack from the rear suspension system, making sure it reacts quickly and predictably to both the road surface, as well as any steering actions you might make. Most noticeably, you should replace the flimsy Panhard rod (a.k.a. the track bar) with a more sturdy unit with firmer bushings, or better yet, Heim joints. An adjustable Panhard rod allows you to correct rear axle assembly positioning beneath your Camaro, to ensure the car is tracking straight (rather than "crab walking" through the course). Replacement lower control arms with firmer bushings also help keep the rear end properly located.

Though it's less important from a handling standpoint, installation of

a stronger, adjustable torque arm helps improve braking and acceleration into and out of corners, which can help you explode toward the next gate, rather than rolling into the throttle to avoid possible tire spin. This is especially important if your Camaro's engine has been significantly upgraded, making tire spin likely.

Another helpful tuning aid is Global West's VariTrac adjustable lower control arm mounts. These mounts change rear suspension geometry, helping the car hook up better for quicker acceleration.

Springs and stabilizer bars are harder recommendations to make, because they depend upon particular course layouts. In general, stock springs and stabilizer bars often provide good performance when combined with the above-prescribed system upgrades. Any changes require a trial-and-error approach. However, it should be pointed out that only linear-rate (nonprogressive) springs should be used, to preserve predictability.

Road Racing

Road racing is uniquely demanding because of the speeds at which things take place. With speeds often well over 100 miles per hour, there simply isn't time for mistakes, so it's absolutely critical that your Camaro's suspension respond quickly, decisively, and predictably to inputs. This requires replacing any

weak parts or parts that allow for uncontrolled movement.

For third- and fourth-generation Camaros, the biggest problem area is the rear suspension. The stock design allows the rear axle assembly to roll, move from side-to-side, front-to-back, and even cock itself at an angle. And the rear axle assembly rarely reacts the same way twice to a given input, because those movements are uncontrolled.

Beyond just removing play from the system, though, the car needs to accelerate and brake predictably and controllably, too.

As with autocrossing, a set of soft-compound road racing tires radically improves handling, acceleration, and braking, and should be your first change.

Adjustable shocks—again, preferably double-adjustable units—are a wise investment for each corner, because they allow you to tune your suspension for various tracks and conditions. They also continue to be useful with the following upgrades, since you can always tune the shocks to maximize the overall system performance. Fourth-generation cars have the added ability of being able to run coil-over shocks (third-gens can run rear coil-overs), which allow for ride height adjustments and weight jacking (what NASCAR guys term adding or removing "wedge").

An adjustable replacement torque arm cures the rear suspension's geometry problems, making it easier for your car to put its power to the ground. The replacement arm also cuts down on the rear axle assembly's unwanted movements, which makes the system more predictable.

An adjustable Panhard rod lets you properly locate the rear axle assembly under the car, then rest assured it remains there even when subjected to the highest cornering forces.

Stronger lower control arms (replacements or boxed factory parts) with either Heim joints or Del-A-Lum bushings should remove the last of the slop from the rear suspension.

The front end needs stronger tie rod adjustment sleeves, and the control arms should be treated to higher-rate bushings in the name of predictable movement and reactions.

Another popular upgrade is to replace stock rubber suspension bushings (control arms, stabilizer bar mounts, and Panhard rod) with firmer polyurethane bushings. While the firmer poly bushings minimize unwanted movements of the components, they can actually create suspension bind, and thereby hamper suspension action. They also tend to be quite noisy, which makes them annoying in a street car.

Another unique upgrade for the rear suspension system is Global West Suspension's VeriTrac adjustable rear control arm mount kit. After welding the brackets to the rear axle housing, they provide three mounting positions (stock, plus two lower positions) that alter rear suspension geometry and help you tune your car's suspension for better acceleration and braking performance.

Again, picking springs and stabilizer bars is subject to the track you are running, other equipment your car is fitted with, and, of course, driver preferences. Owners of fourth-generation cars should consider running coil-over shock and spring assemblies, because of the incredible tuning flexibility they provide. Particular spring rates depend on the shock designs and valving, so consulting with the shock manufacturer is the best way to get springs that are "in the ballpark." Owners of third-generation cars likely have better results ordering a set of 1LE or similar extra-firm, linear-rate springs and stabilizer bars to start with, and relying on the adjustable shocks and struts to tune the system.

Suspension Parts and Upgrades

A number of individual components make up the third- and fourth-generation Camaro suspension systems. Any upgrades you make will more than likely be to these "bolt-on" components, rather than to the body/chassis structure itself. Thus, it's useful to know exactly what parts you are dealing with, as well as some of the shortcomings of each, and how you might be able to correct them to better suit your particular driving needs.

Bushings, Front and Rear Control Arms, 1982–1998

Stock rubber bushings, though comfortable for street use, allow excessive movement of the rear axle assembly under demanding driving conditions. Polyurethane bushings are available and are generally considered to be an improvement over rubber bushings; however, polyurethane bushings can cause the suspension to "bind," producing unpredictable action. Some arms are available with racing-style Heim joints, which remove all slop but transmit excessive vibration and shock to the cockpit, thus making them undesirable for street use. A final option, the Del-A-Lum bushing, is similar to a polyurethane bushing in terms of its durometer (resistance to deflection); however, its steel inner sleeve is free to rotate within the bushing to prevent binding.

Center/Drag Link, 1982–1992

The center link is a steel bar approximately 2 feet in length that connects to the Pitman arm, and to which the left- and right-side inner tie rod ends connect. As the Pitman arm swings, it moves the center link, which moves both inner tie rod ends. The center link is supported on the right side of the vehicle by an idler arm. The center link has no moving parts and doesn't normally require service or replacement, unless it is damaged in an accident.

Front Lower Control Arms, 1982–1992

The original front lower control arms for third-generation Camaros are stamped steel with rubber bushings. For most applications they are suitable as-is. However, for racing use, it may be worthwhile to reinforce them by welding similar-gauge sheet metal to box in the bottoms of the arms for additional strength. In addition, there are tubular steel replacement arms available from aftermarket manufacturers that are both stronger as-is and offer a more correct method of lowering the front suspension, by utilizing deeper spring pockets. Note, however, that deeper spring pockets reduce ground clearance at the control arms.

Front Lower Control Arms, 1993–1998

Fourth-generation factory front lower control arms are of stamped steel construction and feature reinforcing gussets that box much of the arm, resulting in an exceptionally strong component. There is no need to modify the arms for most uses, though autocrossers and road racers may gain some peace of mind by providing additional reinforcing in high stress areas, such as the sides of the arms, the shock mounting points, and the stabilizer bar mounting areas.

Front Upper Control Arms, 1993–1998

The stock upper control arms of fourth-generation Camaros are also stamped steel in construction, and are suitable as-is for most uses, though could benefit from additional reinforcing for serious racing efforts.

Fourth-generation car's use a much simpler and less trouble-prone system: a rack-and-pinion steering "box" visible here.

Idler Arm, 1982–1992

The idler arm is a small, L-shaped arm that supports the right-side end of the center link.

Panhard Rod, 1982–1998

The Panhard rod locates the rear axle assembly laterally (side-to-side) beneath the vehicle. One end of the Panhard rod connects to the rear axle housing, and the other end connects to a bracket mounted to the body structure. The stock Panhard rod is of stamped-steel construction in the form of a channel. In stock form, it is unsuitable to anything but mundane commuter driving, due to its weak and imprecise design.

The stock Panhard rod can be strengthened by boxing it, although this won't correct any production tolerance problems. Aftermarket Panhard rods are generally constructed of tubular steel and often feature polyurethane bushings or Heim joints to connect to the rear axle assembly and body structure. Adjustable arms are available and are strongly recommended because of their ability to correct for production variances that can result in an improperly located rear axle assembly. Adjustable arms are also ideally suited to correcting for mislocation of the rear axle assembly that results from lowering the rear suspension.

Rear Lower Control Arms, 1982–1998

Third- and fourth-generation Camaros utilize the same rear lower control arms to keep the rear axle assembly located properly, front-to-

This look at the upper end of the fourth-generation Camaro front suspension system clearly shows the coil-over shock/spring assembly and upper A-arm. While the factory coil-over assembly isn't adjustable (1LE models do come with double-adjustable Koni shocks), aftermarket coil-over units are available that provide ride height or weight-jacking adjustments that allow you to optimize your Camaro's suspension setup for a particular track or driver's preferences.

rear, beneath the car. Unfortunately the stock arms are only channeled stamped steel and are very weak. Heavy-duty replacement arms are readily available, or the stock arms can be upgraded by boxing the open, lower portion.

Shock Absorber/Damper, Front, 1993–1998; Rear, 1982–1998

Shock absorbers don't really "absorb" bumps, they dampen the movements that result from encountering a bump. Valves inside the shock absorber control how quickly the shock rod can move up (rebound) and down (compress) within the shock body. This, in turn, controls how quickly the spring can extend and compress, so the shock effectively acts as a timer, delaying the spring's reaction to a bump. Shocks can be of three basic types: hydraulic twin tube; gas-charged hydraulic twin tube; and

Looking at these two springs (the stock one on the left and a heavy-duty aftermarket rear spring on the right), you might assume the aftermarket spring would lower ride height significantly. The truth of the matter is that the stock spring normally compresses a great deal when installed, whereas the aftermarket spring's compression rate was so high that it hardly compressed at all. The end result: Ride height didn't change, but the ride was noticeably firmer, and both body roll and brake dive were reduced. Incidentally, lowering a Camaro doesn't necessarily improve handling, and it can actually create handling problems.

high-pressure, gas-charged, mono-tube. Additionally, some shocks offer adjustable valving for either rebound or compression, or both, allowing owners to tune suspension to suit the needs of their driving environment or preferences. Several different calibrations have been used during the production run of third- and fourth-generation Camaros, from soft shocks for a plush ride, to super-firm 1LE racing shocks and even double-adjustable Koni racing shocks. Aftermarket shocks are available in different calibrations; adjustable shocks offer the best performance potential because of their tunability.

Strut Cartridge, Front, 1982–1992

A MacPherson strut cartridge is merely a modified version of a shock absorber that does double-duty as a suspension member that helps to locate the wheel.

Springs, Front and Rear

Springs are what hold the car up off its bump-stops, and they're responsible for the "cushion" effect when you hit a bump. A number of different spring tensions (expressed in pounds-per-inch) have been used by Chevrolet during the production of 1982–1998 Camaros, from soft (base) to extra-firm (1LE). Still more are available from aftermarket sources, though most aftermarket springs are firmer than Z28 springs, or are designed to lower your Camaro's ride height.

Stabilizer Bars, Front and Rear

Stabilizer bars are utilized on Camaros to help control body roll (leaning) during cornering. A single bar spans from one control arm to the other, in front, or from one sub-frame rail to the other, in back. As the weight of the body transfers toward one side of the car during a corner, the suspension for that side of the car begins to compress, twisting the stabilizer bar. Meanwhile, the suspension on the other side of the car is attempting to extend, as weight is unloaded from it, again, attempting to twist the stabilizer bar, but in the opposite direction. As the bar resists these twisting forces and tries to remain flat, it pushes the outer wheel back down while pulling the inner wheel back up, effectively leveling the body. If both front or both rear wheels compress or extend, the bar simply pivots in its mounts attached to the body structure.

Thinner-diameter bars offer less resistance to body roll than do larger-diameter bars, while neither alters ride comfort significantly. While different size bars have been used by the factory and still more are available through the aftermarket, the factory bars may be better choices, because most are typically hollow tubing and are therefore lighter (yet just as effective) as solid aftermarket bars.

Steering Box, 1982–1992

Third-generation Camaros relied upon a decades-old basic steering box design that utilizes a recirculating ball steering mechanism to translate the rotary steering wheel inputs to linear movements that change the direction of the front wheels. The system is effective but requires a bulky, heavy, and complex assembly of steering linkage to transmit steering actions from the steering box to the wheels. Third-generation Camaros utilized several different steering ratios, the most desirable of which are the fast-ratio (higher effort) performance boxes used on Z28s and IROC-Zs. Slower-ratio (reduced effort) boxes were used on nonperformance models.

Steering Rack, 1982–1992

Fourth-generation Camaros did away with the need for much of the steering linkage by switching to a rack-and-pinion steering box that is easier for engineers to design an engine compartment around. It also has the advantage of providing better steering "feel." Again, lighter-effort units were utilized by the factory for nonperformance models, while the Z28s and IROC-Zs featured higher-effort units more suited to fast driving.

Tie Rod Adjustment Sleeves, 1982–1992

Tie rod adjustment sleeves work like turn-buckles, bringing the tie rod ends closer together or moving them further apart to adjust front wheel toe settings. The stock tie rod adjustment sleeves are made of stamped steel and were originally designed to work with the 14- and 15-inch wheels and relatively narrow tires that were planned for the early third-generation cars. Sixteen-inch wheels and wide, sticky tires place more stress on the tie rod adjustment sleeves and cause them to flex or even bend, either of which changes the toe and makes steering unpredictable.

The stock adjustment sleeves can be strengthened by welding bracing material around the sleeves. However, the sleeves can't be fully reinforced, because the stock sleeves are retained by constricting clamps that require the sleeves to be flexible in the clamped area. Heavy-duty aftermarket sleeves, available from Global West and other companies, are significantly stronger, and they eliminate the possibility of tie rod adjustment sleeve flex and, thus, maintain the proper toe settings.

Because the steering rack's output shafts connect directly to the tie rod ends, there's no need for an adjuster sleeve. For racing purposes, however, it may be worthwhile to reinforce the stock steering shafts to eliminate the chance that they might bend.

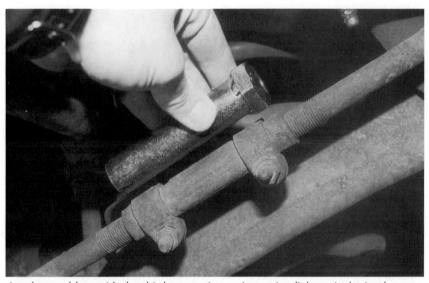

Another problem with the third-generation car's steering linkage is the inadequate tie rod adjuster sleeve. When subjected to the high loads created by large-diameter wheels, wide sticky tires, and high cornering forces, the stock sleeves actually bend. Heavy-duty replacement sleeves eliminate the problem.

Tie Rod Ends

Tie rod ends transmit steering actions from the center link (third-generation) or rack-and-pinion unit (fourth-generation) to the steering knuckles. Stock tie rod ends are made of cast iron and feature a ball-and-socket joint to allow the arm to flex as the suspension causes the suspension to raise and lower, relative to the center link or steering rack. Stock tie rod ends are usually acceptable for even high-performance use, though for racing use it would be wise to have them magnaflux inspected to detect any cracks. It is also possible to replace the stock tie rod ends with Heim joints for more precise steering action in competition use.

Tires

Tires are the last components in your Camaro's suspension system. They provide not only traction for

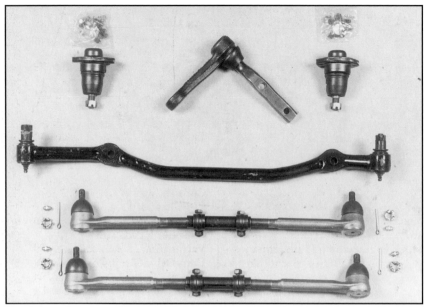

Third-generation Camaros use a complex assembly of steering linkage to transmit your steering commands from the steering box to the wheels. The system uses several ball-and-socket joints that allow for suspension movement, but also allow for imprecise steering.

acceleration, cornering, and braking but also, through their flexible sidewalls, act as springs to soften the ride. Stock Camaros have come with a dizzying assortment of tires from the factory, and countless more are available from numerous tire manufacturers. Prescribing the right tires for your Camaro largely depends upon how you use (or intend to use) your Camaro. No matter what tires you use, however, it is critical that you "tune" them properly by adjusting their air pressure and utilize alignment settings that maximize the tire contact patch with the road surface.

Torque Arm, 1982–1998

Third- and fourth-generation Camaros utilize a torque arm to prevent the rear axle housing from rotating around the axles. The stock arm connects to the snout of the rear axle assembly and runs forward to a rubber-bushed mount attached to the transmission tailshaft housing. Because the stock arm is constructed of stamped steel, it is rather weak and subject to flexing, which allows the rear axle assembly to rotate, affecting the suspension's ability to plant the rear tires and thrust the car forward. Furthermore, the torque arm's front mount on the transmission further limits the arm's effectiveness, because it compounds the flexing problem when the transmission rocks due to engine torque.

As if that weren't enough, the stock arm does nothing to improve traction, because it still allows the rear of the car to squat on acceleration, which effectively lifts the wheels (especially the right rear) off the pavement, reducing traction. While the stock arm could be reinforced to limit its flexing, the rubber front mount would still permit it to twist, and the rubber is necessary, given that the rear axle assembly does move as the suspension compresses and extends. Furthermore, even if you could remove all the flex from the arm, that wouldn't do anything to correct the poor geometry of the stock arm, or its inability to prevent rear end squat.

Aftermarket torque arms, such as those available from Global West and HP Motorsports, don't connect to the transmission, but rather to the body structure, so when the rear end attempts to rise on acceleration, they raise the body, thus planting the tires more firmly against the road surface, increasing traction. The arms also do the opposite during braking—they pull the body down, reducing unsettling and unpredictable weight transfer forward. Both companies' torque arms also permit pinion angle adjustments to control how "hard" or "soft" the power hits the rear tires when you nail the throttle on acceleration. Street tires don't have the traction to handle a sudden application of power, so they require a softer setting. Racing slicks can generally maintain traction when subjected to a sudden application of power, so they can take a harder setting; a softer setting would only serve to slow acceleration by wasting time and delaying full power application.

Track Bar, 1982–1998

See "Panhard Rod"

ENGINE

No matter how well your Camaro handles, no matter how exotic your new brake hardware, no matter what custom touches you've added to its body, enthusiasts always ask about its engine, and probably long before they even wonder about that other stuff.

The engine's disproportionate attention is inevitable, because it's the one part that more enthusiasts equate with power and performance. Never mind that we know that the engine is only a small part of a well-balanced Camaro, or any car, for that matter. It's the part that everyone credits if you're able to outrun your competition: "Man, he must be making some serious power!" even though you might be 50 horses short of what your competitor has but happen to know how to make what you've got work harder.

The good news, of course, is that there's no reason you have to give up any power to anyone. It's technically possible to build an engine for your later-model Camaro that belts out almost unlimited performance. You can start with the stock engine and add performance-enhancing "bolt-on" parts, like a free-flowing air filter, a higher-performance aftermarket computer "PROM" chip, or a less-restrictive "cat-back" exhaust system, or you can rebuild your stock engine with racing parts like a hot camshaft, deep-breathing cylinder heads, exhaust headers, and lightweight, high-compression pistons with special rings. Or you can go all-out and put together a full racing engine that would be more than a match for any NASCAR, Trans-Am, or NHRA small-block V-8. And if the factory's 350-cubic-inch displacement cap seems a bit too restrictive to you, big-block engine swaps are practically a snap.

While it may be fun to dream, for most enthusiasts, finances and

The Callaway SuperNatural 383 LT1 engine is a perfect example of what can be done to a Camaro engine to increase performance and reliability. The SuperNatural 383 develops 404 horsepower, is emissions legal, runs on pump gas, and can sip a gallon of fuel every 25 miles.

practicality are going to dictate sticking with the original engine and finding ways of increasing its power output to acceptable levels. And, as you will find out, there's certainly no shortage of desirable engines under the hoods of late-model Camaros.

Factory Engines

Through the years, nothing has defined a Camaro more than its available engines. In the 1960s, there was the Z28's race-ready 302, the thundering 396 big-blocks in SS models, and the ultra-rare pair of COPO 427s—the L72 425-horse and the ZL1 430-horse big blocks. As Camaro entered the 1970s, a new small block, the LT-1 350, came along with 360 horsepower, proving that big-block power can come in small packages. Though the remainder of the 1970s put horsepower on hold as engineers struggled to cope with unprecedented emissions and fuel economy regulations, salvation came in the 1980s, when engineers learned to harness the power of computerized engine control systems. Once again, horsepower and torque were worth talking about. And unlike in the past, along with power peaks and torque curves, Chevy could shout about excellent

fuel mileage, reliability, and emissions in the same breath. And things only got better in the 1990s, with second- and third-generation "small-block" Chevy V-8s that broke new ground in terms of power, reliability, and efficiency.

To put it bluntly, late-model engines are truthfully the best engines ever offered in Camaros of any generation. But, of course, there's always room for improvement. Everything from the venerable inline four-cylinder that was the base engine for 1982–1985 to the latest late-model engine, the all-aluminum LS1, can benefit from carefully selected upgrades.

V-8 Engines

Tops on performance enthusiasts' minds have always been the V-8 engines on Camaro's option list. The basic rule of thumb has always been that there's no substitute for cubic inches, and as far as Camaros go, the V-8s have had more cubes; thus, they made more power.

Since the debut of the 1982 Camaro, three different generations of small block V-8s have been used to power the Chevy F-body. The first-generation Chevy small-block, which

originally appeared way back in 1955, was used through 1992, but when the fourth-generation Camaro appeared it featured the second-generation small block, the LT1, which was actually introduced in 1992 in the Corvette. In 1998, the smaller, lighter, more efficient, more powerful third-generation small block, the LS1, arrived under the Camaro's new curvaceous hood, just a half-year after the engine first showed up in (where else?) the 1997 Corvette.

While the latter two generations of small blocks have had relatively little to differentiate them from one another, the first generation was produced in a variety of configurations. Most easily pointed to are the numerous induction systems that have fed the engines. Old-tech carburetor-fed systems were used through 1987, and they actually worked quite well, as both the LG4 and L69 "HO"—the latter of which boasted of up to 190 horsepower!—305 engines proved.

The throttle body injection systems were a step up in technology. Available at the dawn of the third generation in the form of the exotic-looking (but silly sounding) RPO LU5 twin-throttle body "Cross-Fire Injection" system, and later on the L03 305 V-8, the TBI systems looked like funny carburetors with large egg-like fuel injectors over their venturis. While the Cross-Fire system was heavily criticized, and was perhaps a bit too far ahead of its time, the later L03 engines were another matter altogether. Though no match for the sequential port fuel injection "Tuned Port Injection" systems that debuted in 1985 on the LB9 305, the L03 was a far less costly system and could easily have been built for more power.

The most efficient induction system design was the aforementioned Tuned Port Injection ("TPI" for short) system that was used from 1985–1992 on the LB9 305 and B2L/L98 350 "Corvette engine," which produced up to 245 horsepower in stock trim. A short-runner version of the TPI system was employed on the LT1/LT4/L99 engine family (and a similar version is available from aftermarket suppliers) from 1993 to 1997. Another variant of the TPI system was incorporated into the 1998 LS1 V-8, but featured several noteworthy

The Camaro has often benefited from having the Corvette as a big brother, especially in the engine department, as seen here with this 1993 Z-28's hand-me-down Corvette LT1. The LT1 and its L99 and LT4 derivatives are known as "Gen-II" small-block Chevy V-8s. They feature a number of improvements over the original small block, including reverse-flow cooling, a more compact design, and very impressive power output and efficiency.

updates, including its medium-length runner intake manifold formed of a "composite" (i.e., plastic) material.

From an enthusiast's standpoint, the TPI engines are the engines of choice, not only because they make more power than the other offerings, but also because there are more performance parts available for them, and they still meet emissions requirements that are required if the cars are to be driven on the street. Second choices would be the carbureted systems, since they can draw upon the four decades of performance parts that have been developed for small-block Chevys. The bottom of the list, unfortunately, belongs to the TBI systems, not because they're bad systems (after all, they're not), but because the aftermarket simply hasn't responded well to them. Still, even the TBI engines can be upgraded, so don't feel dejected if that's what mixes the air and fuel your Camaro thrives on.

And, as we mentioned earlier, there's still no real substitute for cubic inches, so, if or when possible, go for a 350-inch V-8 instead of the 305; it's just easier to make more power thanks to those 45 extra cubic inches the 350 displaces. Naturally, this only really applies to the third-generation cars, since the V-8s in fourth-generation Camaros weren't offered in multiple displacements.

V-6 Engines

Like the V-8 engines available in Camaros over the years, there have been a number of V-6 engines offered, in different displacements, with different induction systems, and, naturally, some are more "performance-oriented" than others.

The initial V-6, the LC1, displaced 2.8 liters (173 cubic inches) and, like the V-8s, was carbureted and rather anemic at only 102-107 horsepower. Along with the TPI LB9 305 V-8, 1985 brought a multiport fuel injection (MPFI) induction system to the V-6 in the name of greater fuel efficiency and reduced exhaust emissions. The fact that the LB8 2.8-liter V-6's power leaped to 135 horses didn't hurt matters any, either.

The V-6 swelled in size in 1990 to displace 3.1 liters in the LH0 MPFI

Another Corvette hand-me-down engine, the LS1, came along in the 1998 Camaro, nearly a year after the all-new 1997 Corvette debuted with the engine in January 1997. With 305 horsepower, the all-aluminum LS1 represents the "third-generation" Chevrolet small-block V-8, but really shares no parts in common with the previous two generations.

V-6, but horsepower only climbed 5 horsepower to 140 horses. Displacement jumped to 3.4 liters, plus different programming in the Engine Control Module changed the MPFI system to a sequential fuel injection (SFI, meaning each injector fired individually, corresponding with the firing order of the engine) system.

While these V-6s were admirable performers—some were even down-right fun to drive—none offered stunning performance, and the difference between them and the V-8 offerings was quite dramatic. In the case of the 1993–1995 Camaros, the V-6 was down 105 horsepower to the LT1 V-8.

The 1996 L36 "3800" V-6 (3.8 liters, or 231 cubic inches) changed many Camaro buyers' views of the economical V-6. With 200 horsepower, the base Camaro coupe's

The 305 versus 350 Engine Debate

Owners of fourth-generation Camaros have it easy. If they're doing a build-up on a production V-8 engine, they are building the 350-inch version. That's because the 350 was standard equipment. But owners of third-generation cars face a dilemma: Should they go with the RPO B2L 350 even though it's only available with the automatic transmission? Or should they go for the RPO LB9 305, which was available with a five-speed and only came in 15 horses shy of the 350 with the dual-cat exhaust?

The problem can seem pretty perplexing at first. But when you start thinking about it, the answer becomes pretty clear—the 350 is the way to go! The 305 only limits the amount of power you are able to produce, given

that the bulk of the parts you are going to stuff into the 305 would work even better in a 350.

Even if you want a manual tranny, it doesn't make much sense to go with the 305. The stock MM5 Borg-Warner T5 five-speed manual gearbox can't handle the stock 350's power and surely breaks up when mated to a hopped-up 305.

The reality is you need to replace a hefty hunk of the drivetrain even if you stick with the undercubed 305. Then you might as well just go for the 350 and get all the power you can. Besides, it's no more difficult—or costly—to rebuild the drivetrain to handle the 350's output than it is to set it up for the 305's.

In short, cubes count, and the more the merrier.

standard-issue V-6 was just 15 horsepower shy of the optional V-8 in Ford's Mustang! Performance was, in a word, impressive. But, considering the engine's lineage, that's not terribly surprising.

The GM "3800" V-6 is derived from the Buick Grand National's (and GNX's) legendary turbocharged, intercooled MPFI 3.8-liter V-6, which put out 245 horsepower in standard 1987 production Grand National trim—and 300 horses for the limited production GNX! While the Camaro made do without the force-feeding equipment, applying the technology lessons learned in the nine years since the engine saw true performance use in the GN and GNX models (the engine never went out of production, and was, in fact, treated to a supercharger in Pontiac Bonneville models in the early 1990s), engineers were able to wring 200 naturally aspirated horses out of the engine, plus improve fuel mileage, emissions, starting, and overall driveability.

If picking a V-6 to fulfill performance duties, the 3800 is a clear-cut winner, but it's not easily adapted to the third-generation cars, because it would require the PCM, wiring harness, accessory mounting brackets and pulleys, accessories, transmission, and other components from the donor car. (Note, however, that Pontiac had installed a version of the Grand National's intercooled turbo 3.8-liter V-6 in the 1989 Trans-Am, so exhaust pieces, motor mounts, and other necessary "accessories" should be available from any GM dealer's parts department.) Aftermarket parts for the Grand National engine can be utilized to fortify the internals if desired, while superchargers available from aftermarket sources provide an instant bolt-on power boost.

Looking at the old 2.8–3.4-liter six-shooters, it's more a matter of choosing the lesser of three evils. The 2.8-liter engine was a peppy, free-revving motor, but lacked serious power, even in MPFI form. The 3.1's longer stroke detracted from the engine's playful spirit, and it was only marginally regained in the 3.4-liter engine. What's worse is that the availability of performance parts for these engines (beyond specific internal parts, like racing pistons and heavy-duty connecting rods) is practically nil, so upgrades beyond free-flowing air filters and exhaust systems is difficult, at best.

Chevrolet V-6s have earned a reputation for exceptional performance in professional motorsports competition, such as NASCAR's Busch Grand National series, before it switched to V-8s. Many of the technologies, techniques, and even the parts that made great racing engines can be adapted to some of the production V-6s.

The Camaro is more than just a performance machine, though. It's a practical, economical, sporty commuter car when equipped with an engine like this 3.4L V-6 in a 1994 fourth-generation model. Third-generation Camaros were available with four-cylinders and two different displacement V-6s through the years.

Inline Four-Cylinder (I-4) Engines

The first four years of the third-generation Camaro's production cycle have the dubious distinction of offering Camaro's only four-cylinder engine ever as base equipment in Camaro sport coupes.

With just 88–92 horsepower, depending on the particular year in

305 Head Headaches

If you've chosen to build or modify a Camaro 305 cubic-inch V-8 engine, you need to be aware that cylinder heads for the larger-bore 350 may present problems—potentially very serious problems—if used on the 305.

Because the 305 has a smaller (3.875-inch) bore than the 350 (4.00-inch), its cylinder head's combustion chamber is designed to match the smaller bore; combustion chambers in 350 heads extend beyond the bore, over the 305's block deck. Depending on the size of the valves installed in the head, the valves may even contact the block deck, which would instantly ruin the valves, and probably the head and block, as well.

In addition, 350s have different airflow demands and characteristics than 305s, so 350 heads may not be ideally suited to making more power on a 305.

Another complication is that there are very, very few heads designed specifically for the 305 and its small cylinder bore. In fact, the only company promoting its 305 heads is World Products, which makes an exceptional cast-iron stock-replacement head that flows significantly better than the stock head.

The shortage of choice heads from which to choose is yet another strike against the otherwise delightful 305 when it comes to rebuild time.

question, the LQ8 and LQ9 "Iron Duke" 151-cubic-inch engines originally developed by Pontiac were barely adequate to move a Camaro at the legal highway speed limit, let alone get your heart racing in the process. Their lackluster performance makes them an unlikely pick for any serious performance endeavors. However, because the engines are members of the "Iron Duke" engine line—which has enjoyed a tremendously successful racing life, and still has a vast array of performance parts available from both General Motors' Performance Parts division and aftermarket companies— there is potential for anyone interested in doing things the hard way.

Determining Your Engine Needs

The stock Camaro engine offerings are excellent for a wide variety of circumstances and serve the car well. But when increased performance comes to mind, the almost limitless upgrades available can make it difficult (to put it mildly) to determine what is best to do in your particular case.

For the sake of simplicity, the following recommendations are limited to the stock engine assemblies and do not encompass engine swaps, which often entail their own volume of specific changes necessary to perform at their best.

Production Camaro Engine Availability

Engine RPO Code	LC1	LG4	LQ8	LQ9	LU5	L69	LB8	LB9	B2L	L03	LHO	L32	LT1	L36	LS1
Year	6/C	8/C	4/C	4/C	8/I	8/C	6/M	8/M	8/M	8/I	6/M	6/S	8/M-S	6/S	8/S
1982 VIN	1	H	F	2	7										
1982 HP	102	145	-	90	165*										
1983 VIN	1	H	F	2	S	7									
1983 HP	107	150	-	92	175	190									
1984 VIN	1	H		2		G									
1984 HP	107	150		92		190									
1985 VIN		H		2		G	I	F							
1985 HP		155		88		190	135	215*							
1986 VIN		H				G	S	F							
1986 HP		155				190	135	190*							
1987 VIN		H					S	F	8						
1987 HP		165					135	190Δ	225*						
1988 VIN							S	F	8	E					
1988 HP							135	195‡	230*	170					
1989 VIN							S	F	8	E					
1989 HP							135	195‡	230Ω	170					
1990 VIN								F	8	E	T				
1990 HP								210‡	245*	170	140				
1991 VIN								F	8	E	T				
1991 HP								205‡	245*	170	140				
1992 VIN								F	8	E	T				
1992 HP								205‡	245*	170	140				
1993 VIN												S	P		
1993 HP												160	275		
1994 VIN												S	P		
1994 HP												160	275		
1995 VIN												S	P		
1995 HP												160	275		
1996 VIN													P	K	
1996 HP													285	200	
1997 VIN													P	K	
1997 HP													285	200	
1998 VIN															G
1998 HP														200	305°

Legend:
4 = Inline 4
6 = V-6
8 = V-8
C = Carbureted

I = Throttle Body Fuel Injected
M = Multiport Fuel Injection
S = Sequential Port Fuel Injection

Δ   Z28 only
*   Z28 (or IROC) w/auto. only
     Z28 (or IROC) w/manual only
‡   195-210 horsepower w/auto; 205-230 horsepower w/manual; 230 horsepower w/manual and dual-cat. exh.
Ω   240 horsepower w/dual-cat. exh.
°   320 w/SS package

While V-6 engines aren't usually much to write home about, the 1996 3800 V-6, which is based on the same engine formerly used in the ominous turbocharged 1987 Buick Regal Grand National, puts out 200 horsepower — just 15 horses shy of the Mustang's base V-8! And with an available supercharger, the 3800 V-6 is a match for any stock V-8 Mustang or Camaro.

Street High Performance

Bowing to the gods who proclaim that "Bigger Is Better," there's no better setup for the street than a stroker 383- or 388-inch small block, whether carbureted or fed by an EFI system. EFI generally rewards you with more torque, increased efficiency, improved reliability, and reduced maintenance, but carbs often surpass at least the stock TPI systems in terms of peak horsepower. Naturally, you should strive to keep your vehicle emissions legal, which likely mandates EFI, just to minimize emissions output.

Barring a stroker package, the production 350 makes the most sense, even if you want a manual transmission. Any modifications made to a 305 would likely make it destroy trannies, too, so why not just start out with the 350, then beef up the tranny for it, instead of just for the 305?

The stock bottom end should be good for 400 or so horsepower, according to Myron Cottrell of TPI Specialties, assuming, of course, that it is in good condition. So, leaving the bottom end alone, Cottrell recommends swapping the cam first, to go for the big gain right off the bat, rather than messing around with little gains here and there, as you would get with new air filters, plug wires, etc.

While you've got the engine torn apart, it's a good time to swap the heads (what's another couple dozen bolts per side at that point?) for either CNC-machined parts or custom-ported units. If you're on a budget, pull your heads and have them reworked with a multi-angle valve job, and new springs, and port-match them to your intake. For the street, valve sizes should be kept relatively small: 2.02/1.60 intakes and exhausts, respectively, are usually sufficient to provide better breathing, without being so big that they kill low-end torque. Headers are easier to install with everything apart, too, so go for a set of metallic-ceramic coated ones, preferably equal length. And you might as well swap the intake base for a better-flowing unit before you get everything bolted back together.

As the intake is going back together, install an adjustable fuel pressure regulator and set it to deliver 45 pounds or so for a baseline, and adjust up or down depending on what you get for driving results.

Next, you should concentrate on helping the engine breathe better. A cold-air induction system with a free-flowing air filter helps feed the engine, while a cat-back exhaust system keeps it from getting plugged up. If you happen to have a carbureted engine, give some thought to switching to an EFI system. A simple throttle-body setup like Holley's Pro Jection unit delivers excellent performance, or Accel has several kits available that offer even more advanced features.

From there, changes become less dramatic. An adjustable fuel pressure regulator lets you optimize the fuel delivery, while a high-quality ignition system makes sure as much fuel gets burned as can be burned. An aftermarket PROM chip or PCM reprogramming computer helps you optimize fuel delivery and ignition timing, among other parameters, to improve engine efficiency with the modifications.

Again, whatever modifications you choose to make, you should strive to be conservative with them, choosing to err on the side of caution. A cam that's too big kills performance quickly, while a cam that's slightly too small still generally provides excellent performance.

Drag Racing

Drag racing requires an engine that can accelerate quickly, has high torque for quick launches, as well as high horsepower for good top speed through the traps. Again, a stroker motor makes an excellent choice, but the production 350 is an outstanding starting point.

For serious drag racing, you can't go wrong rebuilding the bottom end with forged pistons, zero-gap rings, a steel crank, heavy-duty connecting rods, and a heavy-duty oil system, all in the name of increased durability in the face of the tremendous internal stresses the engine has to endure.

A cam swap and freer-breathing cylinder heads make excellent additions, too, while a set of long-tube, equal-length headers yield the most power. In terms of induction systems, you want something that flows well at high rpm (above 5,000). For EFI systems, you want a short-runner intake like the LT1/LT4 unit or the remarkably similar TPI Specialties Mini-Ram intake, which works on first-generation small blocks that require a cooling system crossover. Carbureted and TBI engines should respond well to a tall-profile dual-plane intake, or preferably a single-plane intake. If the engine is for racing only, it may be worthwhile to investigate running a carburetor (unless, of course, you're trying to compete in an EFI class) because they still make more horsepower more easily, and emissions legality won't be a concern then (as long as you don't try to run it on the street).

Drag racing engines place high demands on ignition systems, so don't skimp here. A high-output coil, multiple-discharge spark box, and low-resistance wires should be a minimum, and you probably want a multistage rev-limited timing computer and possibly a retard device if you are running the next item....

Nitrous is almost a given for a serious drag racing engine. The output level you choose depends upon bottom end modifications, but the most efficient nitrous systems have direct port injection, plus their own fuel delivery system, including a dedicated fuel pump.

The stock cooling system should generally be up to the task of cooling your drag racing engine, though addition of an electric water pump drive kit allows the cooling system to keep doing its job after you shut the car off back in the pits.

Autocrossing

Engine output isn't as crucial in autocross racing, so preparations for it should be similar to those for street racing: A good cam, some head work or replacement heads, some intake porting and port-matching or a replacement intake, headers, ignition, etc.

Steer clear of nitrous, superchargers, turbos, and other such toys—tires tend to go up in smoke and increase your lap times.

Road Racing

Road racing places the highest demands on an engine because it has to survive high rpm for extended runs, plus be docile enough to come down to low rpm for tight corners, then accelerate back up to high rpm over and over and over, lap after lap after lap.

The name of the game, then, is durability. If you choose to rebuild the bottom end (and it's a wise idea), install forged aluminum pistons; high-quality rings; rebuild the rods or, better yet, replace them with higher-strength aftermarket parts and top-quality rod bolts. A steel crank that has been cross-drilled for better oil flow and four-bolt main caps held in place with studs (on the center bolts) is a definite improvement as well.

The camshaft needs to meet class rules, but several are available that qualify as stock replacements. Install it with a high-quality timing set (a belt drive allows a great deal of tuning flexibility, but a double-row true roller chain and gear set works fine). Oversize 7/16-inch pushrods improve top-end durability, while roller rockers ensure accurate, nearly friction-free valve actuation. Racing spring retainers and keepers keep the valves in place in the heads, which should be ported and massaged to the fullest extent of the rules and secured by studs. Headers are necessary (rules permitting) for evacuating the exhaust gases, as is a free-flowing exhaust system.

A cold-air/ram-air induction kit and free-flowing air filter should feed an oversize throttle body connected to a ported intake.

The ignition system also needs to be upgraded with a high-output coil, multiple-discharge spark box, and a rev-limiter to keep you from getting too overzealous.

Your oil system should incorporate a high-volume oil pump, a windage tray, an extra-capacity oil pan, an oil cooler, and synthetic oil, while the cooling system should have an aluminum racing radiator and high-flow water pump as minimal equipment.

Engine Parts and Upgrades

The right combination of engine parts can reward you with an engine that performs better than the sum of its parts would suggest. A poor combination, however, could leave you with an engine that barely runs, doesn't run at all, or even worse, might run just long enough to destroy itself.

But assembling a powerhouse engine doesn't necessitate spending a small fortune—nor even a large one—on exotic aftermarket parts. Some factory parts are better than others, and those that come up short can often be modified to perform better. Of course, in some cases, aftermarket parts just work better than any factory part, no matter what modifications you may make. The following information should give you some idea of what you should be thinking about for each of the particular parts you run across in your build-up.

Because most performance enthusiasts are likely to be working on V-8 engines, the following discussion of engine components (grouped by engine "system") is written with the V-8s in mind; however, if you happen to be working on a V-6 or even four-cylinder engine, the information presented is still applicable, though certain specifications or modification procedures may be slightly different for your particular engine of choice.

Short-Block Assembly

The short-block assembly consists of the engine block (i.e., cylinder case) and the parts that fill it, less the camshaft. In other words, you're dealing with the pistons, piston rings, connecting rods, crankshaft, bearings, and

If you're planning an engine rebuild or build-up, a bunch of down-time is saved if you build-up a second engine, such as these used ones seen at the annual Corvettes at Carlisle gathering. You just build the second engine, then spend a weekend swapping out the stock engine for the new one. A bonus is that if you ever want to swap back to the original engine (say for re-sale in 20 years or so), your original engine is unharmed and more-or-less ready-to-go.

other miscellaneous components.

In terms of the Chevy small-block V-8s used in third- and fourth-generation Camaros, the short-block assembly can typically be left well enough alone. In fact, according to Myron Cottrell of Cottrell Racing Engines and TPI Specialties, the factory TPI/LT1 short-block assemblies are typically good for up to 400–450 horsepower, so you can spend your time and money on the parts you bolt to the engine, rather than overhauling the basic engine assembly itself. In fact, he's built numerous 400+ horsepower TPI engines with stock short-block assemblies.

That's not to say there aren't worthwhile improvements to be made to stock short blocks. Depending on what you're planning on doing with your Camaro, there are specific components that may be worth upgrading.

Engine Block

The engine block (also called a "cylinder case") is the foundation of your engine, which means it's critical that it be sound and sturdy. Fortunately, most production blocks are more than suitable for high-performance use.

One of the biggest selling points for many enthusiasts is whether the engine block is a "two-bolt" or "four-bolt" block, referring to the number of fasteners that retain each of the

73

three middle main bearing caps. Four-bolt blocks are generally considered to be stronger than two-bolt blocks, but it has been shown time and again that two-bolt blocks are more than capable of retaining the

Reducing friction is a quick way to free up horsepower. One proven method of reducing parasitic friction that slows your engine is to replace the stock engine accessory pulleys with low-drag pulleys like these HyperTech Power Pulleys. *HyperTech photo*

ECM or PCM: What's the Difference?

General Motors has had two names for its computerized engine control systems over the years. Until 1993, the Electronic Control Module, or ECM for short, controlled only the engine. In 1994, however, GM made two significant changes. First, it changed the computer itself and did away with the ECM's replaceable PROM (Programmable Read Only Memory) chip in favor of a soldered-in EPROM (Erasable PROM) that could be updated with new data downloaded to it via connection to an external computer. The second change was the introduction of GM's new Hydramatic 4L60-E electronically controlled automatic transmission. Given that the new "ECM" now controlled the two key components of the car's powertrain, the control system was renamed the Powertrain Control Module, or PCM for short.

The only significant difference worth remembering about the two is how you upgrade them: The ECM gets a new PROM chip, while the PCM gets new data downloaded to it.

crankshaft in engines that produce as much as 500 horsepower, especially if crank speeds rarely exceed 5,500–6,000 rpm for any length of time. The factory knew this and didn't waste time or money equipping production Camaro blocks with four-bolt mains until the introduction of the third-generation small block, the LS1, in 1998. But then it had an excellent reason—the LS1 block is cast aluminum, which isn't as strong as cast iron, so engineers reinforced the block with not just four-main cap bolts but *six*! Four bolts run from the bottom of the caps up into the block, while two— one on each side—run through the sides of the block into the sides of the caps. Interestingly, the Corvette versions of Camaro engines, the Corvette's L98 (the equivalent of the Camaro B2L/L98 TPI 350) and LT1/LT4 engines—all featured four-bolt main bearing caps.

If you feel your engine requires the added strength of four-bolt main caps because the engine has to endure sustained crank speeds of 6,000 rpm or higher, you may still be smarter to hunt for a two-bolt main engine block. The reason is that factory four-bolt blocks use four parallel bolts—they each run vertically into the block. But with a two-bolt block, you can have it machined to accept four-bolt main bearing caps that feature "splayed," or angled, outer bolts, which make the engine assembly much stronger. Note, however, that not all machine shops are capable of performing the needed processes to install splayed-bolt main caps. Check with the machine shops in your area if this is an appealing process to you.

Another concern is the rear main bearing seal design. The 1987-and-later small-block Chevy V-8s utilize a one-piece seal that is far superior to the two-piece seal used previously. The primary advantage of the one-piece seal is the reduced likelihood for leaks and seepage, though with proper installation, the two-piece seal can be quite reliable. While it wouldn't make sense to avoid a block simply because it has a two-piece seal, if you have a choice between otherwise identical one-piece or two-piece seal blocks, go with the one-piece

seal. However, it's worth noting that if you're going to be strictly racing your Camaro, the availability of affordable aftermarket crankshafts far outweighs the inconvenience of a potential minor oil leak.

If you're building a "first-generation" small block, you also need to concern yourself with the type of camshaft the block was designed for. Most early small blocks used flat-tappet camshafts, but when Chevrolet began incorporating roller camshafts, the lifter valley machining was changed to accommodate the new roller lifters. Older blocks can use roller cams with aftermarket roller lifters, but factory roller cam blocks can only use roller cams.

Lastly, block selection should include the customary inspections, even if it's your original engine block that you're planning to use. As a minimum, you should have the block cleaned and magnafluxed to check for cracks, then measure the cylinder bores for taper and roundness, as well as the presence of any gouges or a ridge at the top of the cylinders. Deck surfaces should be checked for flatness, and main bearing bores should be checked for roundness, size, and alignment. If you're building an all-out race engine, then you should also take the time to verify tappet (i.e., lifter) bore placement.

Crankshaft

The crankshaft harnesses the forces pushing the pistons down in the bores and converts it to rotary motion that can be easily transmitted to the rear axle assembly and put to work turning the tires. In short, the crankshaft is the most essential component of a reciprocating engine assembly—it's what keeps things reciprocating.

Given the high loads placed on the crankshaft "throws," it's essential that the crankshaft be in excellent condition; the slightest defect can lead to disastrous results—an expensive engine in pieces. But this doesn't mean you always need the most exotic crankshaft, you just need one that's well-matched to your driving conditions, and is properly prepared.

Factory production crankshafts have served countless drivers well for years and years, in both stock and modified engines, even under racing conditions. For the first-generation small blocks, there are four crankshafts from which to choose: cast-iron or forged-steel units in either of the two rear main seal designs (one-piece or two-piece). Forged cranks are generally considered to be stronger, but they're also significantly more expensive to purchase, if you don't already have one. They can be identified by a wide (± 3/8 inch) parting line on the unmachined portions of the crank throws (Cast iron cranks have a narrow parting line, by comparison).

Cast-iron cranks, however, when properly machined and balanced, are perfectly suitable for high-performance use, as long as crank speeds are generally kept below 6,000 rpm.

The LT1 and LT4 "Gen-II" small-block V-8s all used the same crankshaft design—a forged-steel, one-piece unit machined for the LT1/LT4 Opti-Spark ignition system. Likewise, LS1 engines use a similar crankshaft design, which is also a forged piece with the specific machining required by the LS1 engine design.

Aftermarket crankshafts are readily available in both cast iron and forged steel. The advantages of aftermarket cranks is the ability to get them in superior metals, with more precise machining and in pretty much any stroke length you need. Additionally, many aftermarket crankshafts can be treated to performance-enhancing machine work, such as "knife-edging" the counterweights so that they slice through the air and oil in the engine as they spin. Also available are lightweight crankshafts that can greatly enhance an engine's ability to rev quickly and thus accelerate the car more quickly, which can be extremely advantageous in competition. Note, however, that lightweight crankshafts typically sacrifice durability in order to provide the performance gains, so they're not necessarily a good choice for a street-based high-performance Camaro.

A popular and worthwhile consideration for an engine build-up is building a "stroker" motor—one with a longer-than-stock crankshaft stroke. While the stock 4.00-inch bore and 3.48-inch stroke combine to make a 350-cubic-inch V-8 (305s

have a 3.825-inch bore), a long-stroke crankshaft with a mild overbore can produce a 383-inch small block that produces more horsepower and torque much more easily than a 350 ever could.

No matter what crankshaft you choose, it or your engine won't last long if you don't prepare the crank properly. Crankshafts should always be magnafluxed to check for cracks that wouldn't normally be visible. A cracked crank isn't good for anything more than an oversize paperweight.

You also need to check the crank for straightness; bent cranks can be straightened, but the process requires special tools that your local machine shop isn't likely to have. And if you're working with a cast-iron crank, it's often less expensive to simply replace the crank than go to the trouble of straightening the bad one. Naturally, you should also check the journal sizes, to ensure they haven't already been turned (reduced in size by machining a small amount, typically .010 inch, from them) excessively. If a crank's journals have been machined more than .020–.030 inch under size, you should start questioning that crank's suitability for high-rpm use;

.020–.030 inch of material is an awful lot of material to remove from the journals. Machining journals may remove any surface-hardening treatment that may have been originally performed, such as Chevy's "Tuffride" process. Naturally, the crankshaft should be balanced, and not just for high-performance use— balance it for any use!

Other steps you may want to consider are enlarging the journal radii, cross-drilling the oil passages, and chamfering the oil passage holes. Lastly, for cars equipped with manual transmissions, you should always install a new pilot bushing in which the transmission's input shaft spins. An old pilot bushing may be slightly out-of-round and could induce chatter or excessive drivetrain noise, among other potential problems. GM and many aftermarket performance parts companies offer a roller-bearing-equipped pilot bushing that virtually eliminates drag and lasts longer, too.

Connecting Rods

Connecting rods link the pistons to the crankshaft. It sounds like a simple job, but it's actually incredibly demanding. Connecting rods

Engine vibrations can literally shake an engine to death. The Vibratech Streetdamper (shown hear installed on a crankshaft) is designed to minimize harmful vibrations, so your engine lasts longer and produces more power. *Vibratech photo*

For racing applications, Vibratech offers its Fluidampr, which is designed to withstand higher rpm and more severe crankshaft harmonics. *Vibratech photo*

must endure incredible forces that continually stretch and then compress the rod during each and every revolution. As the rod pushes the piston up the bore, there are minor compression forces caused by the resistance of the piston and speed with which the crank is thrusting the rod upwards. As the piston reaches Top Dead Center, the piston attempts to keep rising, but the rod must yank it back down as the crankshaft swings downward; this causes the rod to stretch. As the piston reaches Bottom Dead Center, the opposite happens—the piston tries to keep dropping, but the rod starts pushing it back up, causing the rod to compress. Of course, the rod is also compressed by the combustion forces, too. This process repeats thousands of times per minute, and is especially punishing at high rpm.

Factory stock rods are excellent low-performance items, and even work well in mild high-performance applications without much special attention. More extensive work can prepare stock rods for even severe service; stock rods have successfully been used in 9,000-rpm drag racing engines—and lived to tell about it.

But stock rods aren't ideal performance pieces. Compared to most aftermarket rods, stock rods are heavy, which slows down engine acceleration and, therefore, slows vehicle acceleration. Stock rods aren't made from the choicest of materials (1982–1992 rods are cast iron, while 1993-and-up rods are powdered metal, which offers similar strength to forged steel, but at a lower price).

Forged-steel rods, such as the rements and are good choices, but they're not inexpensive, nor are they lightweight. Stock rods, whether of cast, powdered metal, or forged construction, machined to precise tolerances are not cheap or lightweight as well. While the specified length for 305 and 350 V-8 rods is 5.700 inches, mass production tolerances allow for the length to be a few thousandths of an inch longer or shorter, so it's possible to have one rod that's 5.702 inches and another that's 5.698 inches in the same engine. The difference may not sound like much, but it can significantly affect engine operation, because the cylinder with the shorter rod has less compression than the other cylinders. Thus, the long rod pushes the piston further into the chamber, raising the compression over that of the other cylinders. Different compression in each cylinder can cause a severe imbalance that can destroy an engine.

Aftermarket rods, on the other hand, have the luxury of being produced in far fewer quantities for enthusiasts who know their value and are willing to pay for it. Typically, even inexpensive aftermarket connecting rods feature specific design improvements over stock rods, such as larger, stronger rod bolts or even cap-screw-style bolts that allow manufacturers to greatly improve the strength of the "big end" of the rod. Additionally, they can be made of superior metal alloys, and can be treated to machining processes that are either too costly or time-consuming for mass-produced rods. Additionally, aftermarket rods can be specified in different lengths, which can greatly affect engine performance by altering rod angularity and piston velocities. Longer rods tend to help an engine develop more power because the rod spends less time trying to push sideways and more time pushing the piston up or pulling it down as the crank continues its rotation. Plus, longer rods allow pistons to dwell at TDC longer, which keeps the air/fuel mixture compressed longer and, thus, aids combustion because the mixture burns more completely. Shorter rods, however, tend to allow for quicker engine acceleration, but give up some power to do so.

If you're rebuilding your short-block assembly, there are some processes to which you can subject your connecting rods that strengthen them and improve their reliability. Again, the most basic step is to have the rods magnafluxed for crack detection. Cracked rods make excellent paperweights, and if you get enough of them, they're even decent wind chimes.

Next, the rods should be "resized," which ensures that both the small and big ends of the rod have the intended bore sizes and that those bores are round. On the small end, that may entail reaming out the bore and installing a bushing that reduces the opening to the proper size, while the big end can have the cap milled slightly, then the bore rebored to the proper size.

You should never re-use old rod bolts, especially after resizing the big end of a rod. Replacing the stock rod bolts with high-performance rod bolts greatly improves the strength of the rod assembly. Traditionally, bolts with knurled shanks were the top choice for rebuilds, but Automotive Racing Products (ARP) has developed what it calls a "wave-lock" bolt design that is now the choice of top race engine builders in NASCAR, NHRA, SCCA, and other forms of motorsports. Instead of knurled shanks, the ARP Wave-Loc bolts have a series of rounded humps that grip the inside of the rod without damaging it as knurled bolts do.

Next, the rods should be deburred and preferably polished to remove any stress risers that could lead to cracking, particularly along the rod beam (the long, skinny section between the small and big ends). After that, the rod should be shot-peened to essentially pound down any minor surface ridges. Finally, the rods should be balanced, which simply requires finding the lightest rod in a set and grinding material from the heavier rods to make them equal the weight of the light rod.

All of this work runs up the price of using stock rods and makes aftermarket rods—which are typically stronger and lighter, and typically already have all this work done—even more attractive.

Pistons and Wrist Pins

Pistons have the unfortunate duty of compressing the air/fuel mixture, then standing up to the intense heat and pressure that result from that mixture burning after ignition. The pistons may even have to endure the occasional detonation episode, which can be extremely damaging.

Pistons come in three basic flavors: cast aluminum, hypereutectic (high-silica content), and forged aluminum. Cast pistons are strictly low-performance items and aren't suited to high compression, and they won't withstand sustained high rpm (over 5,500 rpm), but they are very stable, in terms of size, and they run very quietly. Most production engines used cast pistons because they were reliable and far less expensive than forged pistons.

Hypereutectic pistons are sort of a middle ground between cast and forged pistons. Made of a high-silica content aluminum alloy, they essentially combine the advantages of cast aluminum (stable size, reliable, cost-effective) with increased strength, which had always been the big advantage of forged pistons. General Motors uses hypereutectic pistons in a number of its production and over-the-counter engine assemblies, because they're essentially a best-of-both-worlds solution.

Forged aluminum pistons have long been the choice for high-performance and racing engines, mainly because of their strength, and they still hold a significant advantage in this regard over pistons made with other processes. But forged aluminum pistons are expensive, and, because they expand a great deal when subjected to heat, they must be installed with fat clearances that allow the piston to move around in the bore when cold, and thus are rather noisy (the noise typically fades as the pistons heat up). Forged pistons can still handle higher temperatures, higher loads, and higher engine speeds, which keeps them the top choice for racing use.

In most cases, when rebuilding an engine you're likely going to utilize aftermarket pistons, simply because they're available in different compression ratios, and different over-bore sizes, and typically they cost less than factory parts. When shopping for pistons, you should pay particular attention to the weight of the pistons you're buying. Factory pistons are notoriously heavier than necessary to minimize the chance of failure, but the extra material also tends to slow down engine acceleration. Naturally, you need to be concerned with compression ratio, which

also requires taking into account the combustion chamber volume of your cylinder heads, the thickness of the head gaskets, the camshaft profile, the fuel you are running, and even the engine design itself.

First-generation Chevy small blocks that are forced to run on pump gas (92/93 octane) won't react well to compression ratios over 10.0:1. Beyond that, the engine detonates under all but the lightest loads, causing the knock sensor (if equipped) to retard timing so drastically that performance is noticeably hampered. Engines without a knock

---

What's a Stroker Motor?

You may have heard the term "stroker motor" before and wondered exactly what it means. In the strictest sense, it means an engine that has had its displacement increased by using a crankshaft with a longer-than-stock stroke length. (A crank with a shorter stroke will result in a "destroked" engine.)

The advantage of a longer crankshaft stroke is that it increases torque by increasing the leverage applied to turning the crankshaft.

The concept of "stroker" motors is nothing new. In fact, Chevrolet has

been building stroker motors for years. The 350—the most popular engine in the world—is nothing more than a stroked version of the 327.

Today, the most popular stroker motor combines a 0.030-inch over-stock 4.00-inch bore 350 Chevy block with a 3.75-inch stroke crankshaft to displace 383 cubic inches. Aftermarket "tuners" like Callaway Cars, TPI Specialties, Lingenfelter Performance Engineering, and Doug Rippie Motorsports all sell 383-inch small-blocks that develop 400 horsepower or more in naturally aspirated form.

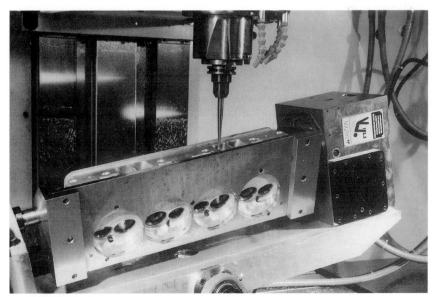

Good cylinder heads are essential for making good power, and thanks to computer numerically controlled (CNC) machining equipment, ports and chambers are exactly alike from cylinder-to-cylinder to ensure even power production. *CNC Cylinder Heads photo*

Quick Test: TPI Specialties ZZ9 Camshaft

Part:	TPI Specialties ZZ9 Hydraulic Roller Camshaft
Approx. Price:	$375
"Before" HP:	345.6 @ 5,000 rpm*
"After" HP:	390.1 @ 5,500 rpm*
Gain:	44.5 horsepower*
Install Time:	Approx. 3 hours
Rating:	****
Pros:	Awesome power! Smooth, good driveability, good economy
Cons:	Expensive. Requires new valve springs for best results ($130)
Comments:	The ZZ9 cam is an expensive part, and cam swaps aren't for the faint-of-heart, but it's hard to argue with the results. Every aspect of the engine's performance either remained as good as stock or improved. This should be your first upgrade!

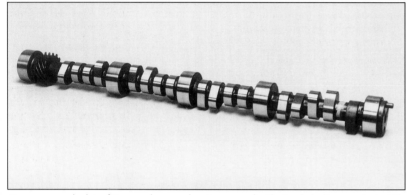

You can spend a lot of time and money horsing around with simple bolt-on parts, but if you want a serious jump in power, tear right into the engine and install a new cam, like this ZZ9 unit from TPI Specialties. Gains of 45 horsepower on an LT1 are possible, and it performs similarly in LB9 and L98/B2L engines, too! TPI Specialties photo

*TPI Specialties Test Figures

Rating System for Quick Tests

****	Outstanding
***	Excellent
**	Good
*	Fair

sensor simply detonate like crazy, potentially destroying the engine with every knock and ping.

Because of the LT1/LT4/L99 engines' reverse-flow cooling system, they are more tolerant of higher compression, since the cylinder heads run cooler. Compression ratios of 10.5:1 are easily acceptable, and even 11.0:1 can be tolerated (though performance may vary depending on fuel quality and other factors).

The LS1 engine was still too new when this book was produced to have aftermarket pistons readily available, but piston manufacturers had begun making custom sets, and once there's a demand, LS1 pistons should be widely available.

A final word on piston design: When possible, it's best to use a flat-top or even dished piston because "pop-up" piston domes can interfere with the travel of the flame front during the combustion process.

The wrist pins (also called piston pins) connect pistons to the connecting rod, and raise another aspect of piston design worth thinking about: the pin type. Some pistons use pressed-in wrist pins and some use floating wrist pins. Pressed-in pins may be pressed into the piston but left floating in the rod's small end, or they may be floating in the piston but pressed into the rod's small end. Floating pins float in both the piston and rod and are typically only used in professional competition engines. For most applications, pins that press into the piston but float in the rod are the best choice. Pins that float in the piston require that the piston pin bores in the piston be machined to receive spiral snap-ring locks to keep the pin from sliding out of the piston and possibly contacting the cylinder wall.

The job of selecting piston pins is often an easy one: Pistons typically include an appropriate pin. Of course,

most piston manufacturers happily sell you (or substitute) the specific pins you want. High-strength piston pins are available, as are lightweight piston pins. High-strength pins are a good idea, even if they weigh a few more grams than a standard pin. Lightweight pins, though, should only be considered for use in competition engines that have them frequently replaced.

Just like any other engine component, pistons and pins need to be prepared properly if they're going to last for many thousands of miles. Used pistons should be thoroughly cleaned, including the ring grooves, which requires a ring groove cleaner that scrapes carbon build-up and other deposits from the grooves. All pistons should be checked for cracks by having them magnafluxed, then they should be deburred to remove any potential "hot spots." Finally, piston and pin assemblies should be balanced to match the heavier assemblies to the lightest assembly's weight.

Piston Rings

Pistons don't completely fill the cylinder bore, because they need some clearance to allow for expansion and an oil film to lubricate the cylinder walls. Of course, if this clearance gap wasn't filled, the engine would hardly develop any compression at all, and therefore it would hardly make any power. Plus, it would burn oil and the oil would quickly become contaminated by gasoline.

Preventing all that is up to the piston rings. Piston rings are little more than seals that fit in grooves on the piston and help seal the piston to the cylinder walls. Most engines utilize three rings per piston. The top ring, the compression ring and is intended to help prevent the compressed air/fuel mixture from blowing out of the cylinders, plus it ensures that the rapid expansion of gases caused by the combustion process isn't lost in the same manner. The second ring helps further limit any pressure losses. The lowest ring groove is occupied by the oil control ring package, which does as its name implies—controls oil, limiting how much is allowed above it.

In the old days, the two top rings were typically just plain iron, but performance top rings are now typically moly-faced, or plasma-coated to improve their sealing and wear properties. Second rings still are typically plain iron, while the oil control package usually consists of steel upper and lower scraper rings, plus a steel expansion ring between the two.

The critical element of piston rings are the end gaps. An excessively large gap allows too much cylinder pressure to blow through. Too tight a gap might result in a broken ring, if the ring expands so much as it heats that the ring ends physically press against each other.

Certain piston ring designs actually provide a "zero gap" by having the ring ends overlap, rather than butting toward each other. Zero-gap rings are the ultimate in cylinder sealing, because they virtually eliminate blow-by, thereby maximizing power.

Oil control packages are available in a special low-tension design to reduce friction, but be wary of such a design, because it can result in excessive oil consumption and unsightly puffs of blue smoke emitting from the tailpipe (just watch stock 5.0-liter Mustangs some day—they use low-tension oil control rings and almost always "puff the blues" when accelerating or starting up), because excessive oil is allowed past the rings.

As with pistons, whenever you rebuild an engine, a set of aftermarket piston rings is desirable, because more sizes and styles are available, and the price is generally more favorable.

Beyond measuring and correcting ring end gaps, there's little that must be done to piston rings to prepare them for use. However, it should be noted that the only correct way to install piston rings on pistons is with a set of piston ring expansion pliers (a satisfactory set costs you about $10 at any Sears tool center).

Cylinder Heads and Valvetrain
Cylinder Head Assemblies

Anyone who follows NASCAR racing knows that cylinder heads are considered to be *the* most critical components, in terms of power production. The better the heads let air and fuel flow in, allow it to burn, and let the exhaust gases rush out, the more power an engine can make. Interestingly, good cylinder heads don't really *make* horsepower, but rather bad heads *restrict* how much power can be made, so good heads just provide less of a restriction.

Most third-generation Camaros featured cast-iron cylinder heads, except for some B2L/L98-equipped cars that sported aluminum cylinder heads. All V-8-equipped fourth-generation Camaros have aluminum cylinder heads. Likewise, most aftermarket heads are made of aluminum.

The particular material from which a given cylinder head is made doesn't affect air-flow through the head, but does affect power production. Aluminum heads run cooler and, thus, allow for less ignition advance before detonation sets in. Less advance allows the air/fuel mixture to be more compressed before it is ignited, so it burns hotter and quicker when ignited, thus producing more power.

Factory heads can be modified to perform quite respectably with some basic rebuilding steps and a few high-performance modifications. First, the heads need to be cleaned thoroughly, then magnaflux-inspected for cracks. Assuming the heads are crack-free, their mounting surfaces should be checked for flatness and milled if necessary (which requires subtle milling of the intake manifold mating surfaces to restore port alignment).

Port-matching the intake ports to the intake manifold runners helps reduce any turbulence caused by differences in port size or shape. Additional massaging of the intake and exhaust ports to remove casting imperfections and smooth the short-turn radius of each port aids flow into and out of the chamber. The valve seats (and valve faces) should naturally be treated to a multi-angle valve job, and bronze valve guides should be installed for trouble-free valve opera-

Stock rockers are fine for stock engines, but when you're trying to make serious power, roller rockers minimize valvetrain friction, plus provide an accurate ratio, rocker to rocker, unlike the stock stamped-steel units. They're also available in oversize ratios to effectively increase the size of your camshaft. *Competition Cams photo*

tion. And screw-in rocker studs should be installed, preferably with the big-block-size 7/16-inch stud to better resist flexing, especially at high rpm.

Aftermarket heads are typically manufactured with the above modifications, or variations of them are often offered as options, which can make replacing stock heads with ready-to-bolt-on aftermarket heads a tempting exercise. But one of the best reasons to go with aftermarket heads is because of their precise machining that not only helps your engine develop more power, but helps it develop more well-balanced power.

Whereas stock heads are cast, and therefore have variations cylinder-to-cylinder in terms of the volume and shape of the combustion chambers and ports, most aftermarket heads are machined by Computer Numerically Controlled (CNC) equipment. CNC machining ensures that each cylinder's combustion chamber and intake and exhaust ports are exactly like those of every other cylinder's chamber and ports. This equality helps equalize power production from cylinder to cylinder, which results in a balanced, smoother-running engine.

Cam-Drive Timing Sets

Cam-drive sets harness the rotation of the crankshaft to turn the camshaft. Timing sets spin the cam at precisely one-half the speed of the crankshaft.

Production cam-drive sets consist of a drive (crank) gear, a driven (cam) gear, and a chain that connects the two. Aftermarket cam-drive sets are available in a variety of configurations: with high-performance true-roller and double-roller chain and gear combinations; in gear-only systems (with either three or four gears); or as belt-drive systems. Each type has its own advantages and disadvantages.

Chain-drive systems are inexpensive and relatively quiet, although the chain is subject to stretch, and that causes erratic timing. Double-row true roller chain-drive sets minimize this possibility.

Gear-drive systems are much stronger than chains, and thus don't stretch. However, because gear-drive systems so accurately transfer the crankshaft's rotation to the cam, they can cause unwanted harmonics to be transmitted, too. And most gear drives are noisy, though more recent designs are quieter and thus less objectionable for street use.

The LT1 air intake ducting is notoriously restrictive, particularly with regard to the large resonance chamber that is designed to cancel out particular "objectionable" sound frequencies for quieter operation.

Belt-drive systems are very quiet, very accurate, easily adjustable, and feature an easily replaceable belt for when the belt eventually stretches.

Because the driven gear mounts to the camshaft with bolts, it is wise to install the bolts with a bolt lock-plate, with bendable ears that prevent the bolts from loosening over time. Such lock-plates are very inexpensive (less than $5) and provide excellent insurance against what could be a serious problem.

Camshaft

The camshaft is your engine's brain. By controlling when the valves open, how quickly they open, how far they open, and how long they stay open, the camshaft ultimately determines not only the engine's power, but also its driveability, fuel efficiency, and emissions levels.

There are four basic types of camshafts: mechanical (i.e., solid) flat-tappet cams; hydraulic flat-tappet cams; mechanical roller cams; and hydraulic roller cams. Chevrolet hasn't used mechanical flat-tappet cams since the early 1970s "muscle car" engines, but it did continue to use hydraulic flat-tappet cams through much of the 1980s, including in a number of Camaro engines.

Roller camshafts, however, offer significant advantages in terms of valve opening and closing rates. Flat-tappet cams have to have gradual camshaft lobe opening and closing ramps in order to allow the tappet (also known as a lifter) to follow the lobe profile. Roller camshafts, though, by virtue of the large rolling wheel on the lifter base, can follow a much steeper ramp, allowing the valve to open and close much more quickly, so the valve can be open at maximum lift earlier and remain there longer than it could with a flat-tappet cam.

To help you visualize it, a typical flat-tappet cam's lobe looks like an egg, but a roller cam lobe looks more like a rectangle with a round bottom. So, while the two valves may only be open the same amount of time (measured in crankshaft degrees), the roller cam allows more air/fuel mixture into the cylinder and more exhaust gases out, thus making more power. Aftermarket roller cams are available for engines originally equipped with flat-tappet cams, but they require the use of aftermarket roller lifters.

Factory cams are, as a general rule, conservative. They perform well but leave a lot of room for improvement, and aftermarket companies have taken advantage of the opening Chevy left them by designing replacement cams that offer substantial power improvements, without sacrificing driveability, emissions, or even fuel economy.

If your engine wasn't originally equipped with a roller camshaft, you should strongly consider installing one. As with flat-tappet cams, mechanical roller cams generally rev to higher rpm before suffering lifter "float" (when the lifter loses contact with the lobe) than hydraulic cams. Also, the hydraulics are quieter and require less maintenance.

Tappets/Lifters

Tappets—or lifters, as they're often called—ride along the cam lobe. As the camshaft spins, the lobe's shape causes the tappet to rise up and down in its bore, which in turn raises the pushrod, thus tipping the rocker arm which pushes the valve open.

Four types of tappets are available: mechanical flat-tappet; hydraulic flat-tappet; mechanical roller; and hydraulic roller. Mechanical tappets (flat or roller) generally sustain higher engine rpm before "floating" off the cam's lobe, which makes them popular choices for racing engines. However, mechanical lifters require a slight clearance between the rocker arm nose and the tip of the valve, and this clearance causes a ticking noise during engine operation as the rocker strikes the valve tip. The vibrations and shock caused by the ticking also tends to loosen the rocker arm, requiring periodic adjustment to maintain proper valve operation.

Hydraulic tappets work similarly to shock absorbers—the oil within them cushions the movements of the valvetrain, and results in much quieter operation. However, because the tappet's pushrod seat takes time to reseat after the lifter crests the peak of the cam lobe, hydraulic lifters lose contact with the cam lobe several hundred rpm earlier than mechanical lifters. Because of the cushioning effect hydraulic lifters provide, they do not induce vibrations into the valvetrain and thus require far less frequent adjustment, and usually extend the life of other valvetrain components, such as pushrods and valve stems.

The particular tappets, or lifters, that your engine uses are dictated by the camshaft you install, as each camshaft is designed to work only with a particular style of lifter.

Old flat-tappet lifters should never be used with a new camshaft, because the lifters already have developed a wear pattern that may cause accelerated wear of the cam lobe. Likewise, if you ever remove old lifters and intend to reinstall them with the same camshaft, make sure that you reinstall each lifter in its original position, since lifters and lobes wear together to form compatible mating surfaces. No such problem exists when using new lifters with an old cam. Nor are roller lifters subject to these rules.

Pushrods

Pushrods have two functions: First, they are responsible for transmitting the lift provided by the tappet up to the rocker arm. Second, a hollow channel inside the pushrod acts as an oil passage to deliver oil to the rocker arm and valve assembly at the top of the cylinder head. One end of the pushrod rests in a cup in the tappet, and the other sits in a similar cup in the rocker arm. Holes in the lifter and rocker arm allow oil to enter and exit the pushrod.

Factory pushrods are 3/8 inch in diameter and made of steel. They are reasonably strong but are not generally able to withstand sustained operation over 5,500 rpm without risk of bending or breakage. Aftermarket pushrods are available in both larger diameters (7/16 inch is a common upgrade) and stronger materials, such as chrome-moly steel.

Large-diameter, stronger pushrods are a worthy investment, and one that increases engine reliability and provides added insurance against failure.

Use of pushrod guide plates is highly recommended. Note, however, that steel guide plates require

The Callaway "Honker" intake duct replaces the stock duct on 1993–1997 Z28 Camaros and greatly reduces restrictions in the system, adding as much as 19 horsepower, according to Callaway Cars tests. A version is also available for V-6 Camaros. *Callaway Cars photo*

hardened pushrods. Plastic guide plates are available and do not require hardened pushrods.

Rocker Arms

Rocker arms convert the pushrod's lift into a downward pushing force that forces the valve away from its seat. They pivot on a rocker arm stud that is either pressed or screwed into the cylinder head.

Production rocker arms on all Chevrolet V-8 engines except the LT4 and LS1 engines, are of stamped-steel construction and do not feature rollerized tips or fulcrums. The standard rocker arm ratio is 1.5:1, meaning that a camshaft lobe lift of 0.300 inch is amplified 1.5 times by the rocker arm, resulting in 0.450 inch of valve lift. However, because of production tolerances, production rocker ratios actually vary considerably. It's not uncommon for an engine to be equipped with one or more rockers that actually measure 1.48:1 and others that may be as high as 1.52:1 or more. While that may not sound like much, a 1.48:1 rocker ratio results in a 0.444 inch of lift from a 0.300-inch lobe, while a 1.52:1 ratio results in 0.456 inch of lift from the same lobe—a difference of 0.012 inch. An inconsistency like that can greatly affect overall engine efficiency and balanced power output.

Aftermarket rockers are typically much more exact in their measurements, so a 1.5:1 ratio means the rocker opens the valve 1.5 times the lobe lift. Nonroller stamped-steel rockers are available, though roller versions—either roller tip, or "full" roller rockers with a roller tip and a roller fulcrum—can greatly reduce valvetrain friction, helping to free up some horsepower and aid in engine acceleration. Aftermarket roller rockers are typically constructed of either cast or forged aluminum.

Because rocker arms multiply the lobe lift, utilizing a rocker arm with a higher ratio—such as 1.6:1 or even 1.7:1—is essentially like swapping the camshaft for a "bigger" cam. For instance, a 0.300-inch lobe lift translates to 0.450 inch of valve lift with a 1.5:1 ratio; 0.480 inch of lift with a 1.6:1 ratio; and 0.510 inch with 1.7:1 ratios. Thus, an hour spent changing the rocker arms could boost valve lift by more than .060 inch! It's interesting to note that some camshafts and/or cylinder heads respond well to a mixed rocker/ratio setup, such as 1.5:1 rockers for the intake valves, but 1.6:1 rockers for the exhaust valves, to allow the cylinders to empty out the exhaust more completely, so as not to contaminate the fresh air/fuel mixture, which would obviously decrease power output. Consult your camshaft and cylinder head manufacturers or machinists for their rocker ratio recommendations.

Rocker Arm Studs

Rocker studs have the seemingly simple job of locating the rocker arm in a fixed position. Stock rocker studs are 3/8 inch in diameter and are either pressed into the cylinder heads or screwed in. All aluminum cylinder heads utilize screw-in rocker studs, and screw-in studs are always preferable, since pressed-in studs can loosen and actually pull out of the head. Heads that have pressed-in studs can be machined to receive screw-in studs.

Studs are available in a larger 7/16-inch diameter, which resists bending and flexing better than thinner 3/8-inch units, and thus result in more accurate valvetrain action. Note, however, that larger-diameter rocker studs do require rockers designed for the larger stud diameter.

For racing applications that see extremely high rpm, it may be useful to utilize a rocker stud "girdle," which is essentially just two long pieces of metal (usually aluminum) that are bolted together, one on each side of the studs, to tie each stud to all the others for additional strength and resistance to flexing.

Valves

All production Camaro engines utilize two valves per cylinder—one intake and one exhaust—to control the flow of air and fuel into the cylinder and the flow of exhaust gases out of the cylinder. Stock valves are typically steel, and the valve-face diameters vary depending on the particular engine.

Stock valves are quite reliable (at modest engine speeds) but often limit performance because of their smallish sizes and their inefficient valve seat and face cuts. While a performance valve job increases the efficiency of stock valves, the size of the valve may still present a restriction to airflow.

Aftermarket valves are available in a variety of materials, the most common of which is stainless steel. They're also available in a range of sizes. The particular size of valve you run technically depends upon the design and airflow capabilities of your cylinder heads, as well as your camshaft specifications. In addition, on small-bore engines, especially the 305s used in third-generation Camaros, large-diameter valves may actually contact the cylinder walls, causing immediate and catastrophic engine damage.

For most performance-built 350-inch engines (gen-one and gen-two but not LS1/gen-three motors), 2.02-inch intake valves are desirable, while 1.60-inch exhaust valves provide excellent cylinder-emptying capabilities. Larger-displacement engines may respond well to larger valve sizes, though the small-diameter valves may serve to keep airflow velocity higher than would a larger valve, so actual airflow (volume) through the valve may decrease with larger valves. Consult your cylinder head manufacturer or machinist for their recommendations.

Both stock and aftermarket valves respond well to a multi-angle valve job that smoothes the flow of air into and out of the cylinders. A triple-cut valve seat and double-cut valve face typically work best when performed properly.

Hollow-stem and other "exotic" valves are not usually necessary, except in maximum-effort competition-only engines.

Valve Guides

Valve guides are replaceable sleeves through which the valves slide. Production guides are steel, but bronze valve guides are popular replacements for performance engines. Other more exotic valve guides are available, but aren't usually necessary in anything but the highest-performance racing engines.

Quick Test: High-Performance Air Filters

Part:	High-performance air filter
Approx. Price:	$50
"Before" Time:	14.93 seconds
"After" Time:	14.81 seconds
Gain:	0.12 seconds
Install Time:	Under 5 minutes
Rating:	***
Pros:	Inexpensive, easy, effective, cleanable/reusable
Cons:	None.
Comments:	A quick upgrade well worth doing. The high initial purchase price is more than made up for by the fact that you never have to buy another air filter. Try to stick with a depth-trapping-type foam filter, which flows better longer than a surface-trapping filter.

Air filters come in two basic flavors: those that trap elements on the filter surface, and those that trap elements throughout the filter's depth.

Surface-trapping filters are generally made of either paper, like stock filters, or an oiled cotton gauze, like many high-performance filters. There are two basic problems with surface-trapping filters, however. First, every dirt particle they trap significantly decreases airflow through the filter, because they have only a relatively small surface area through which to breathe. Second, in hot or humid weather, the paper or cotton fibers can swell, effectively blocking any air from flowing through the filter element, which obviously decreases airflow to the engine.

Foam filters, however, trap dirt particles throughout their entire depth, so they remain free-breathing for far longer, plus the foam fibers don't swell in heat and humidity.

An easy and worthwhile improvement to the stock induction system is to install a low-restriction air filter, like this Accel foam element. It increases airflow, and it provides superior filtration and is even cleanable and reusable, so you'll never have to buy another filter.

Whenever cylinder heads are "rebuilt," the guides should be replaced. Some machine shops are fond of "knurling" the valve guides, rather than replacing them, since the process is less expensive. But knurling actually digs up the inside of the guide and often results in accelerated guide wear when the engine is put into operation.

Valve Seals

Valve seals are used to limit the amount of oil that is used to lubricate the valve stem and valve guide. Two basic types are used: the production-style O-rings, and the performance-oriented "PC" or "umbrella" seals that clamp around the head of the valve guide.

PC-style guides are preferable to the stock O-rings.

Valve Springs

While the camshaft is responsible for opening the valve, the valve spring has the duty of closing the valve, once the lifter/tappet crests the peak of the cam lobe. Valve springs must be matched to the camshaft, to ensure that the springs are not so strong that they actually cause the lifter/tappet to wear the cam lobe.

Valve springs weaken with age and mileage, and new springs should always be used when installing a new camshaft. Get the springs that the cam manufacturer recommends.

When installing valve springs, always ensure that you install them at the specified "installed height," utilizing shims, if necessary, to reduce the spring height or have the head's spring seats machined if the non-shimmed installation height is shorter than specified.

Valve Spring Retainers

Valve spring retainers are metal discs that do exactly as their name implies—they keep the valve springs in place. The valve runs through a hole in the center of the retainer.

Production valve spring retainers are made of steel and are typically adequate for general high-performance and mild-racing use.

Aftermarket retainers are often made of higher-strength, lighter-weight materials and are available for oversize springs.

Because valve spring retainers are retained by angled valve keepers, the angle of the bore in which the keepers rest must match that of the keepers. Production keepers utilize a 7-degree angle, while racing keepers may use as much as 10 or 11 degrees, to better prevent the keepers from pulling through the retainer at high rpm or with exceptionally strong spring pressures.

Induction System Components

The air induction system is responsible for feeding fresh air to the engine, which can be mixed with fuel, then delivered to the engine's cylinders where it is burned to produce power.

Stock Camaro air induction systems are fairly restrictive, and are often cited as one of the primary reasons that otherwise-identical engines produce less power in the Camaro than in the Corvette. But GM's engineers have to meet certain requirements when designing a factory air induction system that you don't necessarily have to preserve when redesigning or replacing your Camaro's stock induction system. For instance, GM engineers equip Camaros with a "resonance chamber" because many customers might find the unmuffled induction system offensively loud. But, if the sound doesn't bother you, you can eliminate the resonance chamber to clean up the airflow to the engine.

The stock air induction system essentially starts with the air filter housing, which has an opening through which air can be drawn in. Ingested air then flows through a filter and into the ducts that ultimately funnel the air to the throttle body (be it a carburetor's, a throttle body injection unit's, or a tuned port injection unit's) and into the engine.

Unfortunately, there are several problems with the stock air induction system that cause it to choke the engine, to starve it for air. The first impediment is the air filter housing itself. Not only is the induction port generally somewhat small (and therefore restrictive), but it typically draws air from a cramped, confined area. What air does make it into the housing must then pass through a highly

The 1994-and-up Mass Air Flow sensors use a different design that is not nearly as restrictive as the old Bosch unit.

restrictive paper-based filter, then find its way into the ducts that lead toward the throttle body. Once in the ducts, the ducts themselves often disrupt airflow with sharp bends, and some systems utilize the aforementioned resonance chambers that disturb airflow because some of the ingested air flows into the chamber(s), then swirls around and exits the chamber, re-entering the duct and disrupting an otherwise smooth airflow.

Fortunately, there are numerous upgrades available that can completely eliminate any restrictions that the stock induction system presents. Easiest for the do-it-yourselfer is to replace the paper-element air filter with a high-performance oil-soaked cotton or foam filter. This simple change immediately increases airflow to the engine. Additionally, the aftermarket filters are typically serviceable. You can clean and re-oil them, and you probably won't have to buy another air filter again. Never run your car without an air filter in place, no matter how tempted you might be by the thought of unrestricted airflow to the engine. It's simply not worth the risk. A single grain of sand can have devastating effects on your engine, internally.

Early (1985–1989) TPI Mass Air Flow sensors used screens at each end of the unit to prevent debris from damaging the thin heated wire that measures the air mass. Unfortunately, the screens severely restricted airflow through the sensor. TPI Specialties found an extra 182 cubic feet per minute by removing the screens! *TPI Specialties photo*

Several companies offer replacement ducts that eliminate not only the resonance chamber but other problems of the stock ducts, too.

Another solution worth investigating for your Camaro is the installation of a "cold-air" or "ram-air" system. Several different designs are available from a number of aftermarket companies, but each works essentially in the same way: At low speeds, the cold-air induction systems allow the engine to more easily draw in air, while at faster speeds, air rushing into the cold air system scoop can actually be "rammed" through the filter, ducts, and into the engine, creating a slightly pressurized situation in the intake manifold that isn't unlike a supercharger or turbocharger's effect. In addition, because the air is generally drawn from outside the vehicle's engine compartment, the air is generally much cooler and therefore is more dense and holds more fuel, which means a stronger burn cycle in the cylinder, and more power.

Some cold-air systems utilize a scoop mounted beneath the front of the vehicle, some use scoops and hoses mounted behind or in place of factory fog lights, and some even use unique "cold-air" hoods with special

hood scoops. Each system is effective, but all require some care on your part when driving in rain or other wet conditions, because water can get in through the scoops and eventually get to the engine.

Mass Air Flow (MAF) Sensor

On 1985-1989 and 1994-and-newer TPI engines, a Mass Air Flow (MAF) sensor is used to measure the amount of air flowing into the engine. That information is then fed to the Electronic Control Module (ECM) or Powertrain Control Module (PCM), depending on the year of the vehicle, which calculates how much fuel to mix with the air to achieve a 14.7:1 air-fuel ratio, which produces the most power, best economy, and the fewest harmful emissions. The sensors measure the amount of air with a thin heated wire. As the air flows by the wire, the wire cools and the computer sends more power to the wire to bring its temperature back up to its original level. The more air flowing into the system, the more power is required to keep the wire hot. Thus, the amount of voltage is directly proportional to the amount of air flowing into the system.

The 1985-1989 MAF sensors used a tubular housing, and the sensor was located inside it. Screens on the housing's inlet and outlet added further protection against debris damaging the sensor (they're very, very fragile), but the screens created quite an airflow restriction: According to TPI Specialties' tests, in stock form the MAF could flow 529 cubic feet per minute, but with the screens removed, flow increases to 711 cubic feet per minute—an increase of 182 cubic feet per minute! With potential gains like that, it's no wonder that removing those screens is a popular hop-up trick, but be warned that doing so does increase your chances of ruining the MAF sensor, requiring you to purchase a costly new one. The 1994-and-newer MAF sensors are of a different design and do not require modifications, as they present only a minimal restriction to airflow.

The 1990-1993 TPI engines utilize a Speed-Density system to calculate the amount of air flowing into the engine. Manifold absolute

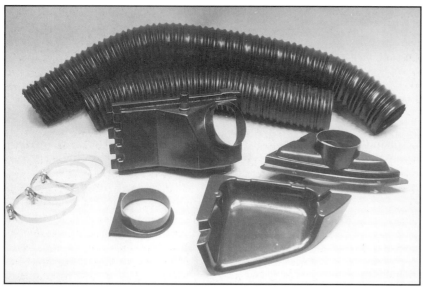

Adding a cold-air induction kit or, better yet, a ram-air induction system lets your engine breathe cooler, denser air, which can carry more fuel and thus make more power. Ram-air systems, like this Random Technologies system for 1993–1997 Camaros, go even further by providing a subtle supercharging effect that forces more air and fuel into the cylinders for even more of a power pick-me-up. *Random Technologies photo*

pressure, manifold air temperature, and exhaust gas oxygen sensors feed data to the ECM/PCM, which it uses to calculate how much air is flowing into the engine. The system is much less costly, but it is less forgiving than mass air systems, because the system relies on "look-up tables"—values stored in the ECM/PCM that tell how much air is entering the system given certain MAP, MAT, and oxygen sensor values. But the stock look-up tables are based on how much air the stock system can ingest.

If you change how much air the engine can ingest—by installing a freer-breathing air filter, housing, and cold air system; swap-in a hotter camshaft; and bolt on some headers to speed the flow of air out of the engine—the actual volume of air flowing into the engine may not be included in the stock look-up tables, so the system won't operate efficiently. In these cases, a replacement PROM chip that is custom-tailored to your engine's air intake abilities is required to restore efficiency and thus maximize power.

Interestingly, speed-density fuel injection systems are more popular in professional motorsports activities that allow fuel injection, because speed-density systems can react more quickly to changes in rpm and engine load. But, again, the system requires look-up tables that are optimized for its particular combination of components, which can be inconvenient (at best) for the average performance enthusiast. Mass Air systems, since they only measure the air flowing into the engine, are much more flexible and still function properly whether you have a stock engine or one equipped with high-compression pistons, a huge cam, headers, and even a supercharger.

Throttle Body Assembly

The throttle body assembly is simply a device equipped with a cable-activated butterfly valve to increase or decrease airflow into the engine. Carburetors have throttle bodies, so do Throttle Body Injection units (big surprise there!), as do Tuned Port Injection systems.

The stock TPI throttle body can flow as much as 668 cubic feet per minute, according to TPI Specialties.

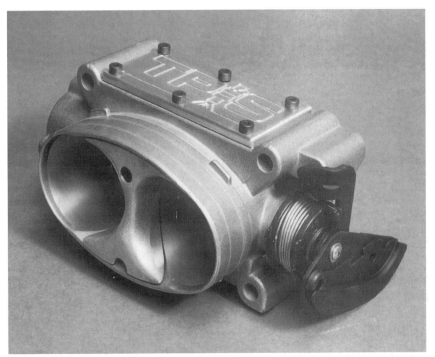

For larger -displacement engines, or ones that are run at high rpm for extended periods of time, a larger throttle body assembly, like this TPI Specialties 52-mm unit, flows significantly more air to keep the engine well fed. A 58-mm version and a huge mono-blade version are also available, flowing up to 1,300 cubic feet per minute! *TPI Specialties photo*

Larger throttle bodies that can flow as much as 1,300 cubic feet per minute are available.

The only real modification that can be made to a stock TPI throttle body is to install an airfoil, which helps streamline the air entering the throttle body, and can result in an increase of 41 extra cubic feet per minute over stock (for a total of 709 cubic feet per minute), according to TPI Specialties' flow-bench testing. Given that these tests measure only air flowing through the throttle body (as opposed to air and fuel, as you would have with a carburetor or TBI unit's throttle body), to compare these "dry test" numbers to the "wet test" numbers of carburetors, you need a carb about 10 percent larger to achieve the same flow rating, since the fuel slows down flow through the throttle body. In other words, you would need an 800 cubic-feet-per-minute carburetor to provide roughly the same flow as a 709-cubic-feet-per-minute stock TPI throttle body outfitted with an airfoil.

With 709-cubic-feet-per-minute flow capability, the airfoil-equipped throttle body should be sufficient for engines producing 400 horsepower or so. More powerful engines require larger-than-stock throttle bodies, such as 52-mm or 58-mm units, which flow 790 cubic feet per minute and 1,000 cubic feet per minute, according to TPI Specialties' tests. The 58-mm unit is acceptable for engines up to 600 horsepower. Above that, TPI Specialties offers a single-blade throttle body unit that flows 1,300 cubic feet per minute and should be good for approximately 800 horsepower.

Throttle Body Airfoil

As mentioned in the previous section on throttle body assemblies, installing a simple airfoil to the inlet side of the stock TPI throttle body assembly can smooth the flow of air into the stock throttle body unit enough to increase maximum flow by 41-cubic-feet-per-minute, for a total of 709 cubic feet per minute flow potential. This typically results in a power gain of 10 to 13 horsepower.

The throttle body airfoil is a simple, effective solution that is strongly recommended for all B2L/L98, LB9, LT1, and LT4 engines. (LS1 engines cannot use an airfoil because of their round, single-blade throttle body assembly.)

Intake Manifold (Plenum, Runners, and Base)

Once air flows through the throttle body assembly, it enters the intake manifold assembly. Engines equipped with carburetors or throttle body injection systems utilize a traditional-style intake manifold, while 1985–1992 tuned port injection engines feature a multipiece assembly that consists of an intake plenum with large curved runners that curl down to an intake manifold base. The LT1 uses a one-piece casting that integrates the plenum to the base with short runners. Lastly, the LS1 features a plastic intake with long runners that curl up over the plenum to feed the cylinders on the opposite side of the engine.

Carburetor and TBI systems can have their intake manifolds ported and port-matched to the cylinder heads to increase flow potential, or replacement intake manifolds are available for even greater flow and power potential.

The 1985–1992 TPI engines can also benefit from traditional porting and port-matching techniques, but they, too, have aftermarket parts available, including different intake plenums, larger-diameter and siamesed runner assemblies, and higher-performance intake manifold bases. Additionally, TPI Specialties offers an LT1/LT4-style "Mini-Ram" one-piece intake manifold assembly that greatly increases horsepower, although it sacrifices some torque.

At this point, the only upgrade possibility for the LT1/LT4 and LS1 intake manifolds is to modify the stock manifold through porting and port-matching.

Manifold Absolute Pressure (MAP) Sensor

The manifold absolute pressure, or MAP, sensor measures the actual air pressure within the intake manifold. You might question that last statement, given that for years and years you've always talked about engine *vacuum*. But, the truth of the matter is that intake manifolds don't experience a vacuum; technically, they just have a pressure that is lower than the surrounding atmosphere but is still actually a pressure (anything below zero pressure is a vacuum).

Speed-density injection systems use a MAP sensor to determine the air pressure in the intake, then combine that data with data from the manifold absolute temperature (MAT) sensor (which reads air temperature, which tells its density) and the oxygen sensor in the exhaust system to determine how much fuel needs to be added to achieve the optimal 14.7:1 air-fuel mixture ratio.

Quick Test: TPI Specialties Airfoil

Part:	Throttle-body airfoil
Approx. Price:	$60
"Before" Time:	14.93 seconds
"After" Time:	14.86 seconds
Gain:	0.07 seconds
Install Time:	Under 10 minutes
Rating:	*
Pros:	Easy installation
Cons:	Expensive for the minimal gain
Comments:	This is an item that looks so right you wonder why GM didn't bother to design the TPI throttle body with an air-foil shape— then you find out why: It's not needed. High-rpm racing engines, especially large-displacement engines, may realize a bigger gain, but for 305–350 cubic-inch engines driven on the street, your money may be better spent elsewhere.

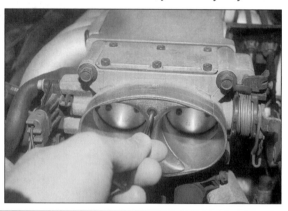

Another quick air induction upgrade is the TPI Specialties throttle body airfoil, which easily mounts to the front of the throttle body, smoothing the flow of air into either of the two throttle butterflies. Gains of roughly 12 horsepower are common.

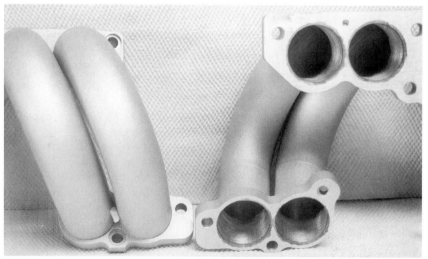

For the original TPI engines, the L98/B2L 350 and the LB9 305, various aftermarket intake runners are available, such as these oversize tubes from TPI Specialties.

Manifold Air Temperature (MAT) Sensor

The manifold air temperature sensor measures the temperature of the incoming air into the engine, because that information tells the ECM/PCM the air's density, which directly relates to how much fuel the air requires in order to achieve a 14.7:1 air-fuel mixture for maximum performance but minimal harmful exhaust emissions.

Fuel System

The fuel system of your Camaro's engine is responsible for the storage and delivery to the engine of fuel that, when burned, produces power.

The fuel system is actually fairly simple to comprehend and work with. A tank stores the fuel, while fuel lines deliver the fuel to either the carburetor or the fuel injection system injectors. A fuel pump pressurizes the system; carbureted systems utilize a mechanical, diaphragm-type pump, while TBI and TPI systems utilize an in-tank electric fuel pump plus a fuel pressure regulator to maintain a constant pressure.

Carburetor

Carburetors were used on the LG4 and L69 305-cubic-inch V-8 engines, as well as a number of V-6 and I-4 engines prior to the 1985 model year. These carburetors can be rebuilt as any old carburetor can, although idle air-fuel mixture screws are blocked off by the factory to prevent tampering. The plugs can, however, be removed for optimal idle air-fuel mixture adjustment.

Metering jets and rods can be replaced with richer or leaner versions to adjust the fuel mixture to account for any performance parts you may have installed.

Other than replacing the carburetors with a factory or aftermarket fuel injection system, there are few other modifications that can be made.

Fuel Injectors

Fuel-injected engines use fuel injector units to squirt fuel into the air flowing through the induction system, before it enters the cylinders. On Throttle Body Injection systems, the injectors are positioned directly above the throttle body bores, while on TPI engines, the injectors are located in the ends of the intake manifold's ports, aimed toward the cylinder head ports.

Just like carburetor jets, fuel injectors are available in different sizes for use with different engines. Fuel injectors are typically rated by the number of gallons per hour the injector can spray.

Injector "on-time" (the length of time it is instructed to spray fuel) is controlled by the ECM/PCM and depends upon the amount of air, the

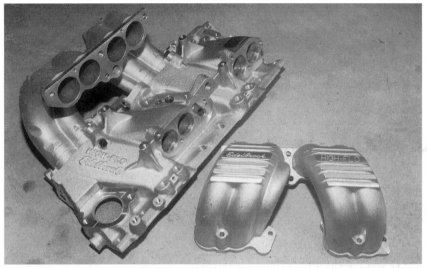

One of the best ways to approach engine modifications is to install performance packages, like Edelbrock's matched intake base and runner set.

Quick Test: TPI Specialties "Big Mouth" Intake Manifold Base

Part:	TPI Specialties "Big Mouth" Intake Manifold Base
Approx. Price:	$475
"Before" HP:	n/a
"After" HP:	n/a
Gain:	22 horsepower*
Install Time:	Approx. 1.5 hours
Rating:	***
Pros:	Good power gain; excellent driveability, trouble-free installation
Cons:	Expensive, requires large-tube or siamesed runners for best results.
Comments:	The stock manifold base has small ports that restrict flow, but the casting is too thin to do much porting. The Big Mouth intake has larger ports and still more material to grind if necessary. But the Big Mouth is more expensive than the Edelbrock intake base, which offers similar performance with mild porting.

* TPI Specialties data.

As in the old days, intake swaps are still a good way to boost engine output. Intakes like the TPI Specialties "Big Mouth" offer oversize ports and hogged-out runners for increased airflow.

air temperature (i.e., density), and other factors.

Interestingly, while it might seem logical to replace fuel injectors when you make performance upgrades to other parts of the engine, as you would have re-jetted the carburetor in the old days, the computer now takes care of that by triggering the injectors to spray fuel for a longer duration of time, if engine demands warrant it. Because the amount of time that injectors spray is adjusted by the computer, there isn't much

need to upgrade fuel injectors. In fact, upgrading injectors could actually kill power and cause fuel mileage to suffer because the injectors have to fire so briefly (since each "shot" from them contains a higher volume of fuel than would a shot from a "smaller" injector) that the fuel can't evenly and fully mix with the air rushing toward the cylinder. According to TPI Specialties, they have used injectors from a stock 305-cubic inch TPI engine on engines over 400 cubic inches with no problems.

Note, however, that fuel injectors do tend to respond well to higher-than-stock fuel pressures, which squirt more fuel through the injector during a given "on-time," plus produce a finer spray for better atomization and even keep the injector itself cleaner.

Fuel Pressure Regulator

A fuel pressure regulator is used in both the throttle body injection and tuned port injection (including B2L/L98, LB9, LT1, LT4, and LS1) engines to maintain a constant, high pressure necessary to produce good fuel atomization when the injectors are triggered on by the ECM/PCM.

Stock fuel pressures vary depending on the engine, but are non-adjustable. Aftermarket fuel pressure regulators typically allow easy adjustment (up or down) of the fuel pressure to optimize engine performance for the given conditions.

The performance improvements from fuel pressure adjustments are surprising and make installation of an adjustable fuel pressure regulator a highly recommended first upgrade.

Fuel Pump

TBI and TPI system fuel pumps are high-volume units mounted inside the fuel tank. They deliver ample supply of fuel to develop 400+ horsepower. The mechanical fuel pumps used on carbureted cars,

Carbureted and TBI cars still respond well to good old-fashioned intake swaps. A high-rise dual-plane intake generally makes more torque and is therefore often a better choice for the street, but a single-plane intake (shown) is usually better for high-rpm horsepower and is thus more suitable to track use. *Dart Heads photo*

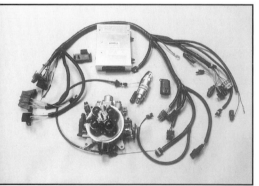

If you want to install a modern TBI or TPI system on an older engine, Howell Engine Technologies offers complete kits that include not only the TPI or TBI units (optionally) but the necessary wiring harness, the ECM, sensors, and even a high-volume electric fuel pump. *Howell Engine Technologies photo*

Holley's Pro Jection 4Di system is an excellent means of replacing a carburetor with a more accurate and easily tunable throttle body injection unit.

Before Chevrolet had the LT1, TPI Specialties had its Mini-Ram short-runner intake that greatly extends the TPI engine's breathing and power abilities at higher rpm, yet only sacrifices a bit of low-end torque to do so. *TPI Specialties photo*

The fuel injectors are, perhaps, the most critical components of your Camaro's fuel delivery system. Dirty or old injectors may not produce a spray pattern that's conducive to proper fuel atomization. Note the irregular spray patterns shown in this TPI Specialties' injector test. Several companies offer flow-tested fuel injectors to correct such problems. *TPI Specialties photo*

however, are low-volume, low-pressure units that are subject to inducing fuel starvation at higher rpm. Installation of an aftermarket low-volume/low-pressure electric fuel pump cures such problems and prevents "vapor lock" on hot days. Use of a fuel pressure regulator is required with electric fuel pumps, and installation of a fuel pressure gauge makes accurate adjustments much simpler.

Fuel Filter

Camaros utilize a canister-style fuel filter mounted in the fuel line between the fuel tank and the engine; it is physically mounted to the underside of the body structure, beneath the left, rear passenger seat. The filter must be changed periodically, as it eventually becomes increasingly restrictive, thanks to the debris it (hopefully) traps.

Aftermarket filters are available that offer superior filtering abilities and reduced restriction to fuel flow.

Fuel Tank

The fuel tanks in Camaros are nothing particularly spectacular—they're just large metal cans that hold 15.5 gallons of your favorite blend of gasoline. Third-generation 1LE Camaros, however, featured a

special dual-pickup fuel sender assembly that helped prevent fuel starvation when cornering with little fuel remaining in the fuel tank. If you road race, this is a worthwhile improvement, though it is of little value on the street, or in drag racing or autocross competition.

Fuel

The fuel you burn in your Camaro's engine determines the amount of power your engine produces, its driving character, and more. All third- and fourth-generation Camaros are designed to run on unleaded gasoline. Leaded gasoline should never be used because it plugs up the catalytic converter and destroys the oxygen sensor.

Because your Camaro's ECM/PCM alters ignition timing to eliminate engine knock—which occurs much more frequently with low-octane fuels—it is wise to use premium fuels whenever maximum performance is desired.

High-octane unleaded racing fuels would theoretically allow the engine to operate at its peak, because all parameters could be optimized by the ECM/PCM for producing power, since engine knock would not be a concern. However, racing fuels are

expensive and hard to find, making them impractical for street use.

Ignition System

Getting fresh air and fuel into an engine's cylinders won't do any good without an ignition system that's up to the task of burning that air and fuel. See how long your engine runs without spark plug wires. (Here's a hint: It won't even start without them.)

The goal of the ignition system, however, isn't just to ignite the air and fuel mixture, but rather to burn it as completely as possible. The more complete the burn, the more power is produced.

Over the years there have been a number of significant advances in ignition systems technologies. Until the mid-1970s, ignition points were still common equipment. Then GM's high-energy ignition (HEI) system did away with points and made high-energy coils common. Then Autotronics Control Corporation revolutionized ignition systems when it introduced its hugely successful multiple spark discharge (MSD) systems that cause the spark plugs to fire multiple times to ensure the air/fuel mixture is burned completely.

When General Motors created the LT1 "Gen-II" small-block V-8 engine for 1992, it replaced the ignition distributor with the Opti-Spark optical crank-triggering system for more accurate ignition timing. And with the LS1 engine, it addressed a long-time problem—insufficient coil-recharge time—by equipping each cylinder of the LS1 with its own individual coil.

When GM introduces a new ignition system, it doesn't take long for someone to figure a way to improve it, so we now have a plethora of performance parts available for your Camaro's ignition system from aftermarket manufacturers, plus a number of modifications that can be made to tune your system.

Ignition Coil

An ignition coil is a remarkable little device. It takes a lowly 12-volt battery signal and steps it up to as much as 60,000 volts or more! All that voltage is needed, however, in order to jump the spark plug gap strongly enough that the spark can touch off a roaring, instantaneous inferno that hopefully burns all of the air and fuel in a cylinder.

Stock coils work well, but when loads are highest and engine rpm are soaring, the coil can't recharge quickly enough or with enough electricity to produce an intense spark across the spark plug gap.

Aftermarket coils typically offer a higher discharge voltage and quicker refresh time, to address those shortcomings in the stock equipment.

Distributor

The distributor is used in "Gen-I" Chevrolet small-block V-8 engines to control where a spark signal is sent (through which spark plug wire) and when. The LT1 does not use a conventional rear-mounted distributor, but rather an optical triggering device that GM called the Opti-Spark system, which is mounted to the front of the crankshaft. The Opti-Spark is essentially a crankshaft position sensor with the ability to pinpoint the crank's position within one degree throughout a full 360-degree rotation. The Opti-Spark sensor tells the ECM/PCM the crank position, and the computer then figures out when to trigger a spark signal, which is distributed through the Opti-Spark system to the ignition wires and, ultimately, to the spark plugs.

LS1 engines use an internal crank sensor, as well as a camshaft

---

Quick Test: TPI Specialties Adjustable Fuel Pressure Regulator

Part:	Adjustable fuel pressure regulator
Approx. Price:	$90
"Before" Time:	14.93 seconds
"After" Time:	14.71 seconds
Gain:	0.22 seconds
Install Time:	Approx. 1 hour
Rating:	****
Pros:	Highly effective, inexpensive, easy installation, improves driveability and throttle response
Cons:	Requires high-pressure fuel pressure gauge (sold separately, $40)
Comments:	An excellent upgrade for any TPI Camaro. Lets you turn pressure up at track for more power, better throttle response, better idle, then decrease pressure to normal for fuel-sipping highway cruising. Another part GM should have included from the factory.

Tests have shown that increasing fuel pressure can aid fuel atomization, improve throttle response, and increase power. This TPI Specialties adjustable fuel pressure regulator installs easily in place of the stock, nonadjustable regulator, and is quickly adjusted with an open-end wrench. TPI Specialties photo

---

One thing that can contribute to a poor injector spray pattern is dirt or debris, allowed to reach the injector by first getting by the canister-style fuel filter. Fuel filters should be replaced periodically to ensure proper engine maintenance.

sensor, to determine crankshaft (and cam) position, then the PCM signals the appropriate coil to fire at the precise moment its spark is needed.

Because the LT1/LT4 and LS1 engine families have no distributor (strictly speaking) to upgrade, only owners of first-generation small-block engines need to read the remainder of this section.

The Camaro engine compartment is a tight place for an engine. As such, engineers had to devise a small-diameter distributor system for use in the Camaro, simply because there wasn't enough space for the bulky standard HEI distributor. As a result, the Camaro distributor is small in size and features a remote-mounted coil. Remote-mounting the ignition coil doesn't adversely affect performance, but the small-diameter distributor cap can allow misfiring to occur because the individual spark plug wire terminals are so close to each other within the cap that the spark energy could conceivably cross from one terminal to another, especially at higher rpm.

Aftermarket companies offer heavier-duty ignition distributors specifically for the Camaro (and its Pontiac sister, the Firebird) that help minimize the chances of misfiring by providing much more accurate operation. Rather than using inferior bushings to prevent the distributor shaft from wearing as it spins in the distributor housing, many aftermarket units feature roller bearings inside a more precisely machined housing that exactly positions the shaft in the center of the housing.

Many aftermarket performance parts companies also offer high-performance, high-quality tune-up parts, like a better distributor cap, rotor, and other parts that improve the reliability and efficiency of stock and aftermarket distributors.

Ignition (Spark Plug) Wires

An ignition wire is the conduit through which a spark pulse travels to reach a spark plug. Stock wires aren't designed for performance use. They typically feature high resistance—as much as 5,000 ohms per foot—which reduces the current available at the spark plug with which to create a spark.

Getting air and fuel into your Camaro's cylinders isn't enough—you need to make sure the mixture is thoroughly burned to maximize efficiency and power. Ignition systems like the Accel 300+ deliver intense spark energy in multiple bursts that help get the most out of every power stroke.

Accel's 300+ ignition system utilizes a version of the company's famous yellow Super Coil to provide the spark energy.

For performance applications, replacement wires offer lower resistance—some as low as 150 ohms per foot—allowing more spark energy to reach the spark plug. Many also employ superior insulating materials that provide increased protection against spark-induction from one wire to another (known as "cross-firing," which has nothing to do with 1982 Camaro "Cross-Fire Induction"

fuel injection systems), plus reduce radio frequency interference, so onboard computers, radios, and communications equipment function properly.

Some wires also provide additional protection against high heat, which is especially useful on engines equipped with exhaust headers, notorious for melting ignition wires. Ignition wires are available in a number of different sizes, and 8-millimeter wires should be considered a minimum. Likewise, because of all of the interference-sensitive electronics in late-model Camaros, you should always use RF-suppression wires that suppress radio frequencies that could disrupt the operation of some vehicle systems, especially radio and stereo equipment.

Spark Plugs

Spark plugs are spark plugs, right? Well, not exactly. Years ago there were few choices in spark plugs—you replaced old spark plugs with new versions of the same things. Today, however, we have an abundance of spark plug choices. There are choices in heat ranges (which we've had for many, many years) and choices in construction materials, electrode designs, tip designs, and

more. There are so many choices and so many claims made about why each one is so much better than the others that it can be a frustrating and tiresome exercise to pick the best plugs for your Camaro.

For years, the factory relied upon standard AC-Delco resistor plugs, but beginning in 1996 it switched to using platinum-tipped spark plugs in order to extend general service intervals to 100,000 miles. (Remember when it used to be amazing to have an engine live to 100,000 miles? Now that's the first recommended tune-up interval!) Platinum plugs actually just use platinum electrode tips, which resist wear much better than do standard plug materials. The result is a plug that preserves its gap and spark quality for longer, thus maintaining optimal performance much longer.

A number of companies produce spark plugs with unique design features, such as a forked tip, grooved electrodes, or other innovative elements. While it is possible that these devices add power to your

Camaro, it's also likely that a fresh set of standard plugs provide much of the same benefits. In other words, the "high-tech" features really don't provide much more performance than a set of new, standard plugs.

How you use your Camaro, and the performance engine equipment that it has, can affect the specific spark plug specifications necessary to maintain optimal efficiency and power. One typical adjustment involves the plug heat range—how quickly or slowly the plug can cool itself. General Motors typically specifies a rather hot plug for production use, given that most vehicles are going to be driven on lots of short, around-town trips that may not always be sufficient to burn the spark plugs clean of soot and carbon. But in racing applications—particularly road racing, where runs are long and cylinder temperatures remain high for extended periods of time—the stock plugs may not cool quickly enough and may actually begin to melt. So, it may be advantageous to switch to a cooler plug heat range than stock.

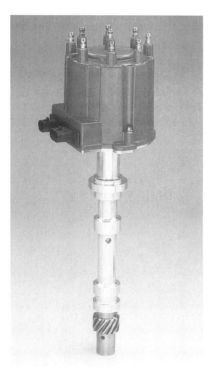

First-generation small blocks relied on traditional distributors to trigger the ignition system and to deliver the spark to the appropriate cylinder's spark plug. While the stock distributor was adequate for mundane driving, it simply wasn't accurate nor durable enough. Accel's Billet F-body distributor has both those bases covered, though, assuring you that your engine's timing is accurate. *Accel photo*

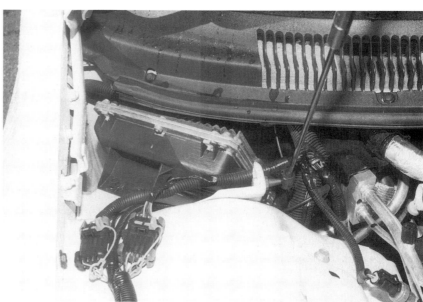

One of the most important parts of your Camaro's engine is its electronic "brain," which was known as an Electronic Control Module (ECM) on models through 1993, then for 1994 changed to a Powertrain Control Module (PCM) because it was given control over transmission functions, too. The 1982–1992 ECMs are located inside the car, under the dash, above the passenger's footwell. All ECMs feature replaceable PROM chips, which contain the "look-up tables" for fuel and ignition curves, among other data. In 1993, the ECM (and later PCM) moved to the engine compartment, on the right inner fender panel, near the cowl, as shown here. PCMs do not have removable PROM, but do feature an Erasable PROM that can be reprogrammed to achieve the same effect as swapping a PROM in an ECM.

There would rarely be a reason to switch to a hotter-than-stock plug, especially if you upgrade other aspects of the ignition system.

Ignition System Accessories

High-performance and racing activities often place special demands on an ignition system and may benefit from the use of certain aftermarket ignition products designed to increase spark output, and thus maximize engine power and efficiency. The most common of these are multiple-discharge spark systems and rev-limiters, but there are others, depending upon your application.

Multiple-Discharge Spark Systems

Aftermarket multiple-discharge spark boxes, as their description implies, deliver a series of spark puls-

When trying to tune your engine to develop maximum power and efficiency, it's helpful to use a diagnostic system that lets you see what the ECM/PCM is doing as you drive. The Diacom Plus system runs on an Intel PC computer (laptop is best) and actually displays the sensor data being fed to the ECM/PCM, so you can see exactly what's happening. And in case you prefer to keep your eyes on the road, the system can be set to "trap" data and store it for later review. Such a system is invaluable when making big modifications that require custom fuel and ignition curves.

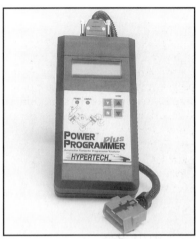

In order to reprogram the 1994-and-up PCMs, you need a special computer like this HyperTech Power Programmer Plus. It connects to the ALDL diagnostic port and swaps out the old EPROM data for new, performance-tuned data, or vice versa if you want to switch back to stock specs. *HyperTech photo*

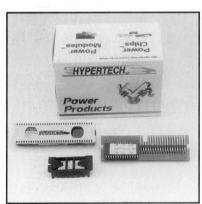

Depending on how you look at things, the old ECMs were either harder or easier to work with, since you simply swapped a stock PROM chip for a performance chip like these from HyperTech. The hard part of the job was often just getting to the ECM to make the swap. *HyperTech photo*

Something that makes swapping ECM PROMs a lot easier is the little black box, the PromPaq II switch box. With slots inside for up to four PROMs, you use a simple keyed switch to select the stock chip, a mild aftermarket chip, a nitrous-optimized chip, or a so-called "valet" chip that only lets the engine create minimal power for parking attendants or maybe your lead-footed son or daughter.

A look inside the PromPaq II reveals a HyperTech chip installed, a small "valet" chip, and two open "slots," one of which would normally be occupied by a stock chip, if you so chose to keep it for economical cruising.

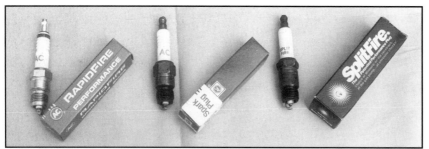

These three spark plugs represent a few of the many choices you have in order to keep your engine running right and healthy. From left to right, they are: AC RapidFire, AC resistor plug (standard), and SplitFire.

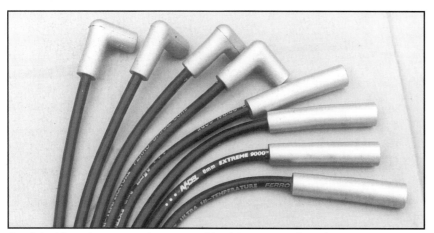

Stock ignition wires can soak up a considerable amount of spark energy just transporting the energy to the spark plug. High quality wires should present as little resistance as possible, in order to deliver as much spark energy as possible for the strongest possible spark. These Accel Extreme 9000 Ultra-Hi Temp Spiral Core 8-mm spark plug wires have just 500 ohms resistance per foot (compare that to 5000 or more ohms per foot for stock wires!) and are made specifically to withstand high-heat environments, including around exhaust headers.

This close-up shows how each of the three plugs differs from the others. Note the AC RapidFire plug is now in the middle of the three. The standard AC plug (left) has a conventional electrode and tip, while the RapidFire plug uses a "fluted" electrode and a standard tip. The SplitFire, on the other hand, utilizes a forked grounding tip and a standard electrode.

es in rapid succession to more completely burn the air and fuel in a cylinder. While the initial pulse ignites the air and fuel and is therefore responsible for burning most of the air and fuel, follow-up sparks can ignite pockets of air and fuel that may have escaped the initial burn cycle, resulting in greater overall efficiency. In addition, many of these multiple-discharge spark boxes deliver a single, extended-duration spark discharge at higher rpm, rather than multiple discharges, because high engine speeds do not leave sufficient time to fire a plug multiple times, but a longer-duration single spark can provide the same benefit.

Installation of a multiple-discharge spark box is a recommended upgrade for all forms of driving—street, drag racing, autocrossing, and road racing.

Rev-Limiters

Whether racing or just playing around on the streets, it can be all too easy to get wrapped up in the moment, and forget to keep an eye on the tachometer to avoid exceeding the engine's redline (maximum recommended rpm). Over-revving the engine can damage a number of internal engine components, including bearings, connecting rods, pistons, pushrods, and more. A rev-limiter can

High-Performance Stock Bottom End

There's an old saying about working on cars: If it ain't broke, don't fix it. And according to Myron Cottrell, of TPI Specialties, when it comes to your late-model Camaro's engine, if it isn't puffing smoke, making funny noises, or suffering from high mileage, the short-block assembly is one of those areas that doesn't really need fixing.

You see, Myron spends the better part of every day—including weekends—working with late-model Chevrolet engines. Sometimes they're in his race cars, sometimes they're on his engine dynos. And more often than not, they're sporting a stock, GM-built bottom end, including the stock crankshaft, stock connecting rods, stock pistons, stock bearings, and more. Still, despite all this stock hardware, some of the

engines Myron has modified have put out well over 400 horsepower with essentially just "bolt-on" items. And nearly every one of them has lived to rev another day.

Myron says the stock bottom ends of TPI Chevy V-8 engines are generally good for around 400 horsepower, though the exact figure obviously varies depending on mileage and engine condition.

What's nice about this, is that if you're planning on hopping up your Camaro's engine, it's nice to know that: 1) Your engine should stay together, and 2), you don't have to waste time and money rebuilding a part of the engine that's already working well—instead, you can spend that money on more power parts to bolt onto the engine.

eliminate excessive engine rpm as a concern, by preventing the engine from exceeding a specific rpm, which is typically user-programmable. When the engine reaches the specified maximum rpm, the rev-limiter begins dropping spark pulses, to keep the engine from speeding up (or even sustaining the speed it has).

Sophisticated rev-limiters offer different rpm settings for different situations. In drag racing, for example, it's often useful to perform a burnout, to heat and clean the tires. Then, when staged, awaiting the green light, a different maximum rpm is needed. Finally, during the run, a still different rpm is needed to both maximize power, without sacrificing engine components or reliability. While some systems only provide a single maximum rpm, others allow you to accommodate multiple settings.

Timing Retard Systems

Timing retard systems are used to retard the timing at certain times, such as when running nitrous oxide, or simply when running extended runs that cause the engine to run hot. Some systems utilize a computer to delay timing events, and most of these types of units allow you to specify the degree of retard to dial-in. Other systems utilize a fixed secondary triggering mechanism in the distributor; when running off the primary triggering system, the timing is as you set it, but when you switch over to a secondary ignition system, the timing is altered by a few degrees.

Back-Up Ignition Systems

NASCAR fans are probably familiar with drivers suddenly slowing on the race track, only to pick up speed again as though nothing had happened. When asked about it, the driver or crew chief often mutter something about having to switch ignition systems. What they're referring to is the practice of equipping a car with a back-up ignition system that features duplicates of the failure-prone components of the ignition system—the coil, multiple-discharge spark box, rev-limiter, and other components, essentially everything except the distributor and spark plug wires. A toggle switch is used to

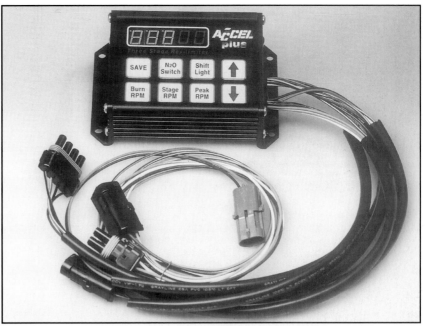

Racers know the value of rev-limiters—to protect your engine from spinning so fast that it could literally throw itself apart. Drag racers, in particular, have unique rev-limiting needs, since they have different "maximum rpm" for their burnouts, for staging, and for the race itself. A multistage rev-limiter, like the Accel Plus Three-Stage unit shown, allows users to specify different maximum rpm for each of three settings, and the settings can be selected at the simple push of a button. *Accel photo*

There are several conditions that may warrant using a timing retard device, like this Accel Plus Timing Retard Module. Racing engines that turn extremely high rpm can build high cylinder pressures that require retarded timing; superchargers, turbochargers and nitrous oxide will all do the same thing on street engines, too. *Accel photo*

The Accel 300+ ignition box is pre-wired for quick, easy installation.

select which ignition system is used. Some systems are available with the secondary ignition system triggering mechanism advanced or retarded a few degrees to allow the system to not only serve as a back-up system but as an on-track performance tuning device, as well.

Exhaust System

An efficient exhaust system is essential for a performance engine, because an engine can't draw in new air and fuel unless the old, burned exhaust gases are removed from the cylinders.

Stock Camaro exhaust systems use cast-iron exhaust manifolds plus steel exhaust pipes as the conduit through which it expels exhaust gases. A catalytic converter (or two) attempts to clean up emissions by chemically altering the exhaust gases, converting them into harmless elements, some of which are even beneficial to the environment. A single exhaust pipe carries gases aft to the muffler, which is mounted transversely between the rear axle assembly and the fuel tank.

As with most things on the Camaro, the stock exhaust system works reasonably well but isn't designed for peak performance. Unfortunately, there are few modifications you can make to an exhaust system legally, given the Environmental Protection Agency's hard-line stance against any modifications that may alter or defeat the operation of emissions control devices, so the only viable options available are to replace components with EPA-approved replacement parts.

Exhaust Manifolds/Headers

All third- and fourth-generation Camaros come equipped with cast-iron exhaust manifolds to direct exhaust gases away from the engine. Cast-iron manifolds are quiet and last virtually forever, but they're quite heavy and are not terribly efficient.

Aftermarket tubular exhaust headers, on the other hand, typically flow much better, since each cylinder has its own primary header tube; thus, pulses of exhaust gases from individual cylinders don't have to fight for space in the single runner of the stock manifold. Long, equal-length primary tubes tend to work better than shorter (i.e., "shorty") tubes of unequal length, because the longer equal-length tubes deliver each exhaust pulse to the collector tube in the same order as the engine's firing order, so pulses of exhaust gases don't even have to fight for space in the collector. In fact, by preserving the firing order, each exhaust pulse that reaches the collector helps to scavenge the next pulse from the next cylinder by creating a low-pressure zone behind it, which the next pulses rush to fill. In addition, headers weigh less than manifolds. Unfortunately, the two areas in which headers haven't typically excelled were their durability and the noise they allow to escape. However, the noise isn't objectionable (most people actually like it)

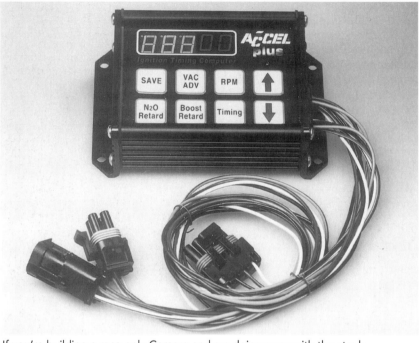

If you're building a race-only Camaro and are doing away with the stock ECM/PCM, you may want to invest in an ignition timing computer to accurately control your ignition system's timing curve. This particular unit is the Accel Plus Ignition Timing Computer. *Accel photo*

Exhaust headers, like these Edelbrock Tubular Exhaust System (TES, for short) pipes are a vast improvement over stock cast-iron manifolds.

One of the biggest pains about running headers is that their fastening bolts always seem to work themselves loose. Stage 8 locking safety bolts are a quick, easy, and attractive way to put an end to that problem.

Generation Gap:
Small-Block Chevy Parts Interchangeability

The two generations of late-model Camaros have featured three generations of "small-block" Chevrolet V-8 engines: The 1982–1992 "Gen-I" engines; the 1993–1997 "Gen-II" LT1; and the 1998-and-newer LS1. When it comes time to build an engine for your Camaro, you therefore have numerous choices of which engine to build, as well as an abundance of high-performance parts from which to choose.

However, despite each engine generation being known as a "small-block" Chevy V-8, there are distinct differences between the generations that prevent parts interchangeability.

The "Gen-I" small-block Chevy V-8 engine has been around in one form or another since 1955. During that time there have been literally tens of thousands of performance parts produced, and, for the most part, almost any of them could be physically bolted to an 1992 Camaro B2L 350 and made to work with little hassle.

The Gen-II small block—which includes not only the Camaro's LT1, but also the Corvette's LT4 and the Caprice/Impala L99—was actually introduced in the Corvette in 1992, but didn't come in a Camaro until 1993. It features numerous improvements over the "Gen-I," including reverse-flow cooling; an intake manifold that lacks both a coolant cross-over and a distributor hole; cylinder heads that lack both coolant cross-over passages and exhaust heat cross-over ports; a different water pump to accommodate the reverse-flow cooling; a different block (to accommodate the new water pump and Opti-Spark ignition system); a new crankshaft casting to accommodate the Opti-Spark system; and numerous other less-significant upgrades. What you're left with for interchangeable parts is a fairly short list: connecting rods, camshaft, exhaust manifolds (they physically bolt on, but won't fit Gen-II-equipped vehicles), oil pans, rocker covers, and assorted smaller items.

The Gen-III small block, the LS1, shares even less in common with the Gen-I. In fact, apart from a few miscellaneous fasteners, the only thing the Gen-III does share with the Gen-I is a dimension: center-to-center bore spacing of 4.40 inches. Otherwise, the LS1 is all-new, designed from a clean sheet with an all-aluminum block; new symmetric-port heads; a new plastic intake manifold; and new crankshafts, connecting rods, pistons, camshafts, oil pumps, oil pan, ignition system, rocker covers, rocker arms, pushrods, and valves—new and different everything.

Keep all this in mind when you're parts shopping and you could save yourself from buying a nifty, but useless, item.

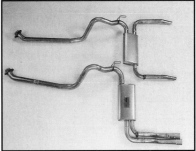

Installation of a free-flowing "cat-back" exhaust system, like these Walker DynoMax 2.5-inch and 3.0-inch systems reduce backpressure, which allows the engine to rid itself of exhaust gases more efficiently. Gains of 15–20 horsepower are not uncommon.

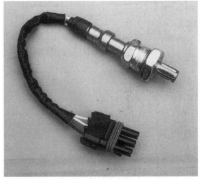

Oxygen sensors monitor the engine's efficiency by measuring the oxygen content of the exhaust gases. If the exhaust is oxygen-rich, the air/fuel mixture isn't rich enough, so the ECM/PCM adds more fuel to the incoming air. Conversely, if the exhaust is oxygen-poor, the computer leans out the air/fuel mixture. This is a heated oxygen sensor from Accel and is highly recommended for vehicles equipped with exhaust headers. The heated sensor reaches operating temperature faster, allowing the engine control system to enter its vastly more efficient "closed-loop" mode more quickly.

nor is it loud, and the advent of metallic-ceramic header coatings has allowed headers to last virtually indefinitely without rusting, corroding, or discoloring.

Metallic-ceramic coatings do more than just make headers (or other exhaust system components) look good, though. The coatings help the header retain heat, which keeps the exhaust pulses hotter for longer, and hotter air moves more quickly than cool air, so the coated headers actually do a better job of expelling exhaust gases than do non coated headers.

Oxygen Sensor(s)

An oxygen sensor measures the amount of oxygen in the exhaust gases, to determine how efficiently the engine is burning the air/fuel mixture. The oxygen sensor's data is used by the ECM/PCM to control the air/fuel mixture; if there is a lot of oxygen in the exhaust gases, the system is running lean, so the ECM/PCM adds more fuel by lengthening injector "on-time." Conversely, if the amount of oxygen in the exhaust gases is low, the system is running rich, so the ECM/PCM leans-out the air/fuel mixture.

There are no repairs that can be made to an oxygen sensor, other than replacement. The only "modification" of sorts is to replace a nonheated oxygen sensor with a heated (three-wire) unit that becomes operational much quicker following cold starts (unheated sensors rely on exhaust gas temperature to heat them). This is especially important for vehicles equipped with headers, since the exhaust gases may cool considerably by the time they reach the oxygen sensor, thereby requiring more time to heat up to true operating temperature.

Catalytic Converters

Catalytic converters are responsible for cleaning up the exhaust emissions by literally converting the gases into other gases thanks to a chemical reaction and the injection of oxygen into the exhaust system, which mixes with the deadly carbon monoxide and converts it to carbon dioxide, which plants and trees need to "breathe."

Ever since catalytic converters were first introduced, in the mid-1970s, they have had the reputation as power-robbing "emissions junk." In fairness to the anticlean-air crowd, the early pellet-type catalytic converters were highly restrictive and killed engine power. But by the 1980s, the pellet-type converters had been replaced by the monolith brick-type converters, which we still have today. Brick-type converters present only a relatively modest restriction to airflow and, therefore, have a minimal impact on an engine's power production. So-called "high-flow" catalytic converters are available from aftermarket sources, but most use merely the same type of brick, just in a larger size and with larger openings and exits.

There are no modifications necessary or permitted to catalytic converters, nor are they replaceable until the chemicals inside the converter have been used up, allowing engine emissions to become dirty again.

While most early Camaros used a single catalytic converters to clean up emissions, a dual-catalyst system was available on TPI engines and became standard on fourth-generation V-8 Camaros. This dual-catalyst system was a terrific power booster, adding as much as 25 horsepower to stock engines.

Cat-Back Exhaust Pipe/Muffler Systems

Since the Environmental Protection Agency (EPA) makes it illegal to alter any emissions devices on a vehicle exhaust system, manufacturers have begun focusing on "cat-back" exhaust systems—systems that replace all the exhaust system parts rearward of the catalytic converter, thus keeping the EPA happy while, at the same time, providing a noticeable power boost and sound-quality improvement.

Most cat-back exhaust systems employ larger-diameter exhaust pipes, typically with smooth mandrel bends, plus a low-restriction muffler with a larger inlet and one or more large outlets. Additionally, most are available in either aluminized or stainless steel to ensure the systems last for many, many years.

Exhaust System Coatings and Wraps

Exhaust system coatings and wraps are designed to improve the performance of the exhaust system by retaining heat, which keeps the exhaust gases hotter inside the tubes and therefore faster-flowing than cooler air. Exhaust system coatings provide the added advantage of protecting the component from rust or corrosion, making it last for many, many years.

Exhaust system wraps, which are popular among racers, do a better job of containing heat within exhaust pipes, particularly inside the header pipes. But wraps are actually considered to be too effective—they trap so much heat inside that the metal from which the exhaust pipes are made changes structurally, and literally becomes so brittle that it breaks apart like glass, requiring frequent replacement of the exhaust headers.

Cooling System

Your Camaro's cooling system is designed to keep a stock engine cool under a wide variety of circumstances, including enthusiastic driving. But if you've modified your engine to create more power, it taxes your cooling system, and if your cooling system isn't up to snuff, your engine could overheat, potentially causing serious internal damage.

Beyond your Camaro's engine cooling system, there are secondary cooling systems for components like automatic transmission fluid, engine oil, power steering fluid, and more. These, too, must be upgraded to handle the extra heat your engine is pumping out.

Radiator

When people think of the cooling system, one of the first two things that usually come to mind is the radiator. Though technically not a part of your engine, your engine

One of the most efficient late-model Camaro exhaust systems is the dual-catalyst exhaust that was optional on some third-generation Camaros and became standard on fourth-generation V-8 Camaros. On third-generation TPI cars, it boosted the LB9's output to 230 horses from 215, while the B2L/L98's output went to 245 from 220.

Catalytic converters have an undeserved reputation of being restrictive performance killers, but, in truth, modern catalysts are quite efficient, flow-wise, especially high-performance units like this Random Technologies Super High Flow converter. *Random Technologies photo*

wouldn't live very long without the radiator, because the radiator is what takes the hot coolant from the engine and cools it off, by sending it through thin tubes (arranged in rows) over which air flows. Additionally, thousands of tiny fins zig-zag back and forth between the rows, absorbing additional heat from the tubes and shedding that heat into the air flowing past them.

Generally speaking, the more rows and columns of tubes a radiator has, the better it can dissipate heat. But there is a practical limit to how thick a radiator can be before it reaches a point of diminishing returns. For instance, a four-row (technically it's four columns of roughly 20 rows of tubes each) radiator is generally considered to be the widest radiator useful in a street car. Any wider and the radiator becomes so thick that it actually acts as a wall, preventing air from flowing through it. Even if air could flow through it, the air would be so hot from the heat given off by the first four "rows" of tubes that the fifth row couldn't dissipate any heat.

The radiators installed in third- and fourth-generation Camaros at the factory utilized plastic end tanks that act as large reservoirs to hold coolant before and after it flows through the cooling tubes. Unfortunately, the plastic tanks are notoriously problematic, frequently suffering leaks, cracks, and other troubles. The finned radiator core is made of thin steel and has no particular drawbacks, but it doesn't have any particular strengths, either. The number of rows used varies, depending on the engine and options ordered.

Most aftermarket performance or racing radiators are made of aluminum, which both weighs less than steel radiators and dissipates heat more quickly, making it more efficient. Along with the aluminum core, most aftermarket radiators feature aluminum end tanks, which virtually eliminate leaks. The aftermarket units are generally available in various thicknesses ("rows" of cooling tubes), with various cooling tube sizes, and even different fins-per-inch (fpi) counts, allowing you to customize your radiator to suit your exact requirements.

Water Pump

The water pump forces coolant through the engine by means of an impeller driven by the crankshaft. First-generation V-8 engines turn the water pump with either a V-belt or flat serpentine belt, depending on the particular year. Anyone who's ever had a "fan belt" break appreciates the cam-driven water pump of the LT1/LT4 and LS1 engines, which allows the engine to be safely operated without a belt at all, giving you the chance to drive to a service station for a replacement engine "accessory" belt, rather than having to walk to one. Note, however, that your alternator won't be turning, so the engine draws its electricity from the battery, and eventually discharges the battery enough that the car won't continue to run.

The first-generation V-8 water pumps turned in opposite directions, depending on whether the pump was driven by a V-belt or a serpentine belt. V-belts rotated the water pump clockwise, while serpentine belts spin the water pump counterclockwise. This difference means that the water pumps are not interchangeable; the difference is more than just the pulley bolted to the front of the pump.

Whichever direction the pump spins, their efficiency can be greatly increased by installing a solid flow-director disk to the impeller. While this can be a do-it-yourself job (a sheet metal disk the same diameter as the impeller can simply be riveted to the impeller), most aftermarket water pumps feature that modification, along with heavier-duty bearings, and even a lightweight, heat-shedding aluminum housing. And if your water pump has any miles on it, it's probably ready for replacement, so you might as well just replace it with a high-performance pump.

Thermostat

The thermostat controls the minimum coolant temperature once the engine is thoroughly warmed up. A temperature-sensitive spring shrinks when coolant of a specific temperature hits it, thus opening a port through which coolant can flow out of the engine. Different

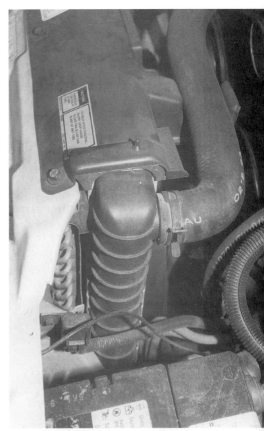

Two more key elements of your Camaro's cooling system are seen here: the radiator and the radiator hoses. Stock radiators are fine for stock or even mildly modified engines, but if you're making any serious power increases, your stock radiator probably won't handle the extra cooling demands. A replacement racing radiator usually handles the job and looks neat in the process. Meanwhile, molded rubber hoses work fine so long as they're not old and weak. You could pick up some polished stainless pipe and replace those flexible hoses with rigid pipe (remember to use lengths of rubber hose to connect the pipe to the radiator necks and engine (water pump or thermostat housing neck) to allow for engine movement due to torque and vibrations.

thermostat temperature ranges use different springs to achieve those temperature settings.

EFI systems, TBI or TPI, are particularly temperature-sensitive, so you should never attempt to run the engine without a thermostat installed. The thermostat itself presents a minimal restriction to coolant flow, and if left unchecked,

Step Up to TPI

The virtues and benefits of running Chevrolet's Tuned Port Injection fuel injection system are as numerous as applications for your Camaro. You really shouldn't be asking yourself, "Should I upgrade to TPI?" but rather, "How soon should I upgrade to TPI?"

Of course, before you can make the upgrade, you have to know a thing or two about how to actually make the swap. And depending on how you go about things, the job can either be easy or hard.

There are essentially two ways to get the parts you need: You can buy a TPI parts car from which you can pirate all the necessary parts, or you can buy a swap kit from companies like Howell Engine Technologies or Accel. Both are effective routes, and each has its own merits.

In the case of buying a parts car, if you can get a good deal and can use or sell the leftover parts, the parts car route may be less expensive.

On the other hand, the aftermarket upgrade kits typically feature improvements over the stock TPI system that increase performance.

There are a few catches to upgrading, however.

First of all, carbureted and Throttle Body Injection Camaro engines utilized traditional flat-tappet camshafts, while most TPI cars used roller cams. That means that the computer programming for TPI systems would be incompatible with the rest of your engine. And since Chevy actually machined engine blocks differently for roller cams than for flat-tappet, you can't just install a TPI roller cam in your nonroller cam block. Fortunately, this problem is easily cured by utilizing a mass air flow-metered TPI system, rather than the speed-density-type system.

To feed the TPI system, you'll need to procure the TPI system's high-pressure fuel pump. You may need to run a fuel return line to the tank, depending on whether your Camaro has one or not.

The TPI system also requires a different air cleaner system. Since you'll likely be using the mass air meter, you can't just plug an air filter on the front of the throttle body assembly like the street rodders. Your remaining options are to get the factory pieces or purchase aftermarket systems. Now you see why buying a parts car with the stock TPI system is advantageous.

You're still not done, though.

Carbureted cars don't have oxygen sensors, so you'll need to either graft one into your existing exhaust system or replace the system with a TPI car's pipes.

The brains of the TPI system, of course, are the Electronic Control Module, or ECM. And while your Camaro may have an ECM, it's not necessarily compatible with your TPI system's hardware. Specifically, GM changed ECM designs in the mid-1980s. The early systems utilized a simple PROM chip, while the later systems used a more durable cartridge-style PROM. Surprise! The two aren't compatible. So, depending on the design of your ECM, you may need to replace it. Either way, you want to get a TPI engine wiring harness for all the proper connections.

Then, of course, there are numerous minor parts that need to be changed: various brackets, cables, hoses, the distributor (TPI systems require a small-diameter distributor), and more.

Naturally, some of the original TPI parts, like the manifold base or the runners, can be replaced with high-performance aftermarket parts at the time of the swap.

So, is all this trouble and expense worth it? The answer depends.

If you're looking for peak power numbers to brag about, carbureted systems still tend to make more power, but not the stock carbureted system, though, so TPI won't help you there. And if you're looking for simplicity, it's awful hard to beat a carb on that count.

But if you value cleaner engine emissions; improved throttle response; increased fuel efficiency; a broader, flatter torque curve; more reliable engine operation; and other advantages of the TPI system, then it's a great way to go!

If you've got a non-TPI Camaro, you've got several options of how to upgrade to the efficient EFI system, but you've also got some "hidden" costs to consider. Still, the benefits typically outweigh any disadvantages, making the induction system swap well worthwhile.

This Milodon Hi-Volume Water Pump, with its rear cover removed, shows the impeller disc installed. The disc directs the flow of coolant better, considerably reducing cavitation within the pump and air pockets within the engine for more efficient cooling. You can modify your stock pump with a simple piece of round sheetmetal riveted to the impeller. *Milodon photo*

coolant could literally flow through the engine so quickly that it wouldn't have time to absorb enough heat to cool the engine, so the engine could easily overheat. Conversely, it may flow through the radiator so quickly, too, that whatever heat the coolant may have picked up can't be dissipated, so the coolant never cools and actually ends up causing the engine to overheat. Either way, the end result is a problem.

Because the ECM factors data from a coolant temperature sensor when calculating fuel mixture, you need a thermostat that allows enough heat in the engine to prevent the EFI system from operating in the cold warm-up mode, but not get so hot that the engine becomes prone to detonation. In the old days, a 160-degree-Fahrenheit thermostat was the ticket for V-8 engines, but at 160 degrees, the EFI system thinks the engine isn't quite warmed up yet. A 170-degree thermostat, on the other hand, is only marginally higher but prevents an extended, mixture-richening "warm-up" mode operation.

Hoses

The cooling system hoses—both the upper and lower radiator hoses, as well as heater hoses—represent some of the weakest spots in your Camaro's cooling system. Over time, the hoses can become brittle and crack, releasing coolant. Or, they could become so weak that, rather than cracking, they simply burst on the spot, spewing as much coolant as your engine can pump out.

From the factory, Camaros are equipped with rubber cooling system hoses, and these should be inspected regularly for cracks and replaced approximately every three years or so.

An upgrade for rubber hoses is silicone hoses. They are stronger and tend to last longer than rubber hoses and can prove quite reliable, even in competition use.

Even better than silicone hoses, however, are braided steel hoses, which are exceptionally strong and can withstand higher pressures. Just don't confuse braided steel hose covers for actual braided steel hoses.

Finally, it is possible to replace the bulk of the hoses under your Camaro's hood with rigid tubing, using only short sections of hose to connect the rigid tubes to the radiator, water pump, thermostat "gooseneck," etc. Rigid tubes can also make quite a fashion statement if anodized or powder-coated.

Coolant

Coolant is probably what comes to most people's minds when they first think of cooling systems. The coolant is the blood of the system, traveling through the engine, picking up heat as it goes, then going to the radiator to dissipate that heat before returning to the engine to pick up more heat.

The factory fills Camaros with a near 50/50 mixture of anti-freeze and water. Unlike most things that are mixed together, a mix of anti-freeze and water actually lowers the mixture's freezing point, while raising its boiling point at the same time. The usually ideal 50/50 mix typically freezes at around -30 degrees Fahrenheit and boils at roughly 250 degrees Fahrenheit. Straight water, by comparison, freezes at 32 degrees Fahrenheit and boils at 212 degrees Fahrenheit.

If you happen to live in a warm climate, you may be able to mix water with a product called Water Wetter, which helps improve the ability of water to absorb and dissipate heat, plus raises the boiling point of

the water. However, in colder climates, use of this product could allow the "coolant" to freeze in the engine, which could cause cracks in the block or cylinder heads.

Note that until 1995, Chevrolet used ethylene-glycol anti-freeze mixed with water. The mixture was a fluorescent lime-green color and needed to be changed every two years or so to maintain optimal efficiency. Beginning in 1995, a new, orange-colored anti-freeze was used, which is designed to last for up to 100,000 miles before needing to be changed. The two types of coolant cannot be mixed, or internal engine damage may result.

Fan(s)

Radiators need to have air flowing through them to cool the coolant flowing inside their tubes. But, given the fact that Camaros breathe cool air from underneath the front of the car and not from a front-mounted grille, the air-flow through the radiator may not be sufficient at even moderate speeds to effectively cool the coolant. A fan alleviates this problem by pulling air through the radiator.

The stock, dual electric fans used on production Camaros are excellent units that draw a good deal of air through the radiator. Unfortunately, they don't come on until late, when the coolant is quite hot. This HyperTech Cool Fan Switch will activate the fans at much lower coolant temperatures to keep the engine cool, rather than lettering it build up excessive, power-robbing heat. *HyperTech photo*

Third- and fourth-generation Camaros have relied on electric fans mounted directly to the radiator, and those fans typically work very well, when they're on. That's the catch:

Quick Test: 170-degree Thermostat

Part:	TPI Specialties 170°F Thermostat
Approx. Price:	$15
"Before" Time:	14.93 seconds
"After" Time:	14.85 seconds
Gain:	.08 seconds
Install Time:	Approx. 30 minutes
Rating:	***
Pros:	Very inexpensive; reduces detonation
Cons:	Requires PROM or fan switch to activate electric fans at lower-than-stock temperatures to experience full benefits. Decreases heater/defroster output in colder climates/weather.
Comments:	At less than $15, this is an item you simply shouldn't pass on. It keeps your engine cooler, which reduces the chance of detonation and thus allows more ignition timing for more power. Even without the PROM or fan switch, the thermostat is quite useful as long as the car is kept moving.

Because electronically fuel-injected engines run such a fine line between rich and lean air/fuel mixtures, they are extremely temperature-sensitive. The hotter an engine runs, the less timing it can handle before detonation occurs. Changing to a cooler thermostat helps reduce operating temperatures, but it is easily possible to run the engine so cold that it never gets out of "warm-up" mode. A 170-degree-Fahrenheit thermostat like this HyperTech PowerStat allows the computer to sense the engine is thoroughly warmed, but still keeps operating temperatures low enough to develop excellent power.

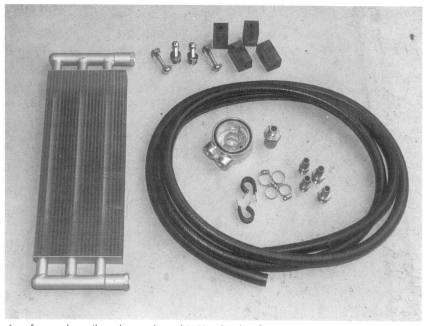

An aftermarket oil cooler, such as this Hayden kit, functions just like a radiator. Hot oil flows inside the miniature radiator; as air rushes through the radiator, it whisks away heat! Kits like this are good insurance against oil breakdown, which could lead to bearing or ring failure.

Your cooling system has components that do more than just remove heat from engine coolant. An oil cooler, like this coolant-to-oil unit installed on 1LE and R6P-equipped Camaros, works quite well and is easy to install.

The stock setting for the fans is often too high for performance use, allowing the engine to build and retain too much heat. Fortunately, a replacement thermostat control switch from a company like HyperTech turns the fans on at lower temperatures. Likewise, most aftermarket PROM chips and EPROM reprogramming computers are programmed to activate the fans at lower coolant temperatures.

Oil System

Most people assume your engine's oil system is only responsible for lubricating the engine, but the oil actually has five critical duties: It cleans the engine, by picking up dirt or other particles and hopefully depositing them in the oil filter; it cools the engine, just as coolant does, by absorbing heat and dissipating it to the air flowing around the oil pan; it seals the piston rings to the cylinder walls, thereby helping to maximize compression; it protects metal components from corrosion and rust; and, it lubricates, to prevent wear between the parts. With all that to do, it becomes clearer why a high-performance engine needs a high-performance oil system.

Oil Pan

The most visible part of any oil system, unless you have a horrendous oil leak, is the oil pan. Stock Camaro pans for all engines (except the LS1 and certain V-6 engines) are made of stamped steel and typically hold four quarts of "liquid gold," and the filter holds another half quart. (Despite what the *Beverly Hillbillies* song says, fresh motor oil isn't black, it's gold.) The stock pan also features a simple baffle designed to keep oil trapped in the deepest part of the pan, the sump (though the baffle does little to keep the oil pump pickup submerged in oil).

A variety of aftermarket oil pans are available that provide both increased oil volume, plus feature better baffling to prevent the oil pump from only sucking air. In addition, an aluminum oil pan tends to muffle sounds better, quieting the engine, and it dissipates heat better.

Because the Camaro has such a low ride height, care must be taken when selecting an oil pan that the sump area won't accidentally contact the ground, which could tear open the pan, spilling oil everywhere, and causing the engine to starve for oil and possibly seize.

Oil Pump

The oil pump draws the oil from the oil pan through a pick-up tube with a coarse screen attached to the end of it, to prevent large debris from being ingested. The pump then sends the oil to the oil filter and then off to the rest of the engine through various oil passages called galleries.

The pump itself features steel gears inside a cast-iron housing. The size of the gears determines the volume of oil the pump can process in a given period of time. Oil pressure is determined by a number of factors, including a bypass spring mounted in the oil pump cover. Other factors that influence oil pressure are the oil filter and the sizes of the oil galleries within the engine.

Windage Trays and Scrapers

Oil that isn't in the oil pan sump can't be drawn in by the oil pump and, therefore, won't do the engine much good. Additionally, because oil has weight, excess oil on parts like the crankshaft can slow down the crank's rotation.

Parts like windage trays and crankshaft scrapers are designed to alleviate these problems. The windage tray, which mounts to special extended main bearing bolts, acts like a baffle to prevent oil from sloshing up onto the crankshaft as you race around or hit the brakes. A crank scraper, on the other hand, actually skims oil off the crankshaft counterweights as it rotates.

Neither windage trays nor crankshaft scrapers are utilized in production engines, nor are they necessary, but they do provide minute benefits if you are compelled to free up every last horsepower trapped within your engine.

Oil Coolers

Because oil flows through the engine and absorbs heat, it gets hot, and when it gets hot, it thins out, decreasing its ability to clean, seal, and especially lubricate the engine. This is especially critical for engines that are operated for extended lengths of time, such as those used in road racing and even just street driving.

An oil cooler can considerably improve your oil's ability to do its various jobs. Factory-installed oil-to-water (actually it was engine coolant) coolers were available at various times throughout Camaro production, as part of various options, including RPO R6P, RPO 1LE, and SEO B4C. The factory cooler utilized an adapter that mounted between the oil filter and the engine block. Coolant from the radiator flowed through the adapter, cooling the oil. It's a simple system, and it works. But it does have its problems.

First, the oil is only in the adapter for a brief period of time, which means there isn't much time for the oil to dissipate its heat to the adapter, from which the heat can then be absorbed by the coolant. Second, if your engine begins to run hot, during an extended race for example, the oil is allowed to heat up. Third, if the oil was running cool on its own, the coolant actually heats up the oil.

Most aftermarket oil coolers are oil-to-air coolers, instead. As with the factory system, an adapter is installed between the oil filter and

the block, but this adapter sends the oil out of the adapter through a hose to a miniature radiator that should be mounted in an area that gets decent airflow. As with the cooling system radiator, the oil cooler radiator absorbs heat from the oil as the oil flows through tubes in the radiator. That heat is then transferred to a series of fins between the tubes, and ultimately dissipated to the air flowing through the radiator. The cooled oil then flows back to the adapter through another hose. Some coolers are even thermostatically controlled to prevent the oil from becoming too cool.

Oil Filters

Oil filters are remarkably unremarkable, usually. You change your filter when you change your oil, then forget about it until the next oil change. But not all filters are created equally.

Stock filters are sealed metal canisters with a mesh-type filter material inside, through which the oil must flow. As the oil flows through the mesh, dirt and metal particles are trapped in the mesh, so only "clean" oil flows out of the filter. Unfortunately, standard replacement oil filters do only a decent job of cleaning the oil. For one thing, the mesh can let smaller particles through that can still damage your engine. Another problem is that stock replacement filters can be quite restrictive to the flow of oil, especially as the filter traps more and more contaminants, blocking the mesh. Finally, because the stock filters are relatively small, they can quickly become plugged up with dirt and debris, allowing your oil to bypass the filter entirely if the filter becomes too much of a restriction.

Aftermarket serviceable oil filters are available that you can periodically clean and reuse. This can be advantageous because it allows you to easily see the kinds of contaminants that are in your engine's oil, and thus gives you important diagnostic information. For instance, the presence of a lot of metal particles could indicate abnormal wear in your engine. (Stock replacement-type filters can be cut open and inspected, but the process is messy

Another worthwhile trick for your oil system is to replace the small, stock oil filter, represented here by the Fram PH30 unit, with a much larger unit designed for GM pickup truck applications, like the AC PF35 or PF1218. Their increased size presents more filtering media, plus they hold more oil, increasing overall oil supply for the engine.

and time-consuming, and the folded mesh makes inspection difficult.)

In addition, some filters offer superior filtering properties, allowing the filter to trap much smaller particles than a stock replacement filter.

Oil

Finally, the most important part of your engine's oil system is its oil. It is the lifeblood of your engine, and without it, your engine comes to a grinding halt in a hurry.

It goes without saying that you need to ensure that your engine always has an ample supply of clean, cool oil to properly perform, so you need to perform oil changes every 3,000 miles for street use, or after every race for competition use.

But what oil should you use? Any good-quality engine oil generally does the job, though there are advantages to using synthetic oils, like Mobil 1. Synthetic oils are scientifically engineered to better withstand heat extremes, both hot and cold. They don't break down and thin out as much in extreme heat, so they protect your engine better. Plus, they flow more easily in extreme cold weather, allowing oil to flow to your engine's vital parts more quickly than could conventional oil, which would leave your engine unprotected. And tests have shown that the bulk of an engine's wear occurs during the first minute or so following start-up, so anything you can do to speed up oil delivery dramatically reduces wear.

Synthetic oils have also been shown to result in increased power production at high rpm, although the increase is minimal and not realizable at normal engine speeds.

Oil Additives

In recent years, a number of oil additives have hit the shelves of auto parts stores claiming to do everything from eliminating engine wear to restoring engine performance. While there is generally some truth to the claims being made, the advertisements rarely provide the whole truth behind the claims.

The bottom line on engine oil additives is that a properly maintained engine that's in good condition shouldn't need any of those additives. As proof, just look to professional motorsports teams from NASCAR, NHRA, SCCA and IRL or CART competition: If the additives provided true, valuable benefits, you can bet those teams would be using them to gain an edge on their competition.

Nitrous Oxide

Nitrous oxide is a popular and effective power booster for stock and race engines alike. Nitrous oxide (also known as laughing gas, because of the effect it has on people if inhaled—which you should never do without medical supervision) increases engine power in two ways: First, it super-oxygenates the air-fuel mixture, allowing it to hold more fuel, so the combustion process produces more heat, which translates into more power; second, nitrous oxide tends to cool the air/fuel mixture, which both allows the air/fuel mixture to hold more fuel and also helps to reduce hot spots in the cylinder that could lead to detonation.

Easy-to-install bolt-on nitrous kits are available for third- and fourth-generation Camaros from a number of manufacturers and can generally boost power anywhere from 75 to 150 horsepower for a stock engine. Modified engines can often handle additional power boosts, up to around 250 horsepower, while full-race motors with heavy-duty reciprocating assemblies may be able to withstand as much as 400 nitrous-generated horsepower or more!

Carbureted and TBI-equipped Camaros can usually utilize a normal injector plate that gets sandwiched between the intake manifold and the carb or throttle body assembly, while TPI cars typically utilize a plate that mounts between the throttle body assembly and the intake plenum. More exotic systems utilize injectors that feed directly into the intake manifold runners, aimed toward the intake valves.

Nitrous kits are easy, cost-effective, and safe methods of increasing engine output for short periods of time, such as is needed during a drag race. However, you must be cautious about how much extra power you attempt to make with a nitrous kit, because it is possible to over-stress parts and cause them to fail, or to increase wear. When in doubt, it is best to be conservative with nitrous system jetting and careful in its use, limiting nitrous use to 15 seconds or less, and only at full throttle.

Additionally, it is often beneficial to employ timing retard devices in conjunction with nitrous oxide systems; because nitrous-oxide-assisted engines create higher cylinder pressures, ignition timing should be retarded. But since you only use nitrous sporadically (and never on the street!) you don't want to hamper engine performance during the 99 percent of the time that you're not running nitrous through the engine. Ignition accessories systems that activate when the nitrous activates retard the timing only when it's needed, allowing engine timing to be optimized for whatever kind of driving you're doing.

Forced Induction Systems

Stock Camaro engines are "normally aspirated," meaning that the only fuel and air they can get into their cylinders is whatever they can suck in. But by pressuring the induction system, it is possible to force-feed the engine more air and fuel than it would normally use. With more air and fuel in the cylinders, the combustion process generates more power.

Probably the quickest power picker-upper is a nitrous oxide system. Injecting nitrous into an engine oxygenates and cools the air/fuel mixture, allowing it to hold more fuel. The more fuel that can be put into the engine, the more power the engine can make. This Nitrous Oxide Systems kit for TPI Camaros is adjustable to deliver between 90 and 125 additional horsepower. Larger kits are available for competition engines. *Nitrous Oxide Systems photo*

Tuning Talk

Your Camaro's Electronic Control Module (ECM, or PCM for 1994-and-up models) is a remarkable device that can adjust fuel mixtures and ignition timing to always deliver optimal performance even as parts begin to wear. The engine may not deliver as much power with a worn set of plugs as with a fresh set, but the performance the ECM gets out of those worn plugs is as much as the plugs can give.

But even the ECM can't work miracles. At some point, things wear enough that performance suffers noticeably. Hopefully, before your Camaro reaches that point, you are going to spend a little time doing some preventive maintenance—a tune-up.

Despite all the high-tech gadgetry under your late-model Camaro's hood, the time-honored tradition of tuning a performance engine hasn't really changed all that much over the years. You still need to start with good old-fashioned diagnostic work, replace worn or failed parts, then adjust everything properly.

Diagnostics

In the old days, if you wanted to thoroughly check out an engine, you needed an assortment of instruments, including a timing light, a compression gauge, a vacuum gauge, a fuel pressure gauge, and a tachometer. If you weren't scared to death of electronics, you might use a voltmeter and ohmmeter to check out a couple things, too.

Perhaps somewhat surprisingly, most of those tools are still needed to tune your late-model Camaro's engine. Some of those old standbys need to be updated—like a new voltmeter that offers a number of different scales to accommodate low-voltage sensor systems, as well as ultra-high voltage ignition systems, and the fuel pressure gauge has to read a lot higher—but they are basically all be there. It's also helpful to utilize a few new tools, like the Diacom Plus interface kit from Rinda Technologies that displays on a PC (or laptop) all the relevant sensor data your Camaro's ECM/PCM is receiving. Overall, though, the types of tests you are doing aren't all that different from what needed to be done on old muscle-car engines.

One of the best first steps is to perform a compression test on each cylinder to check for any signs of internal damage. If you have access to a leak-down tester, that would be an even better tool to use, given its superior diagnostic abilities.

Next, it's useful to hook the car up to a Diacom computer to see if sensor readings fall within specs, as well as to look for trouble codes that may have been set.

Then check the usual things—timing, vacuum, oil and fuel pressures, etc.—to round out the basics. Make sure that all test data is neatly recorded so you can refer back to both now and at the time of your next tune-up, to gauge wear. Compare all data to specs given in a shop manual for your particular Camaro's model year and engine.

Unlike in the past, you need to check the function and adjustment of an assortment of sensors, such as the throttle position sensor, oxygen sensor, coolant temperature sensor, manifold absolute pressure sensor, mass air flow sensor, manifold air temperature sensor, and others to ensure they are functioning as they should be.

The diagnostic end of a tune-up is far more time-consuming, and a little bit trickier than in the past. Fortunately, tune-ups don't need to be performed nearly as frequently on late-model Camaros as on Camaros of the muscle-car era.

R and R Time—
Repair and Replace, That Is

Once you've subjected your Camaro's engine to a full battery of tests and analyzed the data, you need to correct the problems pointed out. In

Basic tune-up principles still apply, at least on first-generation small blocks. Checking the base timing is essential to proper engine operation, since the computer doesn't have a method of sensing crankshaft position in the early engines. Incidentally, 1985–1992 TPI cars generally respond well to base ignition timing of 8–12 degrees BTDC (before top dead center). Gen-II (LT1) and Gen-III (LS1) small blocks have distributorless ignition systems that can only have timing altered through PCM reprogramming (a new PROM for 1993 ECM-equipped cars).

some cases, parts need to be replaced. With a little luck, all you need are small items like PCV valves, air filters, fuel filters, and probably spark plugs and ignition wires. But if compression or leak-down tests reveal internal engine problems (bad rings, bad valve seats, etc.), then you need to take care of those items, too. Replace what's needed, then run more tests to confirm that your fixes actually cured the problem.

Adjustment Period

More than likely, replacing parts only gets you half way to a properly tuned engine. More than likely, you need to make some kinds of adjustments to compensate for some normal and expected wear of certain components.

Gen-II and Gen-III engines have their timing controlled solely by computer, so there's no need to worry about setting base timing for them, but the Gen-I engines still require the base timing to be set properly to give the ECM a useful reference point. You probably also have to make adjustments to the fuel pressure (for which you need to install an adjustable fuel pressure regulator), Throttle Position Sensor, valve lash settings, and more.

For this phase of a tune-up, it's helpful to have a handy reference manual. Two good books come to mind: Howell Engine Technologies' *Service Manual for Corvette, Camaro and Firebird Fuel Injected Engines* and Ben Watson's *How To Repair and Modify Chevrolet Fuel Injection*. The former is available directly from Howell Engine Technologies, while the latter is available from Classic Motorbooks (phone: 800/860-6600).

TPI cars are subject to throttle body coking, just behind the throttle blades. The best method of cleaning is to remove the throttle body assembly and clean it with a soft-bristle toothbrush and carb cleaner spray. Proper adjustment of the throttle position sensor (TPS) is also required for good engine operation. Refer to a shop manual for the proper steps.

There are two basic kinds of forced induction systems: turbochargers and superchargers. Each has its strengths and weaknesses, and use of them should be considered carefully, because they place added stress on engine assemblies and could cause failures. Additionally, each generally requires specific combinations of parts to be most effective, which could require you to rebuild your entire engine.

Turbochargers

Turbochargers utilize exhaust flow to turn an impeller. As the impeller spins, the shaft to which it is connected spins. On the opposite end of the shaft is another impeller, which, naturally, spins as the shaft spins. This second impeller blows additional air into the engine. As more air enters the engine, more fuel is mixed with it, and the cylinders become fully filled with fresh air and fuel (the pressurization also helps to evacuate exhaust gases, too!), so the combustion process produces higher-than-usual levels of power.

However, because turbochargers are driven by the flow exhaust gases, they require the engine to reach a certain rpm before the turbo builds enough boost to be of value. This spin-up or "spool-up" time is felt and known as turbo "lag." Another problem that stems from the use of exhaust gases to run the turbo is excessive heat. The heat from the exhaust heats the turbo unit, which causes the air flowing through it to the intake manifold to heat up, which makes the air less dense and thus reduces the amount of fuel the air can hold. This problem is compounded by the fact that as you pressurize the air, it naturally heats up. And the problem escalates as the turbo continues to run, since exhaust gases are hotter from the pressurized combustion cycles.

Use of an intercooler helps combat the heat problems, insofar as they do lower the intake air temperature substantially.

It should also be noted that, because the turbo units get so hot, they are extremely hard on the engine oil that is supplied to the turbo. In fact, the Number One cause of turbo turbine failures is improper lubrication, usually due to oil that has thinned out from the extreme heat. Synthetic oils are highly recommended for turbocharged applications.

Also, as with nitrous oxide kits, turbochargers require retarded ignition timing because of the increased cylinder pressures, and they also require reduced compression to avoid detonation on pump fuels.

There are few off-the-shelf turbocharger kits for Camaros these days, though it is possible to "home-brew" one.

Unlike nitrous, which is only used for short bursts lasting a few seconds, superchargers like this Vortech unit boost power continually, as long as the engine is running. A supercharger essentially acts like a big fan blowing more air into the engine; the more air that goes in the engine, the more fuel can be mixed with it. And the more fuel in the engine, the more power it can produce. Power gains of 50 percent or more are not uncommon. *Vortech photo*

Of course, you don't have to stick with engines the factory installed. Here's a 1992 Camaro concept car stuffed full of a ZR-1 Corvette's dual-overhead-cam, all-aluminum LT5 V-8. According to the folks in Chevrolet's Raceshop, this wasn't an easy swap, but it sure made for one awesome Camaro!

And proving that big-block fun didn't cease when the fourth-generation Camaro came along, Chevy put together this outrageous 572-inch, all-aluminum, cross-ram injected, 720-horsepower big block in a 1993 Z28 that was dubbed the "ZL1," after its legendary namesake. The car was simply awesome on the Road America road race course, reaching speeds well over 175 miles per hour!

Superchargers

While turbochargers are part-time power builders, superchargers run full-time and always keep the intake tract pressurized because they run off of the crankshaft via a drive belt. This extra drag on the engine does result in a minor parasitic power loss, but the benefits of a supercharger far outweigh that minor drawback. Otherwise, turbochargers and superchargers are essentially similar in design.

Because superchargers do not suffer from lag, as do turbos, they are easier to tune an engine for, plus they are easier to set up a chassis for and to drive, since power application is smooth and consistent, not sudden, bordering on uncontrollable.

Additionally, superchargers do not suffer the same heat problems caused by running off the exhaust gases, though they are still subject to

the intake air temperature rising as a result of pressurization.

As with a turbocharger, using an intercooler results in a fairly dramatic drop in intake air temperature, which allows the air to hold more fuel and thus make more power. Use of synthetic engine oils is also beneficial for superchargers.

A number of companies offer supercharger kits for late-model Camaros, for both V-8 and V-6 applications.

Superchargers also require retarded ignition timing and reduced compression, due to the increased cylinder pressures generated by the unit.

Engine Swaps

Some people just aren't satisfied with bolt-on improvements. To them, spending time and money upgrading a small-block Chevy V-8 (or worse, a V-6 or even a four-banger)

is just a waste. These people want to start out with something already astounding and then improve on that. For these people, there's the wonderful world of engine swaps.

The most common type of engine swap for late-model Camaros is the installation of a mega-inch big-block Chevy V-8. While substantially larger than a small-block Chevy, the big-block engines (Mark IV 396, 427, and 454, plus the Gen-V 454, 502, and 510, plus derivatives of each) offer much more performance per dollar, more bang for the buck—particularly when it comes to torque.

Fortunately, swapping a big block into the third- and fourth-generation Camaro compartments can be accomplished fairly easily. The hard part is hooking them up to everything needed to make them run.

Big-block Chevrolet V-8s use the same motor mounts as a small

A more practical swap is this 1992 Camaro—another Chevy Raceshop creation—that features a 510-inch fuel-injected Gen-V big block! Suprisingly, this swap was fairly straight forward.

block and can nestle snugly between the strut towers of the third-generation cars with little effort, and into a fourth-gen with only a few minor headaches.

Unfortunately, there isn't much room for exhaust system clearance, but several aftermarket companies offer headers that fit third-gen cars without any problems; fourth-generation cars, at this point in time, still require a custom system, but several companies offer weld-together header kits for just such occasions.

Another sticky point is the ignition system. Since a big block is bigger than a small block, there is less room

at the firewall in a third-generation Camaro, which mandates that the big block be run with the reduced-size Camaro distributor, which, fortunately, is a drop-in install. Despite their protruding cowl, fourth-generation cars accept a variety of distributors with only a few modifications to the underside of the cowl, or no modifications at all, depending on the particular distributor used.

The induction system also has minimal room, but a low-profile intake manifold with a four-barrel carb and low-profile air cleaner should fit beneath the hood of a third-gen Camaro no problem. The

fourth-generation cars require a hood scoop for carb clearance, though aftermarket or custom fuel injection systems may fit under the stock hood, depending, again, on the particular system used.

Since all Chevrolet engines use the same bellhousing bolt pattern, a suitably strengthened stock transmission (manual or auto) works behind a big block, though the auto is often far easier to install.

Big blocks aren't the only engines that have been transplanted into third- and fourth-generation Camaros, though. Another impressive (albeit costly) engine swap places a Corvette ZR-1's LT5 dual-overhead cam engine in a third-generation Camaro. Considerable modifications were necessary to both the engine's oil pan and the car's front cross-member, however, and virtually everything must be fabricated.

And a few years back when Buick's turbocharged and intercooled V-6 Grand National Regal was kicking butt on the streets and drag strips, a few resourceful folks went and swapped the GN drivetrain into a Camaro. Then Pontiac went ahead in 1989 and did it on the assembly line with a special edition Turbo Trans-Am, which made the swap into a Camaro an even easier deal, since you only have to order a bunch of factory parts.

Who knows what other concoctions are out there waiting to be brewed? Whatever they may be, though, the Camaro engine bays are ready and willing recipients.

DRIVETRAIN

CONTENTS

Your Camaro's drivetrain—its transmission, rear axle assembly, and related parts—are its engine's link to the pavement. It's what turns your engine's power into motion. And unless your drivetrain is suitably strong and properly matched to your performance needs, you're going to find yourself watching your competition race off into the sunset, leaving you in their dust.

Of all the vehicle systems, the drivetrain is perhaps the easiest to understand. Despite certain mysterious parts (just try to figure out how an automatic transmission works sometime—it's mind-boggling), basics of how the spinning crankshaft turns the transmission's gears, which turn the driveshaft, which turns the pinion gear that rotates the ring gear, which spins the axles, is pretty straight forward. You've got a simple flow of power through the system that just happens to make a 90-degree turn at the rear axle assembly.

Things, of course, are a bit more complicated than that simplistic view. You've got to think about clutches for manual transmissions and torque converters for automatics, about torque-multiplying gear ratios in both the tranny and the rear axle assembly, about pinion angles, and about Positraction and even wheel studs. If you step through the system one piece at a time, it is easy to figure out just what you and your Camaro need to consistently go faster, race after race.

Driveline Durability

Unfortunately, third- and fourth-generation Camaros are not exactly known for having "bulletproof" drivetrain assemblies. In pure stock form, the transmissions, driveshafts and rear axle assemblies are—at best—adequate for the job. But if you start piling on power parts, like hotter camshafts, headers, wider and stickier tires, and especially superchargers or nitrous

Third- and fourth-generation Camaros break no new ground with their traditional drivetrain layout—front engine, mid-mounted transmission, driveshaft, and live rear axle assembly. *Chevrolet photo*

The first link in the drivetrain, after the engine, is the flywheel, or flexplate as it's known for vehicles with automatic transmissions. Aside from using a performance flywheel/flexplate, it's a good idea to either safety-wire the flywheel bolts or use special bolt locks like those available from Stage 8 Fasteners (shown) to prevent the bolts from loosening over time.

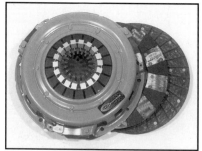

Manual transmissions use a clutch to transfer power from the flywheel to the transmission's input shaft. The stock clutch assembly is adequate for low-performance use, but for racing or other high-performance use—or if you've upgraded the engine's power output—you need a heavy-duty clutch. This dual-disc Centerforce unit nearly doubles clamping force, without increasing pedal effort substantially. *Centerforce Clutch photo*

oxide, the drivetrain parts can break as often as you change your underwear (which might be more frequent, too, given the scary driving that can follow certain drivetrain failures). The simple problem is that the stock Camaro drivetrain components were engineered to work well with the stock equipment, but there wasn't much "tolerance" built into the system for changes.

More engine power stresses the transmission—especially in drag racing conditions, where shifts are typically fast and furious, and at high rpm. Sustained high rpm can cause a stock, steel driveshaft to literally spin itself to pieces, and stickier tires wrench every ounce of life from a rear axle assembly, since the tires may still be gripping when internal rear

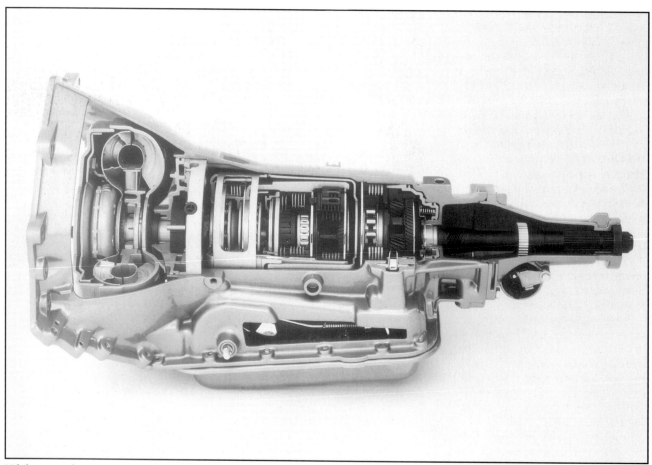

While manual transmissions physically mesh gears together by using shift forks to push one toward another, automatics force transmission fluid through various passages under pressure to control gear selection and operation. With several multidisc clutch packs, planetary gears, bands, and sprags, automatics are much more complicated, but they provide smoother, more accurate, and repeatable shifts, and, of course, don't require the driver's attention to change gears. The 1994-and-newer 4L60-E (shown) uses electronic solenoids and servos to control the hydraulic circuits, which allows the powertrain control module (PCM) to optimize gear selection and transmission function to engine and driving requirements. Upgrading tranny performance then is as easy as downloading new "parameters" to the PCM. *Chevrolet photo*

end damage occurs, rather than slipping before it does to instantly "unload" the stresses in the rear end.

Transmissions

In terms of transmissions, the third-generation Camaros were equipped with a number of different units. Automatics were either the "light-duty" 2004R four-speed automatic, or the "high-performance" or "heavy-duty" 700R4 (later called the 4L60) four-speed auto. Early units used nonlocking torque converters, while later units featured a lock-up converter for more efficient operation in light-throttle, high-gear cruising.

In terms of manual transmissions, a four-speed manual was the sole box available for 1982, and continued on as the base manual through 1984. GM used both Borg-Warner Super T-10 and Saginaw four-speed gearboxes, which are each excellent in their own right. The Super T-10 works well in performance applications, but it and the Saginaw both lack a fifth (overdrive) gear, which limits their suitability for street use.

The Borg-Warner T5 five-speed appeared in 1983 as option MM5. In 1985, the T5 became the sole manual gearbox available. While the MM5 RPO code and Borg-Warner's T5 designation didn't show it, two different T5 five-speed gearboxes were used. The first was a light-duty design used from 1983 through 1987. Unfortunately, these tended to fail quite regularly and prompted GM to switch to B-W's stronger "heavy-duty" T5, which it used from 1988 through 1998, though only in V-6 applications from 1993–up.

Beginning in 1993, when the fourth-generation Camaro debuted, the Camaro finally received a truly sturdy manual gearbox—the Borg-Warner T56 six-speed. Ironically, the transmission was developed by Borg-Warner for GM (specifically for the Camaro/Firebird "F" platform), but Chrysler beat GM off the production line with the T56 by bolting it up behind the Dodge Viper's beastly V-10 engine.

In 1994, GM upgraded the four-speed automatic from the 4L60 (essentially just a name change for the 700R4), to the 4L60-E. That little "-E" was an important change, because it

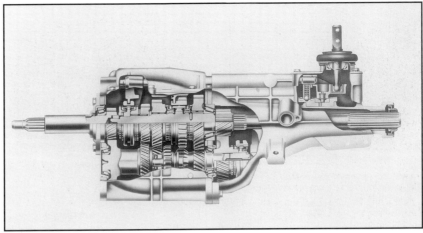

The Borg-Warner T5 five-speed transmission, which has been used in Camaros since 1983, was never designed for high-performance use and was only rated for up to 300 pounds per foot of torque. In fact, "first-design" T5s, used from 1983 through 1987, weren't even designed to handle that much. *Chevrolet photo*

The T5 was an excellent fit for the third-generation chassis, however, thanks to its compact, simple design. Note the hydraulic clutch linkage, the cross-member to which the tailshaft is secured. There is no external shift linkage to require adjustment or repairs, because the T5 featured an internal rail shift mechanism. *Chevrolet photo*

meant that the transmission now took commands from the Powertrain Control Module (PCM), which also controlled the engine. Electronic sensors monitored transmission fluid temperature and pressures, as well as vehicle speed, and fed those to the PCM, which compared them with various readings from engine sensors to determine the proper gear to use and shift characteristics.

The 700R4/4L60 and the later 4L60-E are well suited to stock engines, to approximately 350 horsepower and pounds-feet of torque. Above that, however, it's advisable to have a professional performance transmission builder fortify the internals to handle the added power.

In terms of strength, the late-style T5 is designed to handle only 300 foot-pounds of torque at best (depending on gearing, see sidebar, "T5 Five-Speed Gearing and Torque Capacities"), whereas the worst T56 was still rated for at least 60 foot-

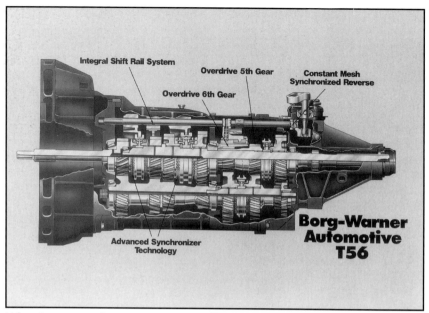

When it comes to factory transmission offerings, this is the unit to have for most performance situations—the Borg-Warner T56 six-speed manual gearbox available from the factory in V-8 equipped fourth-generation Camaros. *Chevrolet photo*

pounds more. But even the highest T56 rating of 450 foot-pounds is easily surpassed with current aftermarket engine components, which still leaves the T56 as a potentially weak link.

If your Camaro is blessed with a high-output engine that develops 400 foot-pounds of torque or more, you will likely find yourself straining the manual transmission to the point of failure. In such a case, you need to turn to the aftermarket for solutions. Richmond offers a serious-duty five-speed transmission that works well in Camaros but requires different clutch systems and other modifications to install. A better—and more common—choice is the Tremec five-speed, which is based on the T5, but with substantially upgraded internal components and a wider choice of gear ratios, allowing you to custom-tailor the transmission's performance to your application and engine and rear axle combination.

Driveshafts

Stock steel driveshafts have the simple function of connecting the transmission's output shaft to the pinion gear of the rear axle assembly, and they do this exceptionally well in stock vehicles that are driven on the street only. But they're not high-performance pieces, and that can become painfully clear on race tracks where they're likely to endure sustained high rpm use and extreme torsional (twisting) forces during acceleration.

Because balancing imperfections increase exponentially in relation to rpm, even the slightest imbalance becomes a serious strain at high rpm. And since steel driveshafts weigh more to start with, imbalances tend to weigh more, too, so the risk of the driveshaft warping becomes very real at high rpm. All that weight takes its toll on acceleration, too, since it adds to the weight the engine must overcome in order to rotate, which is especially critical on acceleration.

GM took a huge step toward correcting this problem with the 1LE driveshaft, which was made of aluminum. Substantially lighter, the aluminum shaft would allow the engine to accelerate faster, plus it could handle higher rpm for longer sustained runs. But even the 1LE driveshaft isn't perfect.

Aftermarket companies manufacture aluminum and even composite driveshafts that are balanced to more exacting specifications, which allows them to withstand yet higher rpm.

Of course, any driveshaft needs good universal joints to function properly, and aftermarket companies are the best places to turn for them. With large, heavy-duty needle bearings and heavy-duty construction throughout, performance U-joints are cheap insurance against driveshaft failure.

In order to withstand the torque produced by the LT1 engine used in the fourth-generation Camaro through 1996, the T56 was designed with sturdy gears, synchronizers and other internal components. Depending on gearing, the T56 is rated to withstand as much as 450 foot-pounds of torque. *Chevrolet photo*

Automatics are significantly larger (and heavier) than manual transmissions. This 4L60-E is mated to the back of a 1998 model's 3800 V-6 engine. Note that there are differences beyond different PCM "parameters" between the V-6 and V-8 automatics. Prior to 1994, GM's transmission was the 700R4 (a.k.a. the 4L60 in 1993), which was essentially the same as the 4L60-E but lacked the electronic controls.

Another thing to consider for your drivetrain is a replacement performance shifter, like this Hurst unit for T5 five-speeds. Aftermarket shifters generally provide shorter, firmer, more accurate shifts that prevent you from "missing" a gear during performance driving situations.

Automatic transmissions get their fluid pretty warm under normal, around-town driving. High-performance use can send temperatures soaring, and that thins out the fluid (which is oil, actually) and can accelerate wear dramatically. Production cars utilize a transmission fluid cooler to help combat heat, but installing an auxiliary transmission fluid cooler should be considered an absolute requirement for racing or high-performance street use. Use of synthetic transmission fluid is also a good idea because of its superior heat-handling abilities.

Rear Axle Assemblies

The problem that stock Camaro rear axle assemblies have always suffered from has been directly related to the size of the ring and pinion gear set. Simply put, the gears in the stock rear ends—of any of the several designs used—have never been big enough to handle much power. Consequently, broken rearends are commonplace among Camaros that are raced or driven hard with only the stock rear axle assembly beneath them. Specifically, the 10-bolt Saginaw rearend, which used a 7.50-inch ring gear through 1984, was upgraded to 7.65 inches in 1985, when it also received stronger 26-spline axles. These should not be confused with earlier GM "10-bolt" rear axle assemblies that utilized stronger 8.5-inch ring gears, since no parts are interchangeable. In 1990, GM again upgraded the "7.5 inch" (it actually was 7.65 inches, but it is commonly still referred to as a 7.5-inch 10-bolt unit) to 28-spline axles, to further improve reliability.

Another rear axle assembly used on a limited basis under certain high-performance Camaros between 1985 and 1992 was the Borg-Warner 7.75-inch 9-bolt assemblies. This unit featured bearing retainer plates instead of the dreaded "C-clips," making them far more suitable for performance use, since a broken axle wouldn't simply shoot out of the rear axle housing, leaving the wounded Camaro to limp home on three wheels. Unfortunately, because the B-W 9-bolt rears were so limited in use, their are virtually no gearsets available to tailor them to your particular application and engine and transmission combination.

GM offered a third differential assembly for Camaros, but, interestingly enough, never on a production model. Formerly available through the GM Performance Parts program (and under the limited run of 1989 20th anniversary Indy Pace Car Turbo Trans-Ams), the Dana 44 rear axle

Right
Another worthwhile upgrade for both manuals and automatics is the use of a higher-rate transmission mount. The stock rubber mount allows the transmission to "move" in response to engine torque; a "harder" rubber or polyurethane mount limits this movement, allowing more torque to be transmitted to the rear wheels instead of being lost to moving the transmission around.

assembly is a top choice and well worth searching out. Some aftermarket companies still offer the Dana 44 for Camaros, or you may get lucky and find one at a swap meet (or look for a wrecked 1989 Turbo T/A, but don't count on finding one). Because the Dana 44 is used in so many other applications (the 1984–1996

Corvette, Dodge's Viper, and others), there are a wide variety of gear ratios, axles, and other components available for them, allowing you to tailor them to your exact needs.

But there are still better rear axle assembly choices available. Two of the most venerable rear axle assemblies ever offered on production

cars—the GM 12-bolt assembly and Ford's 9-inch assembly—are available through aftermarket parts suppliers with all the proper mounting pick-ups to fit neatly beneath a third- or fourth-generation Camaro. And each is well worth the money.

While it's no secret that the 12-bolt GM rear is nowhere near as strong as the 9-inch Ford unit, the 12-bolt is, nonetheless, more than adequate for all but the most extreme Camaro engine/transmission combination. And because the 12-bolt has a more favorable pinion-to-ring gear relationship, the 12-bolt is a more efficient design, costing you less power to

From the transmission, all the torque is sent through a universal joint to the driveshaft. Considering that the 1998 LS1 produces 330 foot-pounds of torque—and that gets multiplied by the transmission's gears—you're asking your stock U-joints to handle an awful lot of power. High-performance/heavy-duty U-joints should also be required equipment.

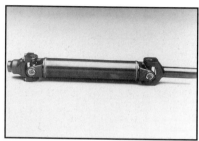

The driveshaft is merely a link between the transmission and the rear axle assembly, but it's a vital one. Standard production driveshafts are made of mild steel tubing and are adequate for casual driving, but can fail spectacularly and dangerously when subjected to high-performance use. The 1LE Camaro's aluminum driveshaft features reduced weight and improved strength. Aftermarket driveshaft can provide even more strength and lighter weight. *Mark Williams photo*

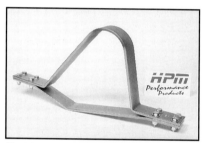

If a U-joint snaps or the driveshaft splits, a driveshaft safety loop keeps the shaft from falling and striking the ground or smashing up through the floorpan. Without a safety loop, your best-case scenario is that the rear of the shaft may fail, causing it to drop down to the ground, snag, and pull the shaft from the rear of the transmission, causing it to lose all its fluid . . . which, when your rear tires hit it, causes you (or a competitor) to spin out. Worst case is that the front of the shaft could swing wildly into the passenger compartment, maiming you or your passenger! This is HP Motorsports' third-generation driveshaft safety loop. *HP Motorsports photo*

Two-piece driveshafts are used in V-6 applications to reduce undesirable harmonics that result because of the V-6's inherent uneven operation. These are much heavier than a single-piece shaft, which means it takes more engine power to turn the shaft, so less is left over to turn the tires. For performance use, use only a one-piece shaft, but be prepared to feel a few more vibrations.

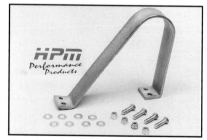

Fourth-generation floorpans are slightly different, requiring a different safety loop design. *HP Motorsports photo*

turn it, thus leaving more power to get through to the wheels. And a vast array of gearsets are available, as are severe-duty limited-slip units, axles, and other components.

The Ford 9-inch rear axle assembly is legendary in the world of automotive performance. It is *the* rearend of choice for NASCAR's Winston Cup cars, NHRA drag cars, and even off-road race trucks. It's economical and unbelievably strong, which makes it a good choice for use under a high-performance Camaro. However, it is heavy and it isn't as efficient as the 12-bolt. But, given the even greater selection of performance components available for the 9-inch, plus its simpler design that allows for faster gear ratio changes (by swapping the removable center sections), it's hard not to recommend it to someone building a serious street or race Camaro.

Clutches

There is nothing inherently wrong with the clutch designs for the 1982–1998 Camaros. In fact, the clutches work exceptionally well. Their only real drawback is their strength—they're not designed for high-performance use, nor do they do well at it.

However, the problem is easily corrected by installation of a high-performance aftermarket clutch pressure plate and disc. Depending on your particular application (whether you're racing or driving on the street, for example) it may be beneficial to consider replacing the stock flywheel with a lighter weight unit, which allows the engine to accelerate faster but gives up some flexibility in around-town use.

It should be noted that 1982 was the only year in which third- or fourth-generation Camaros featured a mechanical clutch assembly. The 1983 and later models all utilized hydraulic clutches. This is particularly important to know if you are attempting to swap in a transmission that is not compatible with a hydraulic clutch assembly, since you would then want to locate parts from a 1982 model to use for the swap.

Torque Converters

Torque converters are mysterious devices to many auto enthusiasts, but essentially they serve the same

The rear axle assembly makes the spinning driveshaft's torque turn a 90-degree corner to spin the rear wheels. As you might expect, this isn't an easy job, and the factory differentials aren't quite up to the task for performance use.

Most third- and fourth-generation Camaros feature what is known as a "10-bolt" rear axle assembly, built by GM's Saginaw division. In actuality, three GM 10-bolts exist: the muscle-car-era 10-bolts, which share nothing with the 1982–1998 10-bolts; the F-body 10-bolt, with a 7.7-inch ring gear diameter; and the F-body 10-bolt with a 7.625-inch ring gear diameter, which is still commonly known as a 7.5-inch 10-bolt. Positraction was optional. A 9-bolt Borg-Warner rear saw limited use, and was substantially stronger, but there aren't any performance gearsets or other parts available for it, which still makes it a poor choice.

function for an automatic transmission as a clutch does for a manual transmission. Torque converters provide a means of transmitting power from the engine's rotating crankshaft to the transmission's input shaft, while at the same time providing a means for the input shaft to stop (when the vehicle stops) without causing the engine to stop in the process.

While the operation of a clutch is easily understood—when engaged, the pressure plate press the disc against the flywheel, causing the input shaft to spin in a one-to-one relationship to the crank—torque converters are a little more difficult to explain and understand.

The shell of the converter is connected to the crankshaft, via the

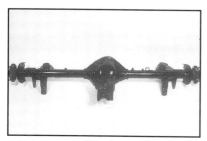

GM knew the 10-bolt wasn't very sturdy, so through its Performance Parts system it offered a Dana 44 rear axle assembly for Camaros, for which a multitude of performance-ratio gears, axles, and other parts are available (through the aftermarket). Unfortunately, the Dana 44 assembly is no longer available through GM, but several aftermarket companies offer it, or you should be able to find one at a swap meet or in classified ads. *Summers Brothers photo*

This cut-away gives you some idea how a torque converter functions. The flexplate spins the outer shell of the converter, which is connected internally to a finned impeller. This "drive" impeller forces transmission fluid within the converter to flow through the "driven" impeller, causing it to rotate, which turns the transmission input shaft to which it is connected. "Lock-up" converters don't rely on fluid to connect the impellers, during lock-up mode only, but instead use an actual physical locking mechanism to eliminate any slippage and thus operate more efficiently.

flexplate (i.e., flywheel). As it spins, impellers inside cause transmission fluid in the converter to spin a corresponding set of impellers that are connected to the transmission's input shaft, forming what is known as a "viscous coupling." Newer torque converter designs implement a "lock-up" feature that actually does provide a mechanical link between the drive and driven impellers, but otherwise there is no mechanical connection between the two sides—only the fluid connects them.

The beauty of the fluid coupling is that at low engine speeds, it's easy for the driven impeller to resist turning (such as when the brakes are applied, holding the vehicle at a stop), even though the drive impeller is free to spin. But when engine rpm increases, the flow of the fluid becomes hard to resist, so the driven impeller begins to spin. The rpm at which the driven impeller begins to spin is known as the converter's "stall speed"—the speed at which either the engine stalls or the driven impeller spins.

Stall speed is an important concept to grasp, because a high stall speed allows drag racers to get into their engine's peak operating range

quicker than a lower stall speed. This is achieved so they can rev the engine higher without fear of the car moving forward until they release the vehicle's brakes, which allows the driven impeller to start spinning even though it may be below the stall speed.

For street use, however, torque converter stall speed isn't necessarily a good thing to alter, because it affects driveability and also raises transmission fluid temperature, which can shorten transmission life.

Auto Trans "Shift Kits"

Because automatic transmissions are controlled by fluid pressures and vacuum (as well as electronics in the 4L60-E), they are tunable by changing those pressures and the way in which the transmission responds to them.

Many aftermarket companies offer "shift kits" that consist of check balls, springs, and minor modifications to the automatic transmission's "valve body," which controls the flow of fluid through the transmission. By raising pressures in some parts of the transmission, and lowering it in others, shifts can be programmed to be "harder" and quicker, or "softer" and slower. Soft, slow

An automatic transmission's valve body is like its brain. Springs and check balls—plus electronic solenoids and servos in the 4L60-E—determine which passages fluid flows through and at what pressures. Changes to a valve body, either through a different design or by installing a "shift kit," can dramatically affect shift quality and timing. *TCI Automotive photo*

700R4/4L60 Gear Ratios (:1)

Gear	Ratio
1st	3.06
2nd	1.62
3rd	1.00
4th	0.70

T5 Five-Speed Gearing and Torque Capacities
(1988–present)

Gear	Ratios (:1)		
1st	2.95	3.35	3.97
2nd	1.94	1.99	2.34
3rd	1.34	1.33	1.46
4th	1.00	1.00	1.00
5th	0.73	0.68	0.79
Rev.	2.76	3.15	3.70
Alt. 5ths	.63-.80	.61-.83	.71-.85
Max. Torque	275 lb-ft	300 lb-ft	225 lb-ft

T56 Six-Speed Gearing and Torque Capacities
(1993)

Gear	Ratios (:1)		
1st	2.66	2.97	3.36
2nd	1.78	1.94	2.07
3rd	1.30	1.35	1.35
4th	1.00	1.00	1.00
5th	0.74	0.84	0.84
6th	0.50	0.62	0.62
Rev.	2.90	3.28	3.28
Max. Torque	450 lb-ft	400 lb-ft	360 lb-ft

shifts are fine for the street, but hard shifts are better for the strip because they're more accurate and you spend less time "between gears," and thus more time accelerating.

Some companies continue to offer traditional shift kits for the 4L60-E transmissions. However, the performance of these units can be considerably upgraded simply by reprogramming the Powertrain Control Module with special tools available from a number of after-market companies.

The Right Gear Setup

One of the hardest concepts of automotive mechanics to grasp is that of gearing on overall performance. Yet the principle is rather straight forward: Gearing should allow the engine to operate at or near its peak efficiency under given conditions.

If thought about in oversimplified terms, this concept becomes a bit clearer. A single-speed transmission would result in a car that was really good at going a certain speed (actually a range of speed), because the engine would thrive at or near its power peak (3,000 rpm, for example). This would directly be multiplied by the single-speed gearbox and the single-speed rear axle and the tire circumference to equate to a particular speed. For example, 3,000 rpm times a one-to-one (1:1) transmission gear results in a 3,000-rpm driveshaft speed; multiply driveshaft speed times a 3.00:1 rear axle gear ratio to determine an axle speed of 1,000 rpm, which must then be multiplied by tire circumference to determine a vehicle speed. A typical 28-inch-tall tire would then yield a speed of 83.3 miles per hour, when all the conversions are computed.

Extrapolating this outward, by adding more gears choices, you come up with certain specific speeds at which the vehicle operates efficiently.

Racers can work with this kind of information to determine the gearing they need to go through certain portions of a race course at a given rpm and vehicle speed.

Unfortunately, that only works for manual transmission and rear axle assemblies, which feature physically changeable gears. Since automatics don't have gears that you can feasibly change on your own, you're left to deal with whatever General Motors has blessed you with. Fortunately, the 700R4/4L60 transmissions have a good gear spread that delivers a wide operating range and good performance throughout that range. (See sidebar, "700R4/4L60 Gear Ratios.")

Differential Types

It's a common misconception to think of an entire rear axle assembly as a "differential." The differential, itself, is merely the device that transfers power to one or more of the axle shafts within the rear axle assembly. The whole idea behind a differential is to enhance a car's cornering abilities, because while cornering, the wheel at the inside of the corner must travel a shorter distance than the wheel at the outside of the corner, so, obviously, the wheels shouldn't spin in a one-to-one relationship.

There are three basic types of differentials available: Open differentials, which power only one wheel at a time and are best suited to low-speed cornering; limited slip differentials, like GM's Positraction units that turn both wheels when traveling straight, but allow the inner wheel to slip somewhat while cornering; and spools, which permanently spin both wheels equally and consequently make turning more difficult.

Camaros have been produced with both open and limited slip differentials. Spools have never been used as production pieces because they cause premature tire wear on the street.

There are advantages to each type of differential, however, depending on your particular application. If your Camaro is solely driven on the street, and you rarely attempt to race anyone (thus ultimate traction is not a high priority), an open differential provides the best driving experience, and longer tire life.

For most Camaro enthusiasts, a limited slip differential is a better choice, because it provides full, two-wheeled traction under straight-line acceleration condition, but still allows some differentiation between the two wheels while cornering, so the vehicle doesn't hop and skip in a turn and won't dramatically increase tire wear.

Spools are strictly for racing use and should never be used on the street. On the track, however, they provide the ultimate in traction because both wheels always provide full traction.

A new type of differential worth discussing is the so-called "Air Locker," which is a special differential design that operates like an open differential under normal conditions but, by pressuring components within the differential with an electric air pump, converts the differential to the equivalent of a spool, doing away with any slip for maximum straight line acceleration. These systems should be especially attractive to

The key ingredient for a rear axle assembly is the differential unit, of which this unit is typical. Differentials transmit power to each rear wheel, though not equally, to allow the inside wheel during a corner to move a shorter distance than the outside wheel. An "open" differential typically turns only one wheel at time, while a "limited slip" (Chevy's term is "Positraction," or "Posi" for short) turns both wheels equally under straight-line driving, but allows some slippage during cornering.

A fairly recent development is the "Air Locker." This system operates as a standard "open" differential under normal use, but uses an electric air compressor to "lock-up" the differential assembly for maximum traction during performance use. It's a trick system that works exceptionally well and provides a "best-of-both-worlds" solution.

A spool or mini-spool (shown) is not a differential. It transmits equal power to each wheel always, and does not allow one wheel to turn faster or slower than the other. This is great for racing because it maximizes acceleration, but it chews up tires and heavily stresses axles and other components during cornering.

Lug nuts can't be ignored either. The type of nuts you use ultimately depends on the requirements of the wheels you use. And if you're purchasing lug nuts for street use, make sure you have a lock nut for each wheel to prevent a thief from absconding with your new rolling stock.

weekend racers, because they really provide a "best-of-both-worlds" system without a lot of fuss. However, it should be noted that "Air Locker" systems are fairly complex to install. Still, the designs are simple and most units have proven reliable under normal use, and are easy to operate.

Axles and Accessories

The last link in the drivetrain starts with the axles, as their splined ends engage with splined receptors in the differential. With the possible exception of the Dana 44 rear axle assembly, all production rear axles should be replaced with high-performance units for competition or high-performance use.

Stock axles are retained within the rear axle housing by C-clips that are inserted into a groove on the axle's end inside the differential. If the axle snaps anywhere, there's nothing to hold that axle in the housing. The result is that the tire—broken axle and all—comes shooting out from under the car, typically damaging the quarter panel in the process, then the bottom of the vehicle slams against the ground and grinds away as the vehicle slows. It's an expensive problem, to say the least, and one you don't want to experience.

Aftermarket axles are typically designed for use with "C-clip eliminators" that hold the axle in place out near the end of the axle tube, right behind the wheel mounting flange, so a break anywhere inside of that point won't result in the wheel coming off. Since the weakest part of the axle is the span between the differential and the wheel bearing (which, itself, is located inside of the

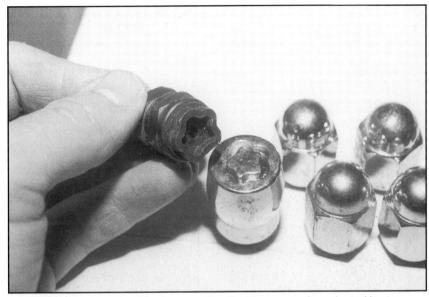

Typical aftermarket wheel locks use a "key" with a protruding clover-like pattern that engages with a similarly-shaped recess in the lock nut's head. Unfortunately, the keys can break or become damaged easily, and the recesses in the lug nut can round over, making them difficult to remove. The lock nut itself is also quite large, which can prevent it from being used with certain wheel designs.

C-clip eliminator), you're covered in all but the rarest occurrences.

A final thought is to upgrade wheel studs. Stock studs are not designed with the high loads that racing imparts, nor are stock studs long enough for use with many aftermarket wheels, which further compromises their strength. A general rule of thumb is that the wheel stud should be at least flush with the top of the lug nut when properly torqued in place. It's even better to have threads protruding beyond the top of the lug nut. These guidelines ensure full engagement of each thread within the lug nut, thus maximum clamping force.

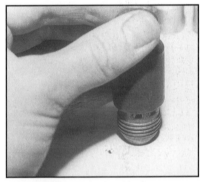

The standard GM wheel lock system does things differently, and better. The key fits around the lock nut, giving it more surface area for a better grip. Even better, the GM lock nut is the same size as a normal lug nut, allowing it to work with nearly any wheel.

CONTENTS

BODY

Chevrolet designers blessed the Camaro with a dramatic, exciting body, and there's really no reason to make any changes to it—few find fault with a stock Camaro's appearance. But there's nothing stopping you from putting your own "personal" styling touches on your Camaro.

Over the years, the aftermarket parts industry has responded to the popularity of the Camaro with a number of replacement body panels, add-on parts, striping and graphic designs, and much, much more. Or you can go the home-brewed route and create your own parts and pieces, paint schemes, and pretty much whatever you want. The only limitations to Camaro body modifications are really just your imagination and your wallet. If you're choosing to create panels on your own, it helps to have the necessary skills, too, though it is possible to come up with the design on your own and rely on someone else to make it a reality.

Factory Stock Body

The third-generation Camaro was in production for 11 model years—practically an eternity in the automotive world. During that decade, GM stylists subtly massaged the Camaro's all-metal body from year to year, often through the incorporation of revised rubber-like front and rear fascias, composite spoilers, and add-on ground effects cladding to come up with rather distinctive base, RS, Berlinetta, Z28, and IROC styling. If you like the look of any one of the production appearances, it's fairly simple, straight-forward work to give your Camaro that look—all you need is the factory's panels, which can be purchased from your local GM dealer (any GM dealer can order the necessary panels). You may get lucky and find a suitable donor car (or cars) in a local salvage yard, which would save you a bundle, though require a bit more preparation work by you or your chosen body man.

The Camaro's body is its most visible element, and so it should come as no surprise that upgrades for the body are quite popular among enthusiasts. While some upgrades are simple, like a new spoiler, others, like the Callaway C8 conversion (shown), radically alter the appearance of a Camaro. *Callaway Cars/David Newhardt photo*

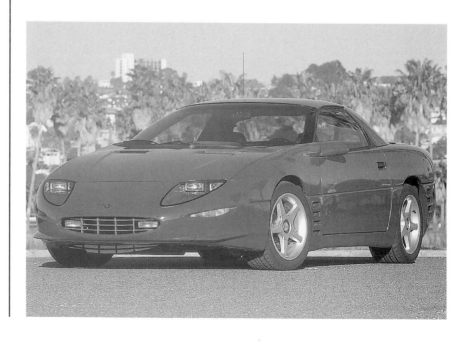

The fourth-generation Camaro debuted in 1993 with a completely new, aerodynamic body that shared no panels with the previous generation cars, and also had no distinguishing panels for the Z28 models versus the base V-6 cars, or even the convertibles. You basically had one style to choose from and that was it. Unlike in the past, though, the new Camaro panels were made from differing materials. The quarter panels, rocker panels, and roof "targa" bar were of traditional sheet metal, but the front fenders, taillamp panel, and decklid were of composite (plastic). While all the panels did shave a few pounds off the previous generation's equivalent panels, the new materials were used to solve technical problems. For example, the front fenders couldn't be made of metal because of their curvaceous shapes. To appease insurance companies, the plastic panels were constructed so that they could be repaired at a lower cost than metal panels. The smaller lighter hood allowed hood support struts to last longer, reduced manufacturing costs, and improved customer satisfaction. This kept purchase prices down, despite all the improvements made to the new cars.

In 1997, Chevrolet revived the "RS" (which had stood for Rally Sport, but now just stood for "RS") for the Camaro, and gave it a special ground effects package and rear spoiler lip for a racier image. Another exciting package debuted on the Camaro order form in 1997, as well—the Camaro SS performance appearance package, which was actually a conversion job handled by Street Legal Performance (SLP), the maker of Pontiac's popular Firehawk Firebird. In addition to a hopped-up engine and revised suspension calibrations, the SS model included an elegant decklid spoiler panel and composite forced-air induction hood styled to resemble the 1966–1967 Corvette Sting Ray "Stinger" hood. It was also available in a special "Anniversary" package that featured Arctic White paint with Hugger Orange hood and decklid stripes

When the third-generation Camaro debuted in 1982, its looks were clean and simple, yet very exciting. In short, it looked great in stock form.

To celebrate the 30th anniversary, Chevy again revived the Heritage stripe package in 1997, and it proved a very simple and attractive improvement for the otherwise plain-looking production Camaros.

During the 10-year run of the third-generation Camaro, Chevrolet tastefully updated the body, culminating with this superb 1992 RS convertible with 25th anniversary "Heritage Edition" hood and decklid stripes, plus an attractive yet subtle set of ground effects panels. *Chevrolet photo*

Proving perhaps just how flexible the third-generation Camaro design was, it even looked great in simple black and white (though not so good if you happened to view it this way in your rearview mirror). *Chevrolet photo*

The basic Camaro body needs little to look much more aggressive, as this 1997 Camaro SS by SLP Engineering shows. With the addition of only a scooped hood and redesigned wheels, the car's look is totally transformed. *SLP Engineering photo*

Realizing that many buyers wanted a bit more than the plain Camaro bodywork, Chevrolet cooked up the 1997 RS package, which featured ground effects skirting and a rear spoiler extension, plus other features. *Chevrolet photo*

similar to those used on first-generation Camaro Z/28s. For 1997, the Camaro also featured a new taillamp treatment that added yellow-amber turn signals, instead of the plain red that had been used since 1993.

In 1998, the big news was Camaro's new nose. A new "big mouth" faux grille gave Camaro a meaner, more aggressive image. The new proboscis also added composite headlamps in place of the mini-quad halogens. A new hood added character lines, and new fenders were needed to mate everything together properly.

The 1998 SS performance appearance package featured the necessary changes related to the new front end treatment, but stylists took the opportunity to redesign the SS hood with a forward-mounted scoop. And, though it had nothing to do with styling, the SS package reverted to being fully assembled on the Ste. Therese, Quebec, Canada F-car assembly line, alongside regular Camaro coupes, convertibles, and Z28s.

As with the third-generation cars, exchanging body panels between the fourth-generation Camaros is fairly easy, with the exception of installing the 1998-and-up panels on a 1993–1997 car, which can still be done but requires many more parts, given the radical restyling.

Aftermarket Body Options

While many people—hundreds of thousands of Camaro buyers, in fact—found the exterior styling of the third- and fourth-generation Camaros more than satisfying, thousands more yearned for more. They longed for that extra something that would set their Camaro apart from everyone else's.

That's where the aftermarket body panel industry stepped in with all manner of replacement hoods (typically formed in fiberglass, which also shaved precious pounds off the cars), ground effects kits, rear spoilers, and even full-blown body cladding kits that radically (too radically in some people's opinions) altered the Camaro's familiar appearance.

For one reason or another, the aftermarket parts industry never saw the third-generation Camaros as a major market, so offerings for those cars continue to be primarily fiberglass hoods (of many designs) and various fiberglass replacement panels. Perhaps due more to market trends more than the fourth-generation's styling, popularity, or even construction, the newer cars have been far more attractive to parts companies, in terms of body panels and restyling kits. In addition, nearly every aftermarket performance "tuner" Camaro features its own unique body package, consisting usually of lower body panel ground effects extensions, a different spoiler treatment, and sometimes even a new hood.

One tuner, Callaway Cars, in particular, went to great pains to redesign the Camaro in the process of developing the company's C8 conversion package. With new front and rear fascias, plus strikingly different side styling, nearly every panel on the C8 differs from a production Camaro. The result is a sleeker Camaro that is totally unique and unmistakable.

General Motors got into the aftermarket body panel market as well, by offering what it called the "F1" body appearance package through GM's Performance Parts operation. Essentially, the "F1" is a close copy of the deceased "RS" package's equipment and is a popular dealer-installed "option" selected by many new Camaro buyers. A version of the "F1" body kit was released for the 1998-and-up Camaro as well.

For the most part, the aftermarket body panel kits are weekend "bolt-on" projects, though prepping and painting the panels adds to the installation time.

Of course, not all of the body upgrades involve replacing or altering the factory body panels. In fact, some of the most popular aftermarket body hop-ups involve only inexpensive items, like tinted headlamp and taillamp covers, bright wheel opening "eye-brows," and gold or chrome emblems to replace the sedate black factory pieces.

Right
A number of different replacement hoods are available for fourth-generation Camaros, too, including this functional ram-air induction hood from SLP Engineering. *SLP Engineering photo*

This 1987 Camaro IROC Z convertible was the first new generation ragtop, and all the hardtop performance options were available for it. Premium suspension components gave it superb road manners and a 350 derived from the Corvette provided thunderous performance. The Corvette engine featured aluminum heads and stainless steel exhaust while the Camaro engine sported iron heads and iron exhaust manifolds.

Body kits are plentiful, allowing you to make your Camaro as radical as you want. Note this convertible's ground effects, rear spoiler, aftermarket wheels, and round headlights instead of the stock rectangular units.

A number of tasteful replacement spoilers or spoiler extensions are available, too, like this SLP "Ultra Z" spoiler. *SLP Engineering photo*

The fourth-generation cars look even better slightly lowered, with aftermarket wheels and a monochromatic paint scheme. *Vortech photo*

One interesting change that never caught on was replacing the large glass hatch with a "targa"-style liftback.

Hood scoops and replacement hoods have long been popular upgrades, and are available in a wide variety of styles.

Spoilers too come in numerous shapes and sizes to suit nearly every taste.

Accessories, like window louvers and aftermarket wheels, can be added to give even a mild Camaro an exciting appearance.

Right
This shot shows several body upgrades from RK Sport, including a replacement spoiler, tinted taillamp lens covers, a rear fascia extension, and chromed exhaust tips, to replace the bland black rectangular tips that come stock on Z28s. *RK Sport photo*

Other popular dress-up accessories include tinted headlamp, turn signal, and fog lamp lens covers, like these from RK Sport. *RK Sport photo*

Performance Benefits

Though not dramatic, there are some real performance benefits—plus a few drawbacks—to installing aftermarket body equipment.

On the positive side, some of the ground effects kit front fascia extension panels provide inlets that can be connected to brake cooling ducts, or duct work that can be funneled to oil coolers, transmission oil coolers, and the like. (It should be noted that, because all third- and fourth-generation Camaros draw air from beneath the front fascia to cool the engine coolant in the radiator, installing an aftermarket fascia extension may cause your car to run slightly hotter.)

The fascia extensions also reduce the amount of air that flows beneath the car and thus reduce aerodynamic lift generated by the air beneath the car. The rear decklid spoilers, if designed properly, yield similar advantages, in terms of planting the rear end of the car more firmly on the ground at high speeds.

Hoods—one of the most popular body changes—can often include cold-air induction inlet scoops, like the hoods from SLP Engineering, which can improve the efficiency of your Camaro's induction system. Some hood designs even create a "ram-air" effect, whereby air is funneled into the engine faster than the engine would normally draw it in, thus allowing the engine to make more power because the additional air can be packed with additional fuel.

A very serious drawback to ground effects packages, however, is that they reduce already precious ground clearance, which likely leads to "grounding out" and scraping the ground effects (particularly the front fascia extension) on the ground on certain transitions from or to an inclined surface.

Finishing Touches

Bolting on new panels isn't much of a trick, which is good news for the do-it-yourselfer. Unfortunately, few of the available panels—or even factory replacement panels—are offered in painted and "ready-to-install" form. This means that whatever panels you buy will likely have to be prepared and painted properly to complete the installation. In some cases, it may be

When it came time to go racing, the Camaro made one of the best-looking racers ever, yet still looked remarkably similar to its street counterpart (something its closest competitor couldn't honestly boast).

Chevrolet has also experimented with some not-so-mild appearances for the Camaro, including this flamed big-block-powered show car. *Chevrolet photo*

Left
Some of the best upgrades, though, are subtle ones, like replacing standard emblems with custom ones. Chevrolet used this ZL1 decal on another show car.

more convenient to have the panels painted off of the vehicle (after trial-fitting them to the car, to locate and drill the necessary mounting holes, etc.). In other cases, it may be necessary to install the panels first, then have the paint work done.

When it comes time to paint, you need to make a few decisions about what type of paint and what type of paint system to use.

General Motors was quick to adopt the base-coat/clear-coat painting system because of its superior finish and body protection. All third-generation cars built between 1986 and 1992 featured a base-coat/clear-coat finish. In 1993, however, facing ever-stricter environmental protection regulations, GM began using a new waterborne paint system, which

not only was kinder to Mother Earth but also provided more vibrant colors and improved protection against fading and certain other elements.

Of course, if you're having your Camaro custom-painted, your choices of paints broadens considerably. Depending on your chosen body man's preferences and skills, he (or she) may guide you toward an enamel finish, a lacquer finish, an acrylic finish, an acrylic-enamel finish and several other possibilities. Each has its own merits, and each has its own demerits, not the least of which may include price, necessary care, and expected life. Naturally, your specific choices may be narrower if you're electing to only paint (or repaint) certain portions of your Camaro, which would then necessitate some

color-matching, which is often far less complex if the painter sticks to the paint type your Camaro originally came from the factory in.

Paint technologies change rapidly, and paint manufacturers frequently introduce new products that have very specific advantages that may be worth considering in your case. Because there's no way of knowing what new paint types and application methods may be available when it comes time to repaint your Camaro, it's highly recommended that you consult with a number of painting professionals and ask them for their suggestions and their warnings.

After you've spoken with a fair number of paint pros, sit down and go through your notes to see what everyone said about each paint type and application method, as well as which painter seemed most responsible and experienced. By all means compare quotes for the cost of the job, but don't let that be your only determining factor, unless you're on a very tight budget. If there's one truism with painting cars, it's that you tend to get exactly what you pay for—at least on the cheap end of the scale. Conversely, paying a lot for a paint job doesn't necessarily guarantee a high-quality paint finish in the end, either. So choose wisely and carefully.

Accessorizing

Though not technically a body "modification," the use of automotive "bras" to protect the front fascia from damage caused by bugs, sand, pebbles, or other flying debris is fairly common on many cars, and Camaros are no exception.

It's important to understand that, while a properly installed and maintained bra typically preserves the paint beneath it, all too often, bras can actually damage the paint more than they protect it.

The Number One problem is that of rubbing. As the wind buffets the bra while you're driving, it can cause the bra to flap. Every time the bra's material smacks against the paint, it rubs a little more paint away. It's easy to understand how considerable paint damage could eventually occur if the problem isn't corrected. Most bras feature adjusting straps to cinch the bra down tighter against

The Magnetic Graphics Alternative

Whether you've got sponsors who demand it, or just want your car to *look* like a race car at the track (hopefully for that psychological edge over your competitors), the thought of permanently applying decals to your Camaro isn't terribly exciting because you not only risk ruining the paint beneath, but should you ever try to remove the decals, you risk public ridicule driving around town in an over-decorated car.

Fortunately, there's a good solution to the problem: Don't apply decals to your Camaro permanently. Instead, apply them to an easily removable magnetic or static-cling substance, which should be available from a local sign-painting shop that handles lettering and graphics on commercial vehicles. Third-generation cars have only metal body panels, so they can use the same sort of magnetic material that building contractors usually use to slap a sign on the door of their trucks. Fourth-generation cars, because of their plastic doors and fenders, need a material that adheres by static cling.

Whichever material youm need, simply apply the decals to the material, and cut along the edges of the decals. Then you are able to drive to the track, arrange the decals for the race, then, at the end of the day, take them off for the drive back home. You will also be able to change decals more easily, such as when you replace particular compo-

nents with parts from another manufacturer, change sponsors, or opt to go for a different contingency prize.

The only thing you need to worry about then is that the panels' surfaces be clean, to prevent scratching.

If you like to go racing and want your Camaro to look like a real race car, you need to decorate it with decals. But you probably don't want the decals on the car for street use. A good solution is to visit a local sign-making shop and purchase either blank magnetic sheet (for third-generation cars with metal body panels) or blank static-apply sheet (for plastic-fendered fourth-generation models), to which you can apply your decals.

the body, but cheaper bras may feature ineffective adjusting straps, or the straps may actually tear from the bra, leaving you with no means of securing the bra properly.

Another potential problem that you need to be aware of is that moisture—from rain or just washing the car—can become trapped beneath the bra, which can eventually cause problems with the paint. Fortunately, most high-quality bras prevent this by utilizing a breathable material, but lower-quality bras may not. Again, it pays to be cautious when you're making your purchasing decisions.

Ultimately, the value of using a bra is somewhat questionable. If your Camaro spends a great deal of time outdoors, the remainder of its body (i.e., the parts not covered by the bra) incurs some fading due to the sun, as well as other damage from wind, water, tree sap, and, of course, the occasional scrape, ding, or dent. So, three years down the road, when you pull the bra off, you may have a fabulous looking front fascia that the rest of the car can't compare with. So, what good has the bra really done?

Perhaps a more important question to ask yourself, though, when considering purchasing and installing a bra on your Camaro is this: For whom are you saving the paint finish? Most people point toward resale value later on, thus the car's next owner is the intended benefactor. But as we've covered, the rest of the car is likely to have numerous battle scars, so the effect on resale value is arguably negligible. And given that few people find bras an attractive accessory, why would you want to drive around in a car many see as uglier than usual, just so someone else later on can enjoy that pristine front end?

Wheels and Tires

We've chosen to cover wheels and tires from a functional, performance-oriented standpoint in the "Suspension and Steering" chapter, but you also need to consider their aesthetic qualities, too. For many people, it actually is the appearance of a wheel and tire combination that is the primary factor in purchasing new rolling stock.

There are literally thousands of possible wheels and tires you could choose from, if you include out-of-production styles and sizes that you might pick up at a swap meet or through classified ads. Of utmost importance when selecting wheels and tires, from both performance and safety standpoints, is whether they properly fit your Camaro. You need to check clearances, backspacing, caliper-to-wheel clearance, and stud-to-nut thread engagement among other possible factors to ensure your new wheels and tires are safe to drive on.

An unsafe combination just isn't worth risking your life or those of your passengers over. Besides, what good are those new wheels if one of them broke lose, punched up all the surrounding sheet metal, and left your Camaro nose-first against a tree, or with its side scraped up close and personal with a guard-rail?

Speaking purely aesthetically, however, you want to consider factors such as the wheel size (both diameter and width), the tire's design, the tire's sidewall height, its tread design, its tread width, and even what your underlying brake hardware looks like.

Third-generation Camaros came from the factory equipped with either 15- or 16-inch wheels, depending on the particular model and options selected, while fourth-generation Camaros used 16-inch wheels on most models but offered 17-inchers on the SS. Various widths, up to 9.5 inches have been used, allowing tire sizes up to 275/40ZR-17 to comfortably fit inside the fenders (careful attention to backspacing and wheel widths have allowed some tuners to run ZR1 Corvette-sized 315/35ZR-17 tires, but clearances are extremely tight with this mammoth tire, so it is not recommended).

Aftermarket wheels are available in 18-, 19-, and even 20-inch sizes. Many people find that a 17-inch wheel with a 40-series tires provides a pleasing combination that fills the wheelwell nicely, provides a good look at any expensive underlying brake hardware, and yet doesn't look "disproportionate." Larger-diameter wheels with lower-profile tires begin to look mismatched with the Camaro body, but this is obviously a debatable issue and one subject to personal tastes and preferences.

Wheel design is another personal choice that may have practical implications. "Laced" or "basket-weave" wheel patterns are still considered to be attractive wheels for Camaros, but they are also substantially more difficult and time-consuming to clean than are more-modern five-spoke wheels.

As this photo of a '94 Camaro Coupe shows, the cars' exterior was very conservative, especially at the rear end.

The wheel finish needs to be considered carefully as well. Aluminum wheels typically come with either a brushed or polished finish that has been clear-coated. While the clear coat looks good in the near term, over time it may decay or become damaged, which can make the affected wheel unsightly. Furthermore, such problems can be difficult and costly to correct. Powder-coated finishes are typically much more durable, though paint is still an effective and reasonably priced method of color coordinating your wheels to the rest of your Camaro.

Another nice upgrade is to replace the standard red and white taillamp assemblies of the 1993–1996 cars with the more distinctive assemblies and their amber turn-signal lenses that were introduced on 1997 models (shown).

The 1998 models brought an all-new front fascia for the Camaro, which also required new fenders, headlamps and a new hood. Many enthusiasts find the "big mouth" simulated grille more reminiscent of older Camaros. This front end can be retrofitted onto older fourth-generation cars but requires the appropriate braces, bracketry, wiring harnesses, and other components, making it most feasible if you were to find a wrecked model in a salvage yard that had been rear-ended.

A minor wheel-related point to keep in the back of your mind is what to do about wheel balancing weights. For the ultimate in performance, you want the wheel and tire assemblies balanced with weights on both sides of the wheel. However, weights on the outside of the wheel do little to enhance the wheel's appearance.

Lighting Options

All third-generation Camaros featured four headlamp units—two high/lows and two high-only beams. The 1993–1997 models featured four mini-quad halogen units, while 1998 and newer models come with composite headlamps that utilize four halogen bulbs. Some models also featured auxiliary fog lights, typically mounted in the "grille" area, one on each side of the front license plate, except in 1998-and-up models that mount small, round fog lights in the air dam itself.

The factory lighting systems—especially systems equipped with fog lights—all provide ample illumination for mundane night driving. If you race, or just want to improve your safety, you should consider adding auxiliary driving lights, because at high speeds it becomes easy to "out-drive" your headlights. That means that your headlights don't illuminate the road far enough ahead of you to give you sufficient time to react to the conditions. In other words, you can easily go so fast that by the time you see something in your headlights, it's too late to avoid hitting it.

It's a common misconception that fog lights and driving lights are the same thing. Fog lights are meant for driving in fog. Period. They are mounted low to hopefully cut beneath the fog, and they spread a broad, short pattern of light. They're not intended for fast driving.

Driving lights, on the other hand, feature a more focused, more intense light beam that can be projected much farther down the road, giving you the needed time (distance) to react to anything they may illuminate.

In many cases, driving lights can be easily installed in place of fog lights in the factory mounting locations. If your Camaro happens to not have factory fog lamps, you can still use those mounting locations, or you may wish to mount your lights beneath the front fascia, but you must be careful not to restrict airflow to the radiator by doing so.

It's important to point out that some states have very strict laws regarding automotive headlamps and auxiliary lights, either restricting their candlepower (brightness), their mounting locations, or even the number of lights you may have on your vehicle. It's always a good idea to consult with local law enforcement agencies prior to making any purchases or installations.

Another RK Sport body enhancement is this solar shield/spoiler combination, which mounts to the top edge of the rear hatch to help prevent the sun's UV rays from fading the interior's carpeting and upholstery. *RK Sport photo*

A final touch is to replace the standard black emblems with more glamorous chrome or gold-chrome emblems, or add additional emblems, such as the "C-A-M-A-R-O" lettering in the corresponding indentations in the rear fascia. *RK Sport photo*

You'll most likely spend more time looking at your Camaro's interior than any other element of it, so doesn't it make sense that it should be equipped the way you like it best?

INTERIOR

Chances are you are going to spend more time looking at your Camaro's interior than any other part of it. It's only naturally, then, to consider upgrading the interior, customizing it to suit your particular tastes. After all, if you aren't happy with the one part of your Camaro in which you spend most of your time, how can you possibly expect to be happy with the car overall?

But there's more to improving your Camaro's interior than blatant acts of vanity. You can also make upgrades that vastly enhance safety and even performance and drivetrain durability. And you don't always need to spend huge quantities of money to experience worthwhile results. The key is thinking creatively and having a course of action in mind before you haphazardly start spinning wrenches and twisting screwdrivers.

Roll Cage

In chapter 3, we discussed the structural importance of roll cages, how they help stiffen the vehicle by giving the suspension a more stable platform against which to operate. But roll cages got their name for protecting occupants of the cars—for preventing the roof from caving in on the occupants in the event the car is rolled on its roof. (Don't laugh—we've seen it done, and it's not a pretty site. Fortunately, it's not exactly easy, either.)

A variety of roll cages are available. Some are bolt-in construction, while some require welding. Some feature just two attaching points, while others have four, six, or more points at which they're secured to the body structure or chassis. Properly welded roll cages always are stronger than bolted-in models, though some sanctioning bodies actually require bolt-in cages, so the choice may not be up to you if you like to compete in sanctioned events.

If you are interested in getting a roll cage for your Camaro, you have several options for the type of finish you want. One of the most popular finishes for bolt-in cages is chrome. Powder-coating is available from

many manufacturers as well. Or you may want to look into having the bars painted to match or contrast with your Camaro's interior or to tie-in exterior colors.

Weld-in cages are considerably harder to finish, given that they have to be assembled in the car from separate pieces and then welded together, which would destroy any finish put on them prior to the welding.

Safety Belts

Another safety upgrade involves the installation of an aftermarket safety seatbelt harness for use during races (they are *not* intended for street use). In addition to coming in an assortment of colors, safety belts are typically available as either four- or five-point harnesses, in reference to the number of points at which the harness connects to the vehicle. A four-point harness has two connections for the lap belt (one per side), as well as two connections for the shoulder belts. A fifth belt keeps the driver from diving beneath the other belts in the system in the event of a crash.

A somewhat minor decision about safety belts involves deciding whether to use the "Y"-style belts, in which both shoulder straps join behind the driver's seat and thus have only one belt that then gets secured to the floor or roll cage, or whether you stick with individual shoulder straps. Individual straps are somewhat stronger but do require a second attachment point.

There are a few options when it comes to mounting your new racing safety belts. First, you can hard-mount them to the floor, which provides a strong, secure assembly but can be inconvenient on a day-to-day basis, especially when you have rear seat passengers in the car.

A second option involves hard-mounting the shoulder straps to your roll cage's cross-brace, if your roll cage has such a provision and sanctioning body rules permit such mounting.

Third, you can mount your belts with heavy-duty quick-disconnect hasps so that you can easily and conveniently install your belts for your racing events, then simply remove them after to get them out of your way for daily driving. Again, consult the appropriate rule books

One of the most noticeable changes was the redesigned instrument panel "tower," which houses the radio and heater/air-conditioning controls. Unfortunately, upgrading older models with the newer parts isn't an easy parts swap because many elements, including the new radio and instrument cluster, tie in to the car's computer.

to determine whether such a mounting method is permissible.

Finally, you need to decide which type of buckle you want—the traditional interlocking buckle or the newer cam style. Both provide equal security, so your decision need only be based on which style you prefer and which you can afford. The complexity of the traditional buckles

is annoying when you're in a hurry to get strapped in, while the more convenient cam-style buckles currently command a much higher price.

Seats

Factory-original Camaro seats provide sufficient support and comfort for typical driving situations, and even serve well in competition use

131

A very worthwhile, and possibly mandatory, upgrade is to add aftermarket safety belts, like these from RK Sport. With a rotary-style "cam lock" system for quick attachment and detachment, these belts keep you safely in the car. As a five-point belt, they feature an anti-submarine belt, too, which prevents you from slipping down and under the belts in the event of a sudden stop. *RK Sport photo*

Though it's impossible to tell in this black-and-white photo, the seat inserts for this third-generation Camaro are day-glow yellow to match accent colors used on the car's exterior. Creative upholstery like this is a great way to customize your Camaro, and it's not too expensive nor even beyond the typical do-it-yourselfer's capabilities.

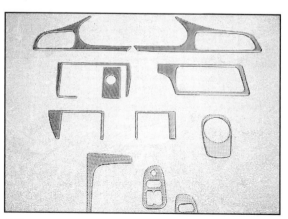

Appearance-wise, the RK Sport carbon-fiber-look appliques dramatically enhance your fourth-generation Camaro's interior. Installation is simple, too, with easy stick-on application. *RK Sport photo*

when a multipoint safety belt harness is used, so there's certainly no need to upgrade your seats, unless you are unhappy with them.

Rather than purchase costly aftermarket seats, many owners opt to recover their original seats in a different fabric or different color to tie in with the exterior paint scheme. This route can provide pleasing results for a modest price and shouldn't be overlooked by anyone customizing their Camaro.

If you do choose to replace your stock seats, you probably want to shop around for the mostcomfortable seats. Though it's tempting to purchase seats by mail order, out of a catalog, or through magazine ads, it's best to actually try the seats. If you're unable to try out the seats you're interested in, perhaps because there isn't a dealer for those seats in your area, then make sure you inquire about return policies—in the event you aren't satisfied with a set of mail-ordered seats.

Naturally, the best way to improve the odds of a seat fitting your form comfortably is to focus on highly adjustable seats that provide lumbar (lower-back) support, adjustable side bolsters, as well as an adjustable seat bottom and back. You should pay particular interest to the length of the seat bottom to ensure that it is long enough to provide ample support for your legs. A short seat cushion leaves your legs tired and worn out after only short trips.

Also spend a good deal of time trying out the headrest portion of the seat. This should be height-adjustable and should be no more than 4 inches

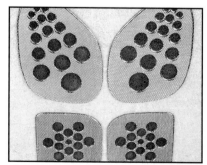

If you're adding the carbon-fiber trim appliques, you won't want to forget about jazzing up your pedal pads with a matching carbon-fiber look. *RK Sport photo*

from the back of your head when you are seated in your normal driving position to properly prevent head and neck injuries during accidents. The headrest must also contact the back of your skull, not your neck. If the headrest is set too low, it acts as a fulcrum, actually worsening injuries.

Some seats offer much more than just an adjustable fit, however. Additional conveniences abound. Some seats feature heated cushions, which are nice in colder climates. Some have built-in speakers. And, of course, they come in different materials and colors.

Leather upholstery provides a supple, rich feel and certainly looks elegant. However, leather is expensive, and it has some drawbacks that should be considered. First, leather can be slippery, which can make it hard to stay squarely behind the steering wheel during performance maneuvers. Leather also tends to get very hot if your car sits in the summer sun long. In winter time, it contracts and becomes brittle, leading to cracks and tears. Leather also requires a fair amount of care to preserve and protect it.

Vinyl upholstery has many of the same drawbacks as leather, but without the high price tag. Vinyl also is considerably easier to care for—mist it with 409 or your favorite household cleaner and wipe it off with paper towels or rags and you're good to go. Vinyl typically looks and feels cheap, but it's almost impervious to spills and stains, so if you're a slob, it might just be a good choice.

Cloth fabrics have few drawbacks and offer many advantages. Aside from being inexpensive and easy for upholsterers to work with, cloth fabrics remain both comfortable and durable in both hot and cold weather, they've got enough

Chevy took custom upholstery to new levels with the seats for the 1993 Camaro Indy Pace Cars. Rather than dying the seat covers, or stitching the different colors onto a base color (such as all-white), the Pace Car seats used a single strand of thread that was different colors where it needed to be and was carefully woven by computerized equipment to create the proper pattern. *Chevrolet photo*

If you're serious about racing, you can help out your Camaro's performance by shedding weight. And the pathetically small back seats are great starting points for an interior diet. You could also remove the jack, spare tire, carpeting, passenger seat, and more if the sanctioning body rules allow.

The 1997 30th anniversary models had a classic look, thanks to black-and-white houndstooth upholstery. *Chevrolet photo*

grip so you don't slip and slide ride off the seat at the first corner you round, and cloth looks good . . . until you spill something. If cloth has a clear drawback, it's that it stains. Scotchgard and other fabric protectants do a commendable job of fending off some stains, but they're not effective against everything. Stubborn stains like the special sauce from a McDonald's Big Mac can be especially tough to clean up, as can the ketchup for your fries, that chocolate shake that shook a little too much, or even just a spilled soda.

It's possible to go outside the norm when recovering seats, too. We've seen cars with seat inserts of wet-suit material, which has a different look and texture, plus is available in vivid, vibrant colors that can really jazz up an otherwise stock interior.

At the other end of the seat spectrum are race-only seats. Usually little more than a metal or heavy-duty plastic shell with only the thinnest

layer of foam and some form of cover material, these seats are extremely light-weight, allowing you to shave considerable weight from your Camaro, or at least to reposition that weight where it works in your favor. These seats, however, should not be considered for anything other than racing use, because they typically won't function with the stock safety belts and may interfere with the proper operation of your Camaro's airbag, if it has one.

However, if the weight savings is important to you for competition purposes, you might want to consider having a set of racing seats that you bolt in at the track, then swap your street seats back in after the races.

A final thought on seats that is worth considering: Power seats are *heavy*! In fact, power seats can weigh nearly twice as much as a nonpower version of the same seat. So, as convenient as they may be, they're every bit as hefty, too.

Instruments

While the windshield and windows let you keep your eyes on the road, your Camaro's instruments let you keep tabs on how your Camaro is operating. The factory instrument packages provide the basic info you need—speed, engine rpm, oil pressure, coolant temperature, and alternator output. Unfortunately, the factory gauges aren't always accurate, and it's risky to chance your expensive engine on questionable gauges; you owe it to yourself to protect that investment by installing additional gauges that allow you to monitor more parameters. Of course, with quality aftermarket gauges, you don't have to leave things to chance.

Not only can aftermarket gauges provide you with far more accurate information, they can provide you with *more* information. Gauges are available to replace the factory units, plus you can get units

By comparison, here's the instrument panel of a typical race car, complete with numerous aftermarket gauges with large faces that are easily read.

that monitor additional parameters, such as engine oil temperature, transmission oil temperature, manifold vacuum, and more. Some gauges, like many aftermarket tachometers, also offer special features such as a memory feature that temporarily stores the highest rpm achieved during a run, or the ability to trigger shift lights so that you don't even have to watch the tach to know when it's time to shift.

Replacing—or rather supplementing—your stock gauges with accurate, high-quality aftermarket gauges is one of the smartest things you can do to your Camaro. When choosing your new gauges, you need to decide whether you want mechanical or electrical gauges. Mechanical gauges typically feature a larger sweep of the needle, which makes at-a-glance readings easier. They also tend to react more quickly to changes, such as rpm, oil pressure, or manifold vacuum.

If you're choosing to add extra gauges, an excellent first pick is an oil temperature gauge. Engine oil temperature is one of the most vital parameters you can monitor, because a sudden change in oil temperature may be your only warning sign of a developing problem. Rather than waiting for the other gauges to tell you a problem has already occurred, you may be able to shut down the engine or alter your driving to prevent serious damage from occurring. Oil temperature also gives you an indication of the oil's condition within the engine. As the oil gets hotter, it thins out. If it gets too hot, it becomes too thin to properly protect your engine's internal components. Likewise, if your oil remains too cold, it is too thick to flow properly to all parts of the engine quickly enough to protect them.

For the same reasons, on cars equipped with an automatic transmission, it's helpful to have a gauge that displays automatic transmission fluid temperature, since automatics are extremely temperature critical. A sustained increase of just 20 degrees in transmission fluid temperature reduces transmission efficiency and cuts the transmission's life expectancy in half. A high-quality gauge can alert you to potential transmission

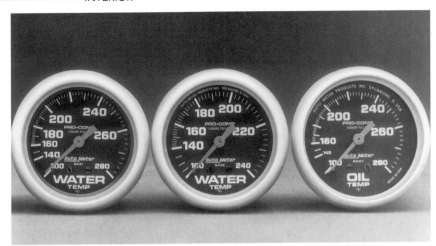

You can add aftermarket gauges, like these AutoMeter liquid-filled Pro Comp gauges, to your Camaro's interior to supplement the factory gauges. Two water temp gauges are shown here; one reads to 280 degrees, while the other only goes to 240 degrees. For strictly street use, the 240-degree unit should be fine. For competition use, the 280-degree unit is the best option, because engine temperatures while racing can exceed the 240 gauge (you just hope they won't). An oil temperature gauge is another must-have gauge. *Auto Meter photo*

Additional gauges worth considering are for fuel pressure (which needs to be mounted outside of the passenger compartment), fuel level (though the stock gauge is usually fine for this function), and, of course, oil pressure. *AutoMeter photo*

troubles before they have time to cause a catastrophic failure or irreparable damage.

A vacuum gauge can be a helpful diagnostic tool as well, because it can indicate problems within the engine by raising, lowering, or merely fluctuating readings. If your Camaro is equipped with a supercharger, you want to get a gauge that shows manifold pressure, since there won't be a vacuum in the vehicle's manifold. Turbocharged engines need a gauge that shows both vacuum (off the boost) and pressure (during boost).

Another excellent gauge to utilize is a fuel pressure gauge; however, mechanical fuel pressure gauges should *never* be mounted inside the passenger compartment because of the fire hazard they represent. Most people choose to install them on the hood, possibly in the cove of a hood scoop, if so equipped.

There are lots of options for mounting the gauges in the interior. Some people have gone to the trouble to butcher their original instrument panel to graft the new gauges into the old IP, but this is a lot of

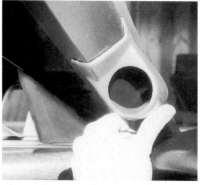

The pods are easily mounted to the A-pillar, but make sure you test various heights to make sure they don't obscure your vision, creating a dangerous blind spot!

While you can mount some aftermarket gauges in those cheap metal gauge panels, there are better options. Plastic gauge pods that mount to the A-pillar (alongside the windshield) are great for putting small (2-inch) gauges right in your line of sight for safe viewing even while racing. They're also available for mounting two gauges.

work and it's hard to make the installations look good. Another good solution is to install them in place of some unused equipment, such as the radio on race cars. Several owners of third-generation cars have installed gauges in place of the usual map pocket (the glovebox area) on the instrument panel, while

1993–1996 fourth-generation Camaros featured a cassette/CD storage compartment at the base of the instrument panel, just above the console, that can easily be blocked off with a piece of plastic, in which you can mount auxiliary gauges. Another nice option is an A-pillar-mounted gauge pod. These plastic pods mount to the roof support pillar in the interior and accept a standard 2-inch-size gauge. A double version is available, as well, that holds two 2-inch gauges. A simple, though less attractive method, is to use the generic metal single-, double-, or triple-gauge mounting frames available from most auto parts stores.

A final mention on instruments must certainly go to the availability of white gauge faces for stock Camaro instruments. With white gauge backgrounds, the gauges are more distinctive and more easily read than the stock version—two very important improvements over the stock equipment.

Shifters

The factory shifters for both the manual and automatic transmissions available in late-model Camaros are meant to be easy to operate, pleasing to the eye, and

inexpensive. They're not designed for performance use, nor are they well suited to it.

The manual transmission shifters feature tall sticks with long throws between gears and a somewhat spongy feel due to their soft bushings that help suppress road and transmission noise that could otherwise be transmitted into the passenger compartment. The primary advantages of aftermarket shifters are their shorter throws and more precise action, both of which tend to decrease the number of missed shifts experienced.

The drawback to automatic transmission shifters is their lack of positive detents when up-shifting manually. With a stock shifter, you can easily knock the shifter from the "1" position up to neutral in a single sweep. In a race, that kind of mistake could be disastrous for your engine, causing it to over-rev. Performance shifters typically feature positive detents that allow the shifter to move only one position at a time, thus preventing you from accidentally slipping into neutral. In addition, most aftermarket shifters feature a "reverse lock-out" feature that requires you to perform some additional movement in order to engage reverse, prior to backing up the car. The additional movement needed isn't troublesome but is merely intended to prevent you from accidentally going into reverse while the vehicle is traveling forward, which would severely damage the transmission and possibly other drivetrain equipment like U-joints, axles, differential gears, and more.

Performance enthusiasts are undoubtedly interested in replacing their Camaro's stock shifter with a performance unit, like this Callaway/Hurst assembly for six-speed-equipped fourth-generation models.

Automatic-equipped models benefit from a good aftermarket shifter, too, to provide positive detents that prevent accidentally shifting into neutral—or worse, reverse!—during competition. *B&M photo*

Installation of an aftermarket shifter is fairly simple for most third- and fourth-generation cars, but may require you to remove a healthy chunk of the console to accomplish.

Stereo Equipment

Production Camaros have always featured some of the nicest-sounding audio systems of any production car. This is especially true of the fourth-generation models, which have benefited from GM's collaboration with Bose to develop an astounding Delco/Bose audio system that features specially tuned speakers and resonance chambers, as well as specific mounting positions for the speakers. But mass production requirements prevent engineers from producing the ultimate audio systems, for a number of factors, not the least of which are cost and interior packaging constraints. Not to mention that most buyers are not highly critical of a vehicle's audio system, as long as it produces reasonably pleasing sounds. Even if engineers did strive to develop the ultimate stereo system, it would be quickly outdated (probably before the car ever debuted) because of the speed with which the audio equipment aftermarket makes technological advances. Today's high-tech system is tomorrow's acoustical dinosaur.

For these same reasons, plus the simple fact that no two people's audio preferences are quite the same, it's impossible to recommend a particular course of action with regard to audio equipment purchases, installations, and upgrades. There are just too many options and too many personal choice decisions.

Generally speaking, however, for fuller, richer sounds you want to replace the entire system, from the "head unit" to the speakers, incorporating one or more amplifiers, equalizers, a cross-over, then some high-performance subwoofers, mid-range speakers, and tweeters.

Security Equipment

When thinking about auto security, you're actually faced with two problems: preventing a would-be thief from stealing your car and preventing disreputable types from making off with portions of it, or your belongings inside it. Though some security systems handle both tasks, your best bet may still be to approach each problem separately and devise independent solutions to maximize your level of protection.

The rear hatch area isn't terribly exciting, but many enthusiasts utilize the deep luggage well for aftermarket stereo equipment or even nitrous oxide systems ... or both!

In terms of outright vehicle theft, there are basically two ways thieves can get your car: They can drive it away or haul it away. Each requires a somewhat different approach to theft prevention, but both share one common truth: Thieves typically like easy targets. Unless they *really* want a specific car, if it's outfitted with one or more security devices, they tend to skip over it for an easy heist.

Drive-off Vehicle
Theft Deterents

The idea behind preventing drive-off vehicle theft, then, is to prevent the vehicle from starting. One of the best means of doing that is something General Motors graciously supplied most third-generation (1989 and up) and all fourth-generation Camaros with: the PASS-Key theft deterrent system, which consists of an ignition key with a special resistor that must be present for the computer to start the vehicle. If the resistor pellet is missing, or an incorrect pellet is used, the fuel, ignition, and starter systems are disabled for a period of roughly three minutes (GM doesn't specify exactly how long the PASS-Key system disables those engine systems) or until the correct key is inserted into the ignition.

This feature is designed to discourage thieves from randomly trying different key/resistor combinations hoping to stumble upon the correct code. Prior to the incorporation of the PASS-Key system, third-generation Camaros had consistently been among the top-10 vehicles stolen each year. PASS-Key nearly eliminated Camaros from the list altogether. It's an excellent system. But it's not foolproof, so it pays to take further precautions. (Systems that provide similar features to the PASS-Key system are available for 1982–1988 Camaros and other vehicles, as well.)

Another excellent device for preventing drive-off thefts is the Prompaq, or the newer Prompaq II, which is essentially a switch box that allows you to install up to four computer PROM chips to control engine performance. By simply turning a key, you determine which PROM the computer takes its commands from. For security purposes, a special "valet" chip is available that limits engine performance, or you can simply leave one PROM socket empty and select that, giving the computer no PROM to read from at all, and thus no way to operate the engine.

But anti-theft tactics need not be sophisticated to be effective. Something as simple as pulling fuses that control the fuel pump and/or fuel injectors can keep your car from starting, so even if a thief gets inside, he's unlikely to get anywhere with it, or would give up long before he would discover the missing fuses.

Another low-tech solution is to install a hidden but easily accessible toggle or key switch that controls power flow to one or more circuits, such as the ignition system or fuel pump. Since thieves depend on getting into a vehicle and away in a matter of seconds, any impediment you can create betters your chances that the thief gives up on your car

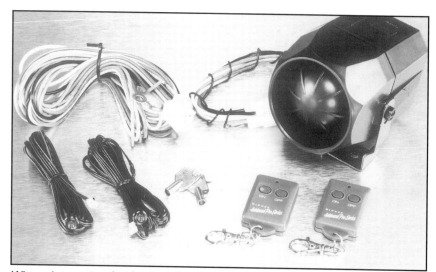

Winner International's Ultra Pro alarm and vehicle immobilizer system essentially accomplishes for non-PASS-Key cars what PASS-Key systems do—it kills the ignition and fuel systems, preventing thieves from starting the car. *Winner International photo*

and moves on. So, given that a thief is battling the clock, they don't have time to look for hidden switches and the like and disable them, so these sorts of devices don't necessarily need to be sophisticated. They just need to slow the thief enough to make him think twice about your car.

Hidden switches can also be useful for another type of drive-off theft—car jackings. In the case of a car jacking, the vehicle is already running, so killing the starter circuit won't do any good. And it's best not to stand in the thief's way if he's trying to steal your vehicle—statistics show that many people who did wound up dead or critically wounded as a result. Instead, it's best to do as the thief instructs, to get out of the car and let the thief drive off. But just because you let them have the car doesn't mean you have to abandon all hope of ever seeing it again.

The basic idea is to allow the car jacker to drive off in the car, get a safe distance from you, then the vehicle's engine would die and not restart. This would cause the thief to jump out and flee the scene.

One company, Jacob's Electronics, produces a product called Stop Thief! that resembles an old floor-mounted headlamp dimmer switch. If you're stopped by a car jacker, all you need to do is inconspicuously tap the switch with your foot, then exit the car. Tapping the switch activates a timer that holds off killing the fuel and ignition systems for a predetermined time, which allows the thief to drive away but not too far before the car becomes undriveable. By doing what PASS-Key does—delaying reactivation of the dead circuits for an unspecified period of time—Stop Thief! also prevents thieves from simply resetting the switch and restarting the car.

You can accomplish similar results by wiring a simple, well-placed but inconspicuous button or toggle switch to kill power to the fuel pump. Residual fuel and pressure within the system should give the thief a few seconds of normal operation before the vehicle acts up and stalls. During that time, you can flee to safety, knowing that your car won't be far away.

A home-grown system could be improved with some form of delay mechanism, which should be available through Radio Shack electronics component stores. The delay would be incorporated to allow a few additional seconds of normal operation before systems lose power.

Steering wheel locks are also excellent deterrents, despite being relatively easy to defeat, because they are one more thing that a thief has to contend with, and those precious seconds could be the ones in which a cop shows up and catches him (or her) in the act.

Preventing Haul-Away Vehicle Thefts

Thieves may use some form of vehicle transporter, such as a tow truck, flatbed, or trailer, to literally tow your Camaro away to a safe location where they can then work on it or strip it for parts. Since the car doesn't actually have to be operating to be stolen, ignition and fuel system disablers aren't going to be effective methods of preventing theft. So you have to be more creative.

At its core, your strategy in this case must focus on immobilizing the vehicle so that it can't be dragged away. Alarm systems typically sense movement of the vehicle and sound a large siren to attract attention and, thus, hopefully discourage the thieves from continuing. But thieves often know how to defeat the expected alarm systems, rendering them ineffective.

One of the best methods of immobilizing your Camaro actually involves utilizing a piece of performance hardware that's intended to help you go faster: a brake system line lock.

Line locks are typically used by drag racers to lock the front wheels without locking the back wheel, so that the car sits still for a pre-run burnout without potentially damaging the car's rear brakes. By simply pressing a button, then stepping on the brake pedal, the front brakes become locked. If wired properly (so that the brake pressure is maintained even with the ignition key is off), the locked brakes could pose a real problem to loading and hauling the vehicle (most professional thieves intent on stealing the entire

Beyond stealing the car, you've got to consider how you protect your valuables inside the car. And the Number One target these days for thieves is the airbag mechanism. The Shield, which works in conjunction with The Club, is an effective deterrent against airbag theft.

vehicle wish to do so with as little damage as possible, to increase the money the car is worth to them). Multiple line locks could be used to lock up all four wheels, if desired, for considerable protection.

A few companies offer brake lock devices made specifically for the job of preventing haul-away thefts.

Even with some method of locking the brakes, you can still better your chances of finding your Camaro where you left it if you practice defensive parking methods, like parking only in highly visible areas (including well-lit areas at night), by turning your front wheels to the full-lock position and making sure the ignition column steering wheel lock mechanism engages, and by leaving the vehicle in park (or first or reverse, for manual transmissions) with the parking brake engaged.

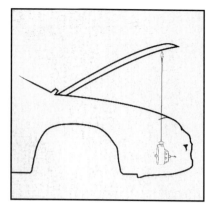

Here's a quick diagram of how the Hood Lock works to protect your valuable engine components. *Winner International photo*

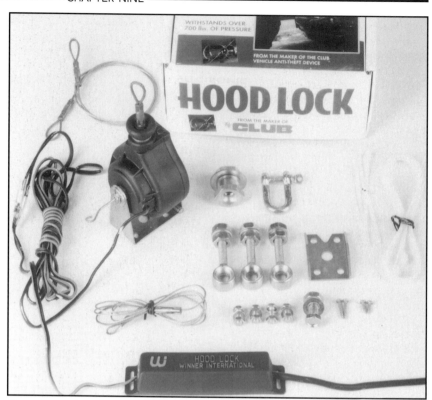

If you have a lot of money invested in engine upgrades, you should consider installing a secondary hood lock kit, such as Winner International's Hood Lock. A steel cable prevents the hood from being raised, even if the car's own hood release cable and latch mechanisms are defeated. *Winner International photo*

Since thieves tend not to like an audience while they work. If your car is within easy sight of large numbers of people, a thief usually leaves it alone. If you turn your wheels to the full-lock position you accomplish several things. First, if the car is parked between other vehicles, it may be impossible to extract it from the parking space without damaging both it and the cars beside it. Second, if the thief wants to haul the car with its front wheels on the ground, he won't be able to. They even make it hard to load on a flatbed transporter, since the car always wants to roll off to a side. Finally, leaving the transmission in first or reverse gear, or "Park" for automatics, can help lock up the rear wheels, possibly preventing it from being towed. It takes only a few seconds to perform all of these steps, and each could be just enough of a problem that a thief would be inclined to give up and move on to easier prey.

Bear in mind, however, that a determined thief can get your Camaro no matter how much you protect it. These suggestions are in no way a guarantee of any sort that they will prevent your car from being stolen.

Preventing Property Theft

As for the crooks who don't want your entire car, but rather just the contents or parts of it, you can make their job a bit tougher, too. A good first-line of defense against such crimes is a set of decals that warn of the presence of an alarm system that responds to movement, such as rocking the car or breaking a window. It's been said over and over again, but it's true: Thieves don't like to work hard. That's why they're thieves. So, decals that alert them to the fact that an alarm goes off should prevent them from messing with your car.

Even with a security alarm system, it's still possible to have your car's wheels stolen right off it in broad daylight. Fortunately, wheel theft can usually be deterred by using simple locking lug nuts. Aftermarket lock nuts are inexpensive and work well, but the most common varieties have two particular drawbacks: their size and the trouble-prone operation of them. The lock nuts tend to feature a large, smooth, round head that makes it hard to remove them with any kind of wrench or pliers—even locking pliers. But the physical size of the lock nuts may prevent them from

fitting on some wheels, particularly state-of-the-art aftermarket performance wheels. And the usual clover-shaped key, which mates with a correspondingly shaped channel in the nut, often doesn't engage well and can even become damaged, making it virtually impossible for you to remove the wheel in the event you get a flat tire or simply want to rotate the tires sometime.

A better solution is close at hand, and affordable, however. And most of you already have it: the factory locking lug nuts. The factory locking nuts are much smaller in size, and the key actually grabs onto the outside of the nut, giving it much more strength and a better grip, so it doesn't accidentally slip off at the least opportune time, leaving you with busted knuckles.

You likely want to protect the contents of your Camaro—its stereo, seats, radar detector, cellular phone, or just packages you bought on a shopping trip. Obviously you can't lock everything down inside the car, and you can't just take everything with you. So what do you do? Well, start by parking in the open, where lots of people are likely to see your car. Thieves don't usually like audiences. They don't like lights either, so parking under bright street or parking lot lights tends to shunt them on to other cars, too.

You can also make your car look less appealing by concealing any loose items in the car, by tucking them under seats, into consoles, or in the glovebox or other storage compartments. If your car originally came with a cargo cover, use it! If thieves don't see anything worth stealing, they probably won't take the time to break in on the off chance that they may find something worth taking.

Cutting Weight

Racers already know that decreasing weight is every bit as good as increasing power, so for them, the notion of putting the interior on a serious diet is a foregone conclusion. In fact, trimming 100 pounds from a vehicle is typically worth one-tenth of a second in the quarter-mile. Camaro interiors are fairly lean straight from the factory, but there are areas where you can shave a few pounds, which might make all the difference between first place and being the first loser.

Some of the easy-to-think-of items that can be shed in the name of weight might be the rear and passenger seats. This alone should be good

This is the ALDL port, and it's your interface with your Camaro's Electronic Control Module (or Powertrain Control Module, for 1994-and-newer models). Located under the steering column, you can connect aftermarket diagnostic equipment, such as Rinda Technologies' Diacom Plus system or HyperTech's Power Programmer Plus, to the ALDL port to monitor sensors or to reprogram the car's computer for more performance!

for roughly 60 or more pounds, but there's more. The jack and spare tire equipment can be quickly removed for another 30 pounds or so. Door panels, carpeting, sound deadener, and plastic trim panels can go, too, slicing approximately another 30 or more pounds from the car. Altogether, there's at least a tenth of a second that can be deducted from your estimated time, provided you deduct the hefty amenities.

CARE AND MAINTENANCE

Whether you've been preparing your Camaro for competition use or just fun-filled daily driving, you've no doubt invested considerable sums of money into the powertrain, suspension, brakes, body, and interior, among other systems. With that in mind, it's only sensible to take a few moments to preserve and protect it against the elements, time, and possible mishaps.

No amount of preparation ever guards against accidents or other unforeseeable problems, but that doesn't mean you should just throw your hands in the air. As the old saying goes, "An ounce of prevention is worth a pound of cure," and with automobiles, that statement can be taken quite literally. An ounce or two of wax or polish serves you well against needing gallons of fresh paint to restore the shine and luster your old paint once had. A few ounces of oil staves off expensive bearing, piston ring, camshaft, and

other engine wear problems. And a cautious, defensive, thoughtful driving style could be all that's required to avoid being between a rock and a hard place, or rather another car and a guardrail.

Ironically, care and maintenance is often one of the areas that few enthusiasts devote enough time to. It's considerably more romantic and exciting to spend an afternoon bolting on a set of new rocker arms than it is to be washing, chamoising, and polishing the car. After all, when you're done, the wash and polish routine leaves your car looking like it did before—and given that you're likely to find a new paint chip or two while you're getting up close and personal with every inch of the bodywork, you may even end up a tad depressed, despite all your hard work. But that's the short-term downside to care and maintenance, and you should never think about your car in a short-term manner.

Washing your Camaro is one of the two most basic steps you can take to care for and maintain it. But even something as simple as washing has a few rules that need to be followed to prevent doing more damage than good.

142

In the long run, that afternoon is likely to add months—if not years—to the life of the paint, which, depending on where you live, could mean the difference between a body that's well protected against rust and corrosion, and one that's highly susceptible to them.

Basically, when talking care and maintenance, you've got two types of tasks to concern yourself with: those that maintain its mechanical components, such as the engine, transmission, brakes, suspension, steering, rearend, and other parts, and those steps that maintain appearance, which could involve almost any part of the car from the body to the interior to underhood, or even the chassis.

Car Care Basics

Sitting there in your driveway, looking at your Camaro, you may find yourself overcome by a wave of helplessness. There's so much work to be done, so many things to do, that you just don't know where to start. The truth of the matter is, you shouldn't really ask "where" to start, but rather "when."

The best way (and time) to start caring for your Camaro is the day you drive it home. Whether it's a new car or a used one, there's no better time to begin caring for it than the beginning. Obviously, your job is considerably easier if you're dealing with a new car. With everything basically shiny and new, your work is merely to preserve that appearance, which tends to fall into the realm of applying coatings to serve as barriers against decay-causing elements. Oils, greases, and, of course, clear paint finishes all have their place, as do trim dressings, silicone sprays, and leather and vinyl protectants. And you won't want to neglect any cloth surfaces that would benefit from the application of a fabric protectant, such as 3M's Scotchgard.

Older cars—even ones only a year old or less—are likely to show some signs of decay. Parts that were once natural cast iron are coated with at least a light coat of surface rust. Unprotected stamped-steel parts have rusted, too, while rubber and plastic parts may have discolored or become otherwise stained. All of these conditions require some

restoration work before preservation steps are of any use. And, consider yourself warned that it's *always* an easier job to preserve something initially than to try to make up for failure to do so later. In other words, you spend far more time restoring a part than it ever would have taken to preserve it in the first place.

The exact order in which you should start protecting your Camaro is ultimately up to you. If you're starting with a brand-new or nearly new car, you can go through it top to bottom, bumper to bumper in a weekend or less. Even if the car is older and already has a thorough coating of surface rust, you can go through the entire car in a couple of weekends, so what gets done when really is inconsequential. And remember that with older cars, you'll likely have some parts that are going to need to be replaced, such as a ratty interior, so those parts won't need to be "preserved" at this point (though the new components should be protected as soon as they're installed, if not before that).

While it may seem contrary to common sense, it may be more logical to tackle the easier projects first, since you can get more of them done—thereby protecting more of the car—in a shorter time than you can one tough project. Once the bulk of the car is taken care of, you can move onto the more time-consuming work without having to worry about the rest of the car degrading further in the process. For example, if the underbody has lots of surface rust but the body and interior are in good shape, then make sure the body and interior stay in good shape while you strip the underbody and repaint it.

Washing 101

It sounds silly, but few people know the *right* way to wash their Camaro, or any car for that matter. Sure, almost any old method cleans off the dirt. But is the car really clean then? And did you actually do more harm than good in the process?

The first thing about the right way to wash your car is that you can't do a proper job without the proper tools and supplies. Supplies-wise, you need to use a solution specifically designed for washing automobiles,

You also need the proper cleaning "tools," like a high-quality wool wash mitt. It's a good idea to actually have two mitts—one for above the "belt line" and one for below—but if you're on a budget, you can use one side of the mitt for the top and the other for the bottom, so long as you mark which side is which. This helps you avoid picking up abrasive grit below the belt line and then dragging it across the paint above the belt line.

because other soaps can be harmful to automotive paint finishes.

Dish soap, for instance, which is a popular choice among many so-called auto enthusiasts, is about the worst thing you can use short of steel wool to wash your car. The reason should be obvious, too: Dish soaps are designed to cut grease on plates, pots, and pans, right? Well, what do you think wax is? It's a form of grease. So, dish soaps remove your car's wax and polish, leaving the paint bare and unprotected from the elements. Of course, if your goal is to remove the wax or polish, such as before re-waxing, by all means wash away. But if you aren't planning on waxing immediately, use a real car soap that won't harm your waxed paint.

Another thing about car soaps: Use a soap-only solution, rather than a soap-and-wax polish combination product. Most women can tell you that all-in-one shampoos and conditioners are rarely as effective as separate products. It's not hard to figure that a soap with some wax particles suspended in it coats some of the dirt on the vehicle's surface, making it harder and harder to remove that grit later. The layer of wax applied by such all-in-one products rarely provides as much protection as a separately

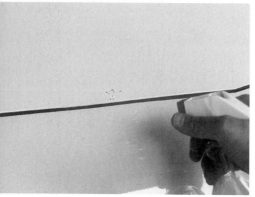

Even though you should wash your car once a week, you should perform touch-up cleaning throughout the week, as needed. A spray bottle filled with water, plus a few cloth diapers, are just the tools for cleaning bug splatter, bird droppings, and other contaminants, but be careful of how much dirt or dust is on the paint surface. If the car is visibly dirty, you're better off washing the whole car, otherwise you risk scratching the paint.

A great way to clean windows of the road film that gradually builds up is to dampen a rag with kerosene and wipe the glass surfaces vigorously. Following up with a coat of Rain-X helps repel water, which makes driving in the wet far more pleasurable.

applied coat of wax or polish. The wax must be substantially thinner in order to be in solution with the soap; thus, less adheres to the body, and whatever does is in a thinner layer.

Okay, so you've got your car wash solution (or concentrate). Now how do you go about getting it on the car? Well, the need for a bucket is obvious, and just about any old bucket will do, though plastic is often a better choice, just in case you happen to bump it against the body.

Your weapon of choice for attacking the dirt, however, should be either a thick horsehair bristle brush, or a plush wool wash mitt. Why these two? Because each has the ability to gently lift dirt from the car's surface and trap it higher up in the mitt or brush's fibers, so that the dirt particles won't scratch or otherwise damage the paint surface as you rub the brush or mitt around. Sponges and wash rags, on the other hand, keep most of the particles in contact with your car's paint finish, scratching it as you drag them around. Nylon bristle brushes, including many do-it-yourself car wash "scrub brushes," can actually be abrasive to paint, even without dirt trapped in them, so they should never be used. High pressure washers,

like those found in do-it-yourself car washes or just your garden hose set to deliver an intense, narrow water jet, can actually blast dirt particles into the paint, rather than wash them away.

Going a step further, whichever you choose—a brush or a mitt—it's a good idea to have two. One can be used for all surfaces above the body side molding or crease line, and one for below. Alternatively, a single mitt can be used if you mark and use one side for the top and the other for below the "belt line." The reason for this is that the body below the belt line gets considerably dirtier, and usually with more sand and abrasive debris that flies off the tires and sticks to the body. If you use one mitt (or brush) for the entire car, you're chances of damaging the top part of the body with the debris from the bottom of the car greatly improves. But by using separate mitts for each area, you prevent contamination as much as possible.

The washing process, from here on, gets pretty simple. With the recommended amount of wash solution in your bucket, fill the bucket with cold water (warm and hot water can cause the paint to expand, potentially damaging it). Then hose down

the entire car, starting at the roof and working your way down to the tires. Use either a hose without a nozzle on it so that the water just rolls out of the hose, or use a misting setting to wet the car gently. The idea is to let the water cascade along the body, lifting dirt up and flushing it away as it flows.

Once the entire car is thoroughly wet, begin washing at the top of the car, washing only one panel at a time, then rinsing with a gentle flow of water before proceeding to the next panel. Wherever two panels meet, you should overlap your washing strokes onto the adjacent panel, to ensure the edges of both panels are cleaned thoroughly.

When the body is washed, you should proceed to the wheelwells and whatever portions of the undercarriage you can reach. In most cases, sponges are the easiest "tools" to use here, since the finish isn't a high priority (it's already subjected to far harsher punishment, anyway). Washing the wheelwells should generally be done at least once a month, to prevent any contaminants from permanently setting.

As for the wheels and tires, you should use a stiff-bristle brush to thoroughly clean the tire sidewalls,

144

though you need to exercise care on the wheels, because a stiff brush may damage any protective coating or other wheel finish. A specific wheel cleaner is helpful for cleaning wheels, or you can use products like Simple Green or Westley's Bleche White. At least once a month you should remove each wheel from the vehicle in order to clean the back of the wheel.

The engine compartment also needs to be cleaned on a regular basis, to remove dirt, dust, and even oil mist. Generally speaking, cleaners such as Simple Green or a foaming engine cleaner do a fair job of cleaning the engine without requiring much effort—you simply spray them on, let them sit a few minutes, then hose them off. Make sure you use a biodegradable product, though. An assortment of rags, sponges, and even small brushes may be helpful in cleaning up the many nooks and crannies under the hood. And be careful not to smear any greases or oils, because you could accidentally create a larger problem than what you set out to clean up.

Lastly, for the finishing touches, you need to clean the door, hood, and rear hatch jams of debris. A mixture of your wash solution and water in a spray bottle makes a convenient way to wet only the necessary areas. Washing and wipe-up can be handled with either sponges or rags, or, perhaps, an old wash mitt.

When the entire vehicle is washed, you should immediately dry it with a genuine chamois cloth to prevent sediment in the water from damaging the body, as well as to prevent the water droplets from acting as magnifying lenses, focusing the sun's rays on the body, literally burning the paint in the same manner that mischievous children light papers on fire with a magnifying glass.

Periodically, you should go over the washed and dried surface with a quality paint cleaner product, which removes the thin layer of film that eventually builds up on every car. Follow the directions of the particular paint cleaner for application instructions and frequency.

Window Washing

Windows present special cleaning challenges. Even with regular washing, windows develop a "film"

Storage Tips

There are a dozen or more ways to ensure your Camaro emerges from storage in the same shape it entered it.

1. Clean it thoroughly, top to bottom, inside and out. And dry it!

2. Fix all paint chips and mechanical defects.

3. Change oil and filter, including automatic transmission, if equipped.

4. Tune-up the engine.

5. Fill up fuel tank and add fuel stabilizer.

6. Leave doors, hood, decklid, etc., ajar to prevent seals from being unnecessaily crushed for extended periods of time.

7. Set moth balls or desiccant pouches in tin pie plates in interior to absorb moisture and prevent mold or mildew.

8. Loosen engine accessory drive belts to keep them from stretching.

9. Double-check antifreeze condition and adjust as necessary.

10. Grease all suspension and chassis fittings.

11. Disconnect/remove battery.

12. Do NOT start occasionally, unless you need to move the car. Starting it periodically only causes more "dry starts" that are hard on bearings, seals, and other parts.

13. Do NOT store on jackstands, but do use junk wheels and tires if possible. Cars were designed to carry their own weight on their suspension, but supporting it on jackstands loads parts of the chassis that weren't designed for that purpose, which can lead to problems.

14. Duct tape plastic whiffle balls to the ends of the exhaust tailpipes to prevent rodents from entering, but allow air to dry out the exhaust system.

15. Leave yourself a note taped or tied to the steering wheel listing any fluids that need to be added or adjustments that need to be made before the car can be removed from storage.

16. If you do store your Camaro in the garage, clear a "safety zone" around the car, and don't allow any yard tools or items into that zone. If necessary, paint lines on the floor to clearly mark where the safety zone is.

17. Cover your Camaro with a high-quality, cotton-lined cover to protect its finish from dust and other contaminants. If possible, store the covered car in an air-tight, moisture-free Car Jacket or Omni-Bag (available from Pine Ridge Enterprises, phone: 800-5-CARBAG) to prevent rust, mold, or mildew from attacking the car while it sleeps.

18. Double-check with your insurance company to make sure your car is protected against fire, theft, and other hazards while in storage.

that is stubborn and hard to remove, unless you know some tricks. One of the best ways to clean the windows is to use kerosene (K-1). Normally, we wouldn't recommend flammable substances as cleaners, but kerosene is an almost ideal glass cleaner. Applied with a typical rag, the K-1 breaks down the built-up grime, making it easier to remove. In the end, the windows are left showroom-floor clean.

But cleaning windows is only part of the problem. Every time a grain of sand hits the windshield, it makes a tiny, almost imperceptible chip in the glass surface. Over tens or hundreds of thousands of miles, all those chips hamper your vision through the glass, especially in bright sunlight, which is now reflected and refracted off the somewhat opaque surface of the glass.

The Eliminator is a glass fiber "pen" that you use to prepare paint chips for touch-up work.

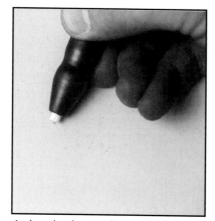

A clean body must be washed, chamoised dry, then cleaned, with an automotive paint-safe degreasing cleaner. This removes any wax that might prevent proper adhesion of the touch-up paint. You should use the glass fiber brush to clean the rust in the chipped paint. Lightly working the glass fiber tip into the chip also scores the walls of the chip, promoting good adhesion of the new touch-up paint, when it is applied.

GM dealers or a body shop can get you all the touch-up paint you'll need. Most bottles have a touch-up paint applicator brush, but a fine-tipped model paintbrush is more accurate. Your goal should be to apply two or three very thin coats of touch-up paint, building the new paint up so that it's slightly higher than the surrounding paint when dry. Extra fine sandpaper can then be used to knock down the high spot, which also helps blend the new paint into the surrounding area. Then wash everything, dry it, and move on to the waxing stages.

And let's not forget about scratches. If a scratch is minor enough, you may be able to remove it with bronze wool (like steel wool, only much, much softer). If scratches or pits are too deep to be effectively removed with bronze wool, you may need to resort to using a glass polishing kit, such as those available from the Eastwood Company. Consider yourself warned, however, that it's easy to overdo it when polishing glass, causing distortions that actually make looking through the glass worse than it was just dealing with the scratch.

Once you've got your glass clean and hopefully free of scratches and pits, you should consider applying a water repellent such as Rain-X, or even a couple coats of wax. The beauty of Rain-X is that it makes light rain showers or mist bearable without wipers—the water just beads up and runs off the treated windows, giving you a clearer view of what's around you.

Paint Chip Repair

Assuming you actually drive your Camaro (and you must, otherwise you probably wouldn't have purchased this book), sooner or later you're going to get paint chips and door dings.

While you're washing your car, getting intimate with nearly every inch of its body, you'll likely notice new chips and dings. Any wound should be repaired as soon as possible to prevent further damage—such as rust or peeling paint—from occurring.

The quick fix is to simply dab on some touch-up paint with a model paintbrush, or the brush that's generally incorporated into the touch-up paint bottle's cap. But this is hardly the procedure for a high-quality repair.

To do the job right, you need to first start out by cleaning the wound with a degreasing agent, then with a glass fiber brush. The degreaser removes any wax or polish that might prevent proper paint adhesion, while the glass fiber brush not only removes any surface contaminants, it scores the surfaces of the wound to improve the adhesion of the touch-up paint.

Next, you need to apply a thin coat of touch-up paint and allow it to thoroughly dry. Then lightly sand it with a very fine sand-paper (test in an inconspicuous spot first), being

careful not to sand an area any larger than is absolutely necessary. Then, clean the surface, dry it, and apply a second thin layer of touch-up paint, and repeat the sanding and painting. Once you have the new touch-up paint level with the surrounding surface, you're almost done. All that's needed then is to use some ultra-fine sandpaper to carefully remove any subtle scratches, then wax or polish the area to protect it.

Waxes and Polishes

Waxes and polishes endow your Camaro's body with a protective barrier against the elements and minor contaminants. Without this layer, your Camaro's paint alone must fend off attacks from wind, water, sand, bugs, airborne pollutants, tree sap, and the occasional small animal that may scamper across the hood. Granted, base-coat/clear-coat paint finishes—which all Camaros built from 1986 and up have—do have that clear coat to serve as a barrier, but any scratch to the paint's surface allows those contaminants to get a foothold that they don't easily relinquish.

While waxes do protect a painted surface, the application of them can be harmful if over-done; because the wax is somewhat abrasive, it gradually removes some paint material each time you wax (just look at your wax applicator pad for the proof—you'll find traces of your car's paint color). If you wax too often, you may literally rub the paint right off your Camaro. Obviously, that would be bad. So, wax sparingly—about once a month is generally sufficient, less often if the car spends most of its time out of the sun, wind, and rain (in other words, if you park in your garage at home, and if it's parked in a covered parking garage while you're at work).

Application of the wax can be accomplished by hand, which many people believe is still the best method. Realistically, however, it's far easier, faster, and convenient to use a dual-action random orbital buffer and the appropriate application bonnets. There are a few caveats that you're advised to follow when using a buffer. First, don't bear down on the buffer, since anything more than a light, even pressure may damage the paint surface. Second, don't leave the buffer in any one place for any length of time—keep it moving to prevent it from generating heat that could cause paint damage. Third, be careful when trying to work the buffer around the mirrors, decklid spoilers, and other such protrusions, to avoid contacting the paint with an unprotected surface of the buffing head or shaft.

Whether you use a paste wax or a liquid wax is up to you, since quality products are available in either form. Again, convenience and speed make liquid waxes a popular choice.

After waxing, it's a good idea to follow up with the application of a high-quality polish, which goes on clear, adds even more protection against the elements and contaminants, and usually does an excellent job of removing any swirl marks left over from the waxing process.

Sealers, Lubricants, and Protectants

Before you can call it a day and tuck your Camaro away in the garage, you need to spend a few last

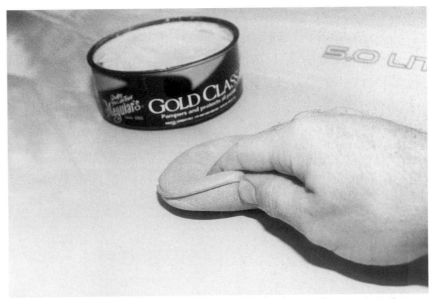

All waxes are slightly abrasive, so you don't want to wax too frequently and cause the paint to wear out prematurely. You can either apply wax by hand, by working the applicator pad in small circular motions, or with a random, dual-orbital buffer. The buffer is faster and easier, but doing it by hand provides a better overall finish.

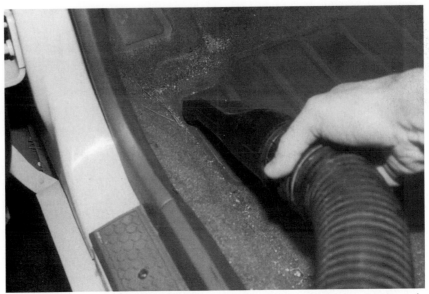

Moving inside, a good first cleaning step is to thoroughly vacuum the carpets and seats. Sand in a carpet actually acts as an abrasive that cuts into the carpet fibers every time you step on the carpet, causing the fibers to rub against the sand. Frequent vacuuming keeps your carpet looking new for years to come.

moments applying various sealers, lubricants, protectants, and other "goops" to various parts to ensure they continue to look and work as you expect them to.

Weatherstrip along the doors, rear hatch, and T-top panels and convertible header should be treated to a moisturizing application of spray sil-

icone. Be ready with a rag to wipe up the excess. If your weather seals are allowed to dry out, they contract or split, or both, creating (or at least worsening) wind and water leaks.

Hood, door, and hatch hinges and latch mechanisms should be lubricated with white lithium grease, which tends to cling to the parts bet-

Next, you want to use a vinyl protectant to wipe down the instrument panel and dash pad, the door panels, console, and other interior parts. It's often less messy to apply the protectant to a rag first, then rub the rag on the component you wish to clean and protect.

Upholstery cleaner made by 3M Scotchgard is an excellent product, and it applies a protective barrier that helps prevent future spills from setting in and becoming stains.

You need to periodically douse the door, hood, and rear hatch hinges with white lithium grease. Lithium grease is thicker than most oils, so it clings to the hinges longer, providing lasting lubrication.

Once the interior is sufficiently clean, it's a good idea to spend some time preserving the weatherstrip by applying a silicone spray to help lubricate it and keep it flexible.

ter than spray-on oils, providing better long-term protection.

Vinyl and rubber protectants have a myriad of uses. Rubber, vinyl, or plastic parts on the body (tires, trim), inside the passenger compartment (dash, door panel inserts, instrument panel bezel), and under the hood (hoses, air cleaner ducts) look markedly better after having protectant products like Armor All or STP Son of a Gun applied. While spraying the products on tires is easy enough, and doesn't make too much of a mess, you may find it's better to apply the products to trim by spraying it on a rag or even a Q-tip first, then use that to apply the protectant to the parts. Here's a tip, though: Never apply vinyl protectants to the rim of the steering wheel, or at least do so only sparingly, to avoid making the wheel slippery, which could cause it to slip in your fingers at a very inopportune time.

There are several excellent cloth fabric cleaners on the market, which can help remove minor stains. After the seats are clean, applying a protectant product like 3M's Scotchgard should help prevent future spills from soaking in before you have a chance to wipe them up. Leather fabrics, on the other hand, require leather cleaners and protectants.

Routine Maintenance

Beauty is only skin deep, someone once said, and with cars, it's often what's underneath that matters most. And just as you need to keep up the exterior of your car, you need to give the powertrain and chassis the needed TLC the mechanical components deserve and require.

The Oil and Filter Change

Perhaps the most obvious maintenance procedure to perform religiously is the time-honored oil and oil filter change. Plan on climbing under your Camaro every 3,000 miles or so to change the engine's life blood and its filter. It has been proven that synthetic oils provide a slight (negligible) power increase over conventional motor oils, but the best reason for using synthetics is their superior protection in extreme temperature conditions, both hot and cold. Synthetics flow better when cold, which

It's also a good idea to check fuel pressure to verify that the engine isn't starving or flooding for fuel. TPI engines can be especially sensitive to fuel pressure adjustment.

Checking throttle position sensor voltage with a digital voltage tester shows you whether the TPS is adjusted properly.

allows them to reach and thus protect components better when the engine is cold. And they don't thin-out ("suffer viscosity break-down" as they say in the television ads) as much as conventional oils in extreme heat, so they provide a better "cushion" between two wear items.

Grease Job

While you're letting the oil drain, take the time to grease all of your suspension and chassis grease fittings.

Remember that many aftermarket suspension pieces, such as high-performance lower rear control arms, torque arms, even Panhard rods, may also have grease fittings, whereas the stock items did not, so grease those new items, too. Again, synthetic products are strongly recommended.

Tire Rotations

Depending on the sizes of your wheels and tires, and whether the tires are directional or not, you may be able to perform some form of tire rotation. If so—even if it's only fronts-to-the-back and vice versa—you should rotate your Camaro's tires every 6,000 miles to lengthen their tread life. If you're able to swap tires not only from front to rear, but from side to side, as well, then you should use either the "fronts straight back, rears criss-cross going forward" or the "rears straight forward, fronts criss-cross going back" method. Whichever you choose does not matter, so long as all of your future rotations follow the same method, to ensure each tire gets used in each position.

Obviously, while you're rolling the wheels around, you've got the

Also take the time to test the battery and alternator output. The battery should show approximately 12.6 volts, while the alternator should put out at least 13 at idle, but no more than 18 volts at any rpm. Unless your system has proper voltage to power the electronics, it won't be getting far for long.

Spark plug wires can be checked for resistance, using an ohm meter. You want less than 100 ohms per foot of wire for the wires to not present any significant resistance to the spark energy trying to reach the spark plug.

You also need to check and adjust the spark plug gap to the distance listed in your shop manual. Slip-type gap gauges, like the one shown here, are *not* the ideal tool for the job, but they get you close. Jacobs Electronics offers a handy and accurate gapping tool if you foresee yourself checking plugs frequently or need to ensure the gap is as accurate as possible.

Spark plugs also need to be checked carefully to determine how efficiently the engine is operating. EFI engines, because of their automatic fuel mixture controls, should look pretty much like this—a white insulator around a clean, but slightly worn tip, plus a basically clean electrode.

perfect opportunity to inspect the tires and wheels for any signs of damage from accidental encounters with curbs and road debris or simple wear. Check tread depth (3/32 inch is minimum legal).

Quick Inspections

While you've got the wheels off, rotating the tires, there are a number of worthwhile inspections you can and should perform on several brake, suspension, and steering system components, as well as a few under the hood.

Having the wheels off gives you easy access to the brake calipers, or the ability to remove any brake drums so that you can properly inspect brake pad wear. Look not only for thickness of any remaining friction material, but also for even wear of the inside and outside pads on each corner, as well as even wear between each front brake and even wear for each rear brake. Uneven wear typically indicates a caliper is sticking on its guide pins, so clean them and apply anti-seize compound to the pins as a lubricant.

You can also inspect the front wheel bearing for any play. Correction may only require a slight adjust of the retaining nut, though a loose bearing that wasn't loose at the last inspection generally indicates that bearing is beginning to wear and may soon fail.

Steering linkage can also be checked for wear by attempting to turn each front wheel by hand. Pay particular attention to tie rod ends, and, on 1982–1992 cars, to the idler arm and center link.

With the car still on jackstands, you can quickly check the condition of the driveshaft universal joints by rocking the driveshaft from side to side. Any slack indicates a worn joint that should be replaced.

The final suspension and steering inspection must take place with the wheels back on the car, and the jackstands removed. Jack up one front wheel by placing the jack under the lower control arm, and, grasping the wheel at the 12 and 6 o'clock positions, rock the wheel up and down to check the condition of the ball joint. If you sense any movement, make sure it isn't a lose wheel

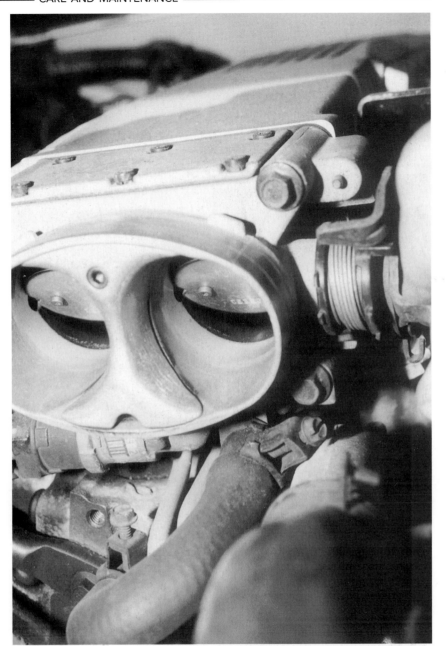

Another inspection to make is the degree of "coking" behind and around the throttle blades. You need to check this with the engine off to prevent accidentally sucking in debris that could ruin your engine.

bearing by grasping the wheel at the 3 and 9 o'clock positions and rocking the wheel back and forth; a wheel bearing features similar play in each direction, while a ball-joint only exhibits wear in the first (top and bottom) test.

A few seconds under the hood can tell you a lot about the general road-worthiness of the engine. You can quickly inspect the engine's drive belts (either serpentine or V-belts) for signs of any cracks, which indicate

they need to be replaced. Also check for proper tension. Since serpentine belts have automatic tensioners, a loose belt indicates the old belt has stretched beyond the tensioner's range of compensation and thus needs to be replaced. Belts should typically last 30,000 miles or three years, though their life span can vary widely due to operating conditions, quality, tension, and other factors.

While you're stooped over checking the belts, check the radiator and

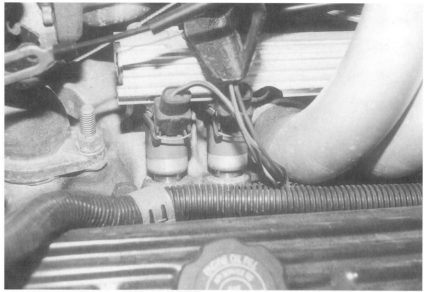

Also inspect your fuel injectors for signs of any leaking O-rings, which seal the injectors to the intake manifold.

The oil filter also needs to be changed to prevent trapped particles from coming loose and working their way back through the engine, where they may cause considerable, expensive damage.

heater hoses. They should be flexible but not soft. Belts should be changed at least every three years or 30,000 miles.

Other Fluids to Change

Oil isn't the only important fluid circulating around in your Camaro's powertrain. You've also got engine coolant to worry about, plus transmission and differential fluids, and even brake fluid! Ethylene-glycol-based (yellow-greenish color) engine coolant should typically be changed every three years to remain effective. Newer silicone-based coolant (orange color) usually goes for up to five years before it begins to weaken.

Automatic transmission fluid takes a beating, thanks to all those slipping clutch packs, so it's especially important to make sure the ATF is changed regularly, along with the ATF filter. Each should be done approximately every 15,000 miles for performance vehicles, which are even more punishing on transmission fluid.

Manual transmissions are far more forgivable, since they don't have "slipping" parts that generate so much heat. Still, manual transmission fluid should be changed approximately every 30,000 miles or sooner. Consult your Camaro owner's manual for the specific fluid required, since different transmissions utilize different fluids. Synthetic fluids are available and should be used, if possible in your case.

Differential fluid has similar changing requirements to those for manual transmission fluid. However, when changing differential fluid, you need a replacement gasket, as well as the Positraction additive for vehicles equipped with limited slip rear axles.

Chapter 4, "Brakes," covered why you need to change your brake fluid at least once a year to ensure optimal braking. If you race your Camaro, you may need to change your brake fluid more frequently, so consult chapter 4 for more specific recommendations.

Another filter that needs regular replacement, normally, is the air filter. Over time, the filter clogs up with dust and debris, which eventually causes the engine to starve for air. A new filter lets the engine breathe deeply for maximum performance.

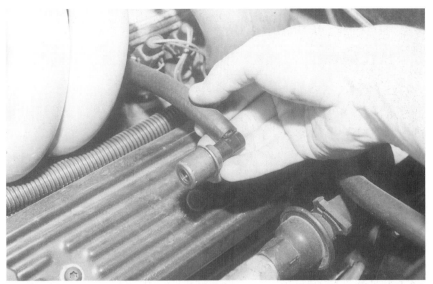

The Positive Crankcase Ventilation (PCV) valve plays an essential role in your engine's operation. If the PCV valve gets clogged, crankcase "gases" build up within the engine, leading to higher emissions output and decreased engine performance.

You've also got to change your Camaro's fuel filter, which, on TPI cars, is located beneath the left rear seat cushion, underneath the vehicle. Note the rear subframe rail, to which the filter's bracket is fastened.

Finally, if you happen to store your vehicle for extended periods of time, such as the winter, you may want to look into a storage shelter like the Cover It garages, which can be used to get the car out of harm's way but won't cost you an arm and a leg all winter.

You should make sure you repack or replace your wheel bearings at least once a year, unless you race often, in which case you should repack them before each race.

Another nice storage accessory is the Carpad protective mat, which primarily is used to contain any fluids that may leak from your car, preventing them from damaging your garage floor or seeping into the ground.

PARTS AND SUPPLY SOURCES

Accel
8700 Brookpark Road
Cleveland, OH 44129
216/398-8300
www.mrgasket.com
Ignition, inductio,n and fuel injection systems and components.

Air Flow Research
10490 Ilex
Pacoima, CA 91331
818/890-0616
Cylinder heads.

American Racing Custom Wheels
19067 South Reyes Avenue
Rancho Dominquez, CA 90221
310/635-7806
www.americanracing.com
Wheels.

American Sports Car Design
324 Home Avenue
Maryville, TN 37801
423/982-3091
www.americansportscar.com
Body kits and components.

AutoMeter Products
413 W. Elm Street
Sycamore, IL 60178
815/895-8141
Instruments/gauges.

Autotronic Controls Corp/MSD
Ignition
1490 Henry Brennan Drive
El Paso, TX 79936
915/857-5200
Ignition systems and components.

BBK Performance Parts
1611 Railroad Street
Corona, CA 91720
909/735-2400
Induction and exhaust components.

Baer Racing
3108 West Thomas Road
Suite 1201
Phoenix, AZ 85017
602/233-1411
Brake systems and components.

BF Goodrich Tire & Rubber
Company
(Contact your local BF Goodrich tire center.)
Tires.

Borla Performance
5901 Edison Drive
Oxnard, CA 93033
805/986-8600
www.borla.com
Exhaust systems.

Callaway Cars
3 High Street
Old Lyme, CT 06371
860/434-9002
www.callawaycars.com
Turn-key Camaro conversions, engine upgrades, body kits, accessories.

Carrera Shocks
5412 New Peachtree Road
Atlanta, GA 30341
770/451-8811
Shock absorbers.

Centerforce Clutch
2266 Crosswind Drive
Prescott, AZ 86301
520-771-8422
Clutches.

Chassis Engineering
1500 Avenue R
Riviera Beach, FL 33404
561/863-2188
Roll cages, suspension components.

Competition Cams
3406 Democrat Road
Memphis, TN 38118
901/754-2400
www.camhelp.com
Camshafts, valvetrain components.

Competition Engineering
80 Carter Drive
P.O. Box 1470
Guilford, CT 06437
203/453-5200
Chassis components.

Crane Cams
530 Fentress Blvd.
Daytona Beach, FL 32114
904/258-6174
*Ignition system and valvetrain
components.*

DG Motorsports
3225 Production Avenue #A
Oceanside, CA 92054
760/433-7413
Body, interior components.

Doug Rippie Motorsports
14070 23rd Avenue North
Plymouth, MN 55447
612/559-7605
*Turn-key Camaro conversions, engine
upgrades, suspension upgrades.*

DynoMax Performance Exhaust
(Contact your local performance
parts dealer.)
Exhaust systems and components.

Earl's Performance Products
189 West Victoria Street
Long Beach, CA 90805
310/609-1602
Brake system components.

Eastwood Company
580 Lancaster Avenue
Box 296
Malvern, PA 19355
800-345-1178
Tools, restoration supplies.

Edelbrock Corporation
Torrance, CA 90503
310/782-2900
*Cylinder heads, intake
manifolds/runners, throttle bodies,
exhaust systems, suspension components.*

Eibach Springs
17817 Gillette Avenue
Irvine, CA 92714
714/752-6700
Suspension springs.

Enkei Wheels
32400 Industrial Drive
Madison Heights, MI 48071
248/585-3100
www.enkei.com
Wheels.

Fel-Pro Performance Products
One Equion Drive
Ashland, MS 38603
601/224-8972
Gaskets.

Firestone Tire & Rubber Company
(Contact your local Firestone tire
center.)
Tires.

Flowmaster Exhaust
2975 Dutton Avenue
Unit #3
Santa Rosa, CA 95047
707-544-4761
Exhaust systems.

Global West Suspension
1455 N. Linden Avenue
Rialto, CA 92376
909-349-2090
Suspension and structural components.

GM Performance Parts
(See your local General Motors
Dealer's Parts Department.)

Goodyear Tire & Rubber Company
(Contact your local Goodyear tire
center.)
Tires.

Griffin Radiator
Piedmont, SC 29673
800/RACE RAD
Radiators.

Hays Clutches
8700 Brookpark Road
Cleveland, OH 44129
216/398-8300
www.mrgasket.com
Clutches.

Hi-Performance Coatings (HPC)
Salt Lake City, UT
800/456-4721
www.hpcoatings.com
Thermal and corrosion protection coatings.

Holley Performance Parts
P.O. Box 10360
Bowling Green, KY 42102-7360
502/781-9741
*Cylinder heads, induction, and ignition
systems and components.*

Hooker Industries
1024 W. Brooks Street
Ontario, CA 91762
909/983-5871
Exhaust systems and components.

Hotchkis Performance
12035 Burke Street
Suite 13
Santa Fe Springs, CA 90670
562/907-7757
Suspension, structural components.

HP Motorsports
5055 S. 36th Street
Omaha, NE 68107
402/731-7301
www.hpmotorsport.com
*Suspension, structural, brake, and
powertrain components.*

Hurst Shifters
8700 Brookpark Road
Cleveland, OH 44129
216/398-8300
www.mrgasket.com
Shifters.

HyperTech
1910 Thomas Road
Memphis, TN 38134
901/382-8888
*Induction, injection, and computer
components.*

Jacobs Electronics
500 N. Baird Street
Midland, TX 79701
800/627-8800
www.jacobselectronics.com
Ignition systems and components.

JBA Headers
7149 Mission Gorge Road
San Diego, CA 92120
619/229-7797
www.jbaheaders.com
Exhaust headers.

Jet Hot Coatings
610/277-5646
Thermal and corrosion protection coatings.

Just Suspension
P.O. Box 167
Towaco, NJ 07082
201/808-0066
Suspension components.

K&N Engineering
561 Iowa Avenue
Riverside, CA 92507
800/858-3333
Air filters.

Kenny Thomas Racing Enterprises
10578 Mahoning Avenue
North Jackson, OH 44451
330/538-0400
12-bolt rear axle assemblies.

Keiper Recaro Seating
905 W. Maple Road
Suite 100
Clawson, MI 48017
313/288-6800
Seats.

Koni America
606/586-4100
Shock absorbers.

Lakewood Industries
8700 Brookpark Road
Cleveland, OH 44129
216/398-8300
www.mrgasket.com
Suspension components.

LG Motorsports
4314 Action Street
Garland, TX 75042
972/272-7753
Engine, suspension, brake, structural, and other components.

Lingenfelter Performance
Engineering
1557 Winchester Road
Decatur, IN 46733
219/724-2552
www.lingenfelter.com
Engine, suspension, brake, and structural components.

March Performance Pulleys
5820 Hix Road
Westland, MI 48185
313/729-9070
www.marchperf.com
Engine pulleys.

Meguiar's
17991 Mitchell South
Irvine, CA 92714
800/854-8073
Cleaning supplies.

Moroso
80 Carter Street
P.O. Box 1470
Guilford, CT 06437-0570
203/453-6571
Numerous components.

Moser Engineering
1616 N. Franklin Street
RR4 Box 22
Portland, IN 47371
219/726-6689
Rear axle assemblies and components.

Mr. Gasket
8700 Brookpark Road
Cleveland, OH 44129
216/398-8300
www.mrgasket.com
Accessories.

Nitrous Oxide Systems (NOS)
5930 Lakeshore Drive
Cypress, CA 90630
714/821-0580
Nitrous oxide systems.

Nitrous Works
1450 McDonald Road
Dahlonega, GA 30533
706/864-7009
Nitrous oxide systems.

NR Automobile Accessories
818/986-8881
www.nrauto.com
White gauge faces.

Paxton Products
1260 Calle Suarte Street
Camarillo, CA 93012
805-987-5555
Superchargers.

Performance Friction
83 Carbon Metallic Highway
Clover, SC 29710
803/222-2141
Brake pads.

Performance Suspension
Technology
P.O. Box 396
Montville, NJ 07045
209/299-8019
www.p-s-t.com
Suspension components.

Random Technology
1313 Temple Johnson Road
Loganville, GA 30052
770/978-0264
High-performance catalytic converters.

Redline Synthetic Oil Corp.
3450 Pacheco Blvd.
Martinez, CA 94553
510/228-7576
Synthetic lubricants.

Rinda Technologies (Diacom Plus)
4563 N. Elston Ave.
Chicago, IL 60630
773/736-6633
Computer (ECM/PCM) interface system.

RK Sport
214 Via El Centro
Oceanside, CA 92054
760/433-1663
www.rksport.com
Engine, suspension, brakes, body, and interior components and accessories.

Russell Performance Products
225 Fentress Blvd.
Daytona Beach, FL 32114
800/394-1120
Brake system components.

Simpson Race Products
2415 Amsler Street
Torrance, CA 90505
310/320-7231
www.simpsonraceproducts.com
Safety equipment.

SLP Engineering
1501 Industrial Way North
Toms River, NJ 08755
908/349-2109
www.slpeng.com
Engine, suspension, brakes, body, and interior components and accessories.

Stencils & Stripes Unlimited
1108 S. Crescent #39
Park Ridge, IL 60068
847/692-6893
Decals, graphics.

Stewart-Warner Instrument Corp.
580 Slawin Court
Mt. Prospect, IL 60056
708/803-0200
Instruments.

Stillen Performance Brake Systems
3176 Airway
Costa Mesa, CA 92626
714/540-5566
Brake systems and components.

Strange Engineering
1611 Church Street
Evanston, IL 60201
847/869-7010
Rear axle assemblies and components.

Summit Racing Equipment
P.O. Box 909
Akron, OH 44309
800/230-3030
*Numerous performance and racing
components.*

TCI Automotive
One TCI Drive
Ashland, MS 38603
601/224-8972
*Automatic transmissions and
components.*

Tire Rack
771 W. Chippewa Avenue
South Bend, IN 46614
888/371-8473
www.tirerack.com
Tires and wheels.

TPI Specialties
4255 County Road 10 East
Chaska, MN 55318
612/448-6021
www.tpis.com
Engine assemblies and components.

VDO North America
188 Brooke Road
P.O. Box 2897
Winchester, VA 22604
540/678-2022
Instruments.

Vericom Computers
6008 Culligan Way
Minnetonka, MN 55345
612/933-4256
users.aol.com/vcomputers
Performance computers.

Vibratech (Fluidampr)
537 E. Delavan Avenue
Buffalo, NY 14211
716/895-8000
Harmonic dampers.

Vortech Engineering
5351 Bonsai Avenue
Moorpark, CA 93021
805/529-9330
Superchargers.

Wings West
845 W. 16th Street
Newport Beach, CA 92663
714/722-9995
Body kits and components.

Winner International (The Club)
32 West State Street
Sharon, PA 16146
800/527-3345
Security systems and devices.

World Products
29 Trade Zone Drive
Ronkonkoma, NY 11779
810/244-9822
www.goracing.com/world/
Cylinder heads.

INDEX